ve

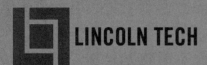
LINCOLN TECH

Lincoln Technical Institute
Automotive Lab Manual
Volume 5

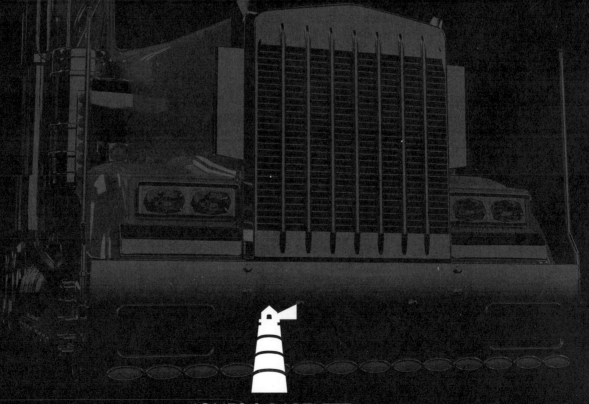

JONES & BARTLETT
LEARNING

World Headquarters
Jones & Bartlett Learning
5 Wall Street
Burlington, MA 01803
978-443-5000
info@jblearning.com
www.jblearning.com

Jones & Bartlett Learning books and products are available through most bookstores and online booksellers. To contact Jones & Bartlett Learning directly, call 800-832-0034, fax 978-443-8000, or visit our website, www.jblearning.com.

Production Credits
General Manager: Douglas Kaplan
Executive Publisher—CDX and Electrical: Vernon Anthony
Managing Editor—CDX Automotive: Amanda J. Mitchell
Editorial Assistant: Jamie Dinh
Vendor Manager: Tracey McCrea
Marketing Manager: Amanda Jo Banner
Manufacturing and Inventory Control Supervisor: Amy Bacus
Composition: B-books, Ltd.
Cover Design: Stephanie Torta
Rights & Media Specialist: Robert Boder
Media Development Editor: Shannon Sheehan
Cover Image: © Masekesam/Shutterstock
Printing and Binding: Edwards Brothers Malloy
Cover Printing: Edwards Brothers Malloy

ISBN: 978-1-284-11188-0

6048

Printed in the United States of America
20 19 18 17 16   10 9 8 7 6 5 4 3 2 1

Contents

Truck Steering-Suspension Systems, DT106

CONTENTS

Truck Steering-Suspension Systems:
Steering Column 1

Student/intern information:

Name _Skyler_   Date _2017_   Class _____

Vehicle used for this activity:

Year _Nov_   Make _oder_   Model _____

Odometer _____ VIN _____

Learning Objective / Task	CDX Tasksheet Number	2014 NATEF Priority Level	2014 NATEF Reference Number
• Identify causes of fixed and driver adjustable steering column and shaft noise, looseness, and binding problems; determine needed action.	H226	P-1	4A1.1
• Inspect and service steering shaft U-joint(s), slip joints, bearings, bushings, and seals; phase shaft.	H227	P-1	4A1.2

Time off _____

Time on _____

Total time _____

Materials Required

- Vehicle with possible engine concern
- Vehicle manufacturer's service information
- Manufacturer-specific tools depending on the concern
- Vehicle-lifting equipment, if applicable

Some Safety Issues to Consider

- Diagnosis of this fault may require test driving the vehicle on the school grounds or on a hoist, both of which carry severe risks. Attempt this task only with full permission from your supervisor/instructor and follow all the guidelines exactly.
- Caution: If you are working in an area where there could be "brake dust" present (may contain asbestos, which has been determined to cause cancer when inhaled or ingested), ensure that you wear and use all OSHA-approved asbestos protective/removal equipment.
- Lifting equipment such as vehicle jacks and stands, vehicle hoists, and engine hoists are important tools that increase productivity and make the job easier. However, they can also cause severe injury or death if used improperly. Make sure you follow the manufacturer's operation procedures. Also make sure you have your supervisor's/instructor's permission to use any particular type of lifting equipment.
- Comply with personal and environmental safety practices associated with clothing; eye protection; hand tools; power equipment; proper ventilation; and the handling, storage, and disposal of chemicals/materials in accordance with federal, state, and local regulations.
- Always wear the correct protective eyewear and clothing, and use the appropriate safety equipment, as well as fender covers, seat protectors, and floor mat protectors.
- Make sure you understand and observe all legislative and personal safety procedures when carrying out practical assignments. If you are unsure of what these are, ask your supervisor/instructor.

Performance Standard

0—No exposure: No information or practice provided during the program; complete training required
1—Exposure only: General information provided with no practice time; close supervision needed; additional training required
2—Limited practice: Has practiced job during training program; additional training required to develop skill
3—Moderately skilled: Has performed job independently during training program; limited additional training may be required
4—Skilled: Can perform job independently with no additional training

© 2017 Jones & Bartlett Learning, LLC, an Ascend Learning Company

Student/intern information:

Name _[handwritten]_ Date _[handwritten]_ Class _[handwritten]_

Vehicle used for this activity:

Year _[handwritten]_ Make _[handwritten]_ Model _[handwritten]_

Odometer _[handwritten]_ VIN _[handwritten]_

▶ **TASK** Identify causes of fixed and driver adjustable steering column and shaft noise, looseness, and binding problems; determine needed action.

NATEF 4A1.1

Time off_____

Time on_____

Total time_____

CDX Tasksheet Number: H226

1. Reference the appropriate manufacturer's service information for the correct procedure to diagnose fixed and driver-adjustable steering column.
2. Diagnose fixed and driver-adjustable steering column:
   a. Start the engine with the transmission in neutral.
   b. Ensure that the steering column is in the center position.
   c. Rotate the steering wheel from lock to lock (rotate the steering wheel all the way to the left and then all the way to the right), observing any noise or roughness in operation: Operational: _[handwritten]_ Requires servicing: _[handwritten]_
   d. If the steering column requires servicing, list the necessary actions or corrections:

   [handwritten]

   _____

   _____

3. Check for any excessive lateral and radial movement.
4. Reference the appropriate manufacturer's service information for the correct procedure to check for unusual noises, looseness, or binding problems from fixed and driver-adjustable steering column. Diagnose fixed and driver-adjustable steering column:
   a. List your tests and observations:

   _____

   _____

   _____

   _____

   b. Within manufacturer's specifications: Yes: _____ No: _____
   c. If no, list the necessary actions or corrections:

   _____

   _____

   _____

   _____

5. Discuss the findings with instructor.

Performance Rating

CDX Tasksheet Number: H226

☐	☐	☐	☐	☐
0	1	2	3	4

Supervisor/instructor signature _____ Date_____

© 2017 Jones & Bartlett Learning, LLC, an Ascend Learning Company

Student/intern information:

Name _____ Date _____ Class _____

Vehicle used for this activity:

Year _____ Make _____ Model _____

Odometer _____ VIN _____

▶TASK Check cab mounting and adjust ride height.   NATEF 4A1.3

Time off _____

Time on _____

Total time _____

CDX Tasksheet Number: H228

1. Reference the appropriate manufacturer's service information for the correct procedure to check cab mounting and adjust ride height.
   a. List the procedure and all safety requirements when checking cab mounting and adjusting ride height:

   _____
   _____
   _____
   _____
   _____

2. Following all procedures and safety requirements, check cab mounting and ride height:
   a. List your observations:

   _____
   _____
   _____
   _____

   b. Within manufacturer's specifications: Yes: _✓_ No: _____
   c. If no, list the necessary actions or corrections:

   _____
   _____
   _____
   _____

3. Discuss the findings with instructor.

Performance Rating

CDX Tasksheet Number: H228

☐ 0   ☐ 1   ☐ 2   ☐ 3   ☐ 4

Supervisor/instructor signature _____ Date _____

Student/intern information:

Name _____ _[handwritten]_ _____ Date _[handwritten]_ ____ Class _[handwritten]_ _____

Vehicle used for this activity:

Year _[handwritten]_ ____ Make _[handwritten]_ _____ Model _[handwritten]_ _____

Odometer _[handwritten]_ _____ VIN _[handwritten]_ _____

Time off_____

Time on_____

Total time_____

▶ TASK Disable and enable supplemental restraint system (SRS) in accordance with manufacturers' procedures.

NATEF 4A1.5

CDX Tasksheet Number: H230

1. On a vehicle equipped with SRS, reference the appropriate manufacturer's service information for the correct procedure to disable and enable the SRS.
   a. List procedure and all safety requirements when disabling and enabling the SRS.

   [handwritten]

2. Have your instructor approve the above procedure.
   Supervisor/instructor's initials: _____

3. Following all procedures and safety requirements, disable the SRS. Have your instructor verify that it is disabled. Supervisor/instructor's initials: _[handwritten]_

4. Following the specified procedure, enable the SRS.
   a. Within manufacturerer's specifications: Yes: _____ No: _____
   b. If no, list the necessary actions or corrections:

   [handwritten]

5. Discuss the findings with instructor.

Performance Rating

CDX Tasksheet Number: H230

☐ 0   ☐ 1   ☐ 2   ☐ 3   ☐ 4

Supervisor/instructor signature _[handwritten]_ _____ Date_____

Student/intern information:

Name_____ Date_____ Class_____

Vehicle used for this activity:

Year_____ Make_____ Model_____

Odometer_____ VIN _____

▶ **TASK** Remove the steering wheel (includes steering wheels equipped with electrical/electronic controls and components); install and center the steering wheel. Inspect, test, replace and calibrate steering angle sensor.   NATEF 4A1.4

Time off_____

Time on_____

Total time_____

CDX Tasksheet Number: H229

1. Prepare the vehicle for steering wheel removal and installation.

2. Ensure that the vehicle is parked on level ground.

3. Run a string line from the rear wheel assemblies to the front wheels, ensuring that the string line aligns with each wheel.

4. If they do not align, turn the steering wheel until the front wheels are aligned with the rear wheels.

5. Check the position of the steering wheel from center: Center: _____ Off center: _____

6. Within manufacturer's specifications: Yes: _____ No: _____
   a. If not within manufacturer's specifications, record the procedure to bring the wheels into correct alignment.

   _____
   _____
   _____

7. Consult the manufacturer's service information and prepare for the steering wheel removal by removing the electrical components and air bag.

   Note: When removing an air bag, consult manufacturer guidelines for the recommended disarming procedure and time frame of battery disconnection before performing any operation.

8. Remove the steering wheel retaining nut from the steering shaft.

9. Once all electrical components are removed, obtain and install the appropriate steering wheel puller and safely remove the steering wheel.

10. With the steering wheel off, inspect the column splines for any imperfections.
    a. Condition of splines: Good: _____ Bad: _____

11. Have your instructor verify removal and your answers.
    Supervisor/instructor's initials: _____

© 2017 Jones & Bartlett Learning, LLC, an Ascend Learning Company

12. Determine any necessary actions:

_____

_____

13. Reinstall the steering wheel being mindful of its center position.

14. Install and torque the steering wheel retaining nut to manufacturer torque specification.
    a. Manufacturer torque specification: _____ ft-lb (Nm)
    b. Actual torque applied: _____ ft-lb (Nm)

15. Reinstall electrical components and air bag assemblies as per the manufacturer's service information.

16. Once all necessary components are on and secure, install the manufacturer accepted scan tool to the 16-pin ALDL connector under the dashboard.

17. Check for any steering angle sensor codes and consult the manufacturer's service information for information regarding the steering angle sensor!
    a. Codes present: Yes _____ No _____

        i.   Record code #1 _____
        ii. Record code #2 _____
        iii. Record code #3 _____

18. If codes are present, perform the manufacturer procedures to repair the problem. List your tests and results:

_____

_____

_____

19. Once the codes are repaired, reconnect the scan tool and clear the codes. Check for any returning codes.

    Note: Some manufacturer scan tools have calibration capabilities for minor adjustments once all critical mechanical adjustments have been made.

20. Discuss the findings with your instructor.

Performance Rating

CDX Tasksheet Number: H229

☐   ☐   ☐   ☐   ☐

0   1   2   3   4

Supervisor/instructor signature _____ Date_____

© 2017 Jones & Bartlett Learning, LLC, an Ascend Learning Company

Truck Steering-Suspension Systems: Steering Units 1

Student/intern information:

Name_____ Date_____ Class_____

Vehicle used for this activity:

Year_____ Make_____ Model_____

Odometer_____ VIN _____

Time off_____

Time on_____

Total time_____

Learning Objective / Task	CDX Tasksheet Number	2014 NATEF Priority Level	2014 NATEF Reference Number
• Identify causes of power steering system noise, steering binding, darting/oversteer, reduced wheel cut, steering wheel kick, pulling, nonrecovery, turning effort, looseness, hard steering, overheating, fluid leakage, and fluid aeration problems; determine needed action.	H231	P-1	4A2.1
• Determine recommended type of power steering fluid; check level and condition; determine needed action.	H232	P-1	4A2.2
• Flush and refill power steering system; purge air from system.	H233	P-2	4A2.3

Materials Required

- Vehicle with possible engine concern
- Vehicle manufacturer's service information
- Manufacturer-specific tools depending on the concern
- Vehicle-lifting equipment, if applicable

Some Safety Issues to Consider

- Diagnosis of this fault may require test driving the vehicle on the school grounds or on a hoist, both of which carry severe risks. Attempt this task only with full permission from your supervisor/instructor and follow all the guidelines exactly.
- Caution: If you are working in an area where there could be "brake dust" present (may contain asbestos, which has been determined to cause cancer when inhaled or ingested), ensure that you wear and use all OSHA-approved asbestos protective/removal equipment.
- Lifting equipment such as vehicle jacks and stands, vehicle hoists, and engine hoists are important tools that increase productivity and make the job easier. However, they can also cause severe injury or death if used improperly. Make sure you follow the manufacturer's operation procedures. Also make sure you have your supervisor's/instructor's permission to use any particular type of lifting equipment.
- Comply with personal and environmental safety practices associated with clothing; eye protection; hand tools; power equipment; proper ventilation; and the handling, storage, and disposal of chemicals/materials in accordance with federal, state, and local regulations.
- Always wear the correct protective eyewear and clothing, and use the appropriate safety equipment, as well as fender covers, seat protectors, and floor mat protectors.
- Make sure you understand and observe all legislative and personal safety procedures when carrying out practical assignments. If you are unsure of what these are, ask your supervisor/instructor.

Performance Standard

0–No exposure: No information or practice provided during the program; complete training required

1–Exposure only: General information provided with no practice time; close supervision needed; additional training required

2–Limited practice: Has practiced job during training program; additional training required to develop skill

3–Moderately skilled: Has performed job independently during training program; limited additional training may be required

4–Skilled: Can perform job independently with no additional training

Student/intern information:

Name_____ Date_____ Class_____

Vehicle used for this activity:

Year_____ Make_____ Model_____

Odometer_____ VIN _____

▶ **TASK** Identify causes of power steering system noise, steering binding, darting/oversteer, reduced wheel cut, steering wheel kick, pulling, nonrecovery, turning effort, looseness, hard steering, overheating, fluid leakage, and fluid aeration problems; determine needed action.

NATEF 4A2.1

Time off_____

Time on_____

Total time_____

CDX Tasksheet Number: H231

1. Reference the appropriate manufacturer's service information for the correct procedure to identify causes of power steering system noises.
   a. List the identified possible noise-producing locations/components and the procedure for diagnosing any abnormal noises:

   _____
   _____
   _____
   _____

2. Discuss the diagnostic procedures with instructor.

3. Following all procedures and safety requirements, carry out the diagnostic process:
   a. List your observations:

   _____
   _____
   _____

   b. Within manufacturer's specifications: Yes: _____ No: _____
   c. If no, list the necessary actions or corrections:

   _____
   _____
   _____

4. Reference the appropriate manufacturer's service information for the probable causes for the steering to bind or for darting/oversteering.
   a. List the identified probable causes for the steering to bind or for darting/oversteering:

   _____
   _____
   _____
   _____

5. Discuss the diagnostic/inspection procedures with instructor.

6. Following all procedures and safety requirements, carry out the diagnostic process.
   a. List your observations:

   _____
   _____
   _____

   b. Within manufacturer's specifications: Yes: _____ No: _____

c. If no, list the necessary actions or corrections:

_____

_____

7. Reference the appropriate manufacturer's service information for the probable causes for reduced wheel cut, steering wheel kick, pulling, and non-recovery.
   a. List the identified probable causes for reduced wheel cut, steering wheel kick, pulling, and non-recovery:

   _____

   _____

   _____

   _____

8. Discuss the diagnostic/inspection procedures with instructor.

9. Following all procedures and safety requirements, carry out the diagnostic process:
   a. List your observations:

   _____

   _____

   _____

   b. Within manufacturer's specifications: Yes: _____ No: _____
   c. If no, list the necessary actions or corrections:

   _____

   _____

10. Reference the appropriate manufacturer's service information for the procedure for inspecting and testing the turning effort, looseness, hard steering, overheating, fluid leakage, and fluid aeration problems.
    a. List the identified probable causes for looseness, hard steering, overheating, fluid leakage, and fluid aeration problems:

    _____

    _____

    _____

    _____

11. Discuss the diagnostic/inspection procedures with instructor.

12. Following all procedures and safety requirements, carry out the diagnostic process:
    a. List your observations:

    _____

    _____

    _____

    b. Within manufacturer's specifications: Yes: _____ No: _____
    c. If no, list the necessary actions or corrections:

    _____

    _____

13. Discuss the findings with instructor.

Performance Rating

CDX Tasksheet Number: H231

☐ 0   ☐ 1   ☐ 2   ☐ 3   ☐ 4

Supervisor/instructor signature _____ Date _____

© 2017 Jones & Bartlett Learning, LLC, an Ascend Learning Company

Student/intern information:

Name_____ Date_____ Class_____

Vehicle used for this activity:

Year_____ Make_____ Model_____

Odometer_____ VIN _____

▶ **TASK** Determine recommended type of power steering fluid; check level and condition; determine needed action.

NATEF 4A2.2

Time off_____

Time on_____

Total time_____

CDX Tasksheet Number: H232

1. Reference the appropriate manufacturer's service information to determine the recommended type and capacity of power steering fluid.
   a. Type of fluid: _____
   b. Capacity: _____

2. Check level and condition of power steering fluid:
   a. List your observations:

   _____
   _____
   _____

   b. Within manufacturer's specifications: Yes: _____ No: _____
   c. If no, list the necessary actions or corrections:

   _____
   _____
   _____

3. Discuss the findings with instructor.

Performance Rating

CDX Tasksheet Number: H232

☐ 0   ☐ 1   ☐ 2   ☐ 3   ☐ 4

Supervisor/instructor signature _____ Date_____

Student/intern information:

Name_____ Date_____ Class_____

Vehicle used for this activity:

Year_____ Make_____ Model_____

Odometer_____ VIN _____

▶ **TASK** Flush and refill power steering system; purge air from system.   NATEF 4A2.3

CDX Tasksheet Number: H233

Time off_____

Time on_____

Total time_____

1. Reference the appropriate manufacturer's service information for the procedure for flushing and refilling the power steering system and for purging air from the system.
   a. List the procedure for flushing and refilling the power steering system and for purging air from the system:

   _____
   _____
   _____
   _____

2. Discuss the procedures with instructor.

3. Following all procedures and safety requirements, flush and refill the power steering system and purge air from the system:
   a. Did the process meet manufacturer's specifications: Yes: _____ No: _____
   b. If no, list the necessary actions or corrections:

   _____
   _____
   _____
   _____

4. Discuss the findings with instructor.

Performance Rating

CDX Tasksheet Number: H233

☐ 0   ☐ 1   ☐ 2   ☐ 3   ☐ 4

Supervisor/instructor signature _____ Date_____

Truck Steering-Suspension Systems:
Steering Units 2

Student/intern information:

Name_____ Date_____ Class_____

Vehicle used for this activity:

Year_____ Make_____ Model_____

Odometer_____ VIN _____

© 2017 Jones & Bartlett Learning, LLC, an Ascend Learning Company

Learning Objective / Task	CDX Tasksheet Number	2014 NATEF Priority Level	2014 NATEF Reference Number
• Perform power steering system pressure, temperature, and flow tests; determine needed action.	H234	P-3	4A2.4
• Inspect, service, or replace power steering reservoir including filter, seals, and gaskets.	H235	P-2	4A2.5
• Inspect power steering pump drive gear and coupling; replace as needed.	H236	P-3	4A2.6
• Inspect, adjust, or replace power steering pump, mountings, and brackets.	H237	P-3	4A2.7

Time off_____

Time on_____

Total time_____

Materials Required
- Vehicle with possible steering concern
- Vehicle manufacturer's service information
- Manufacturer-specific tools depending on the concern
- Vehicle-lifting equipment, if applicable

Some Safety Issues to Consider
- Diagnosis of this fault may require test driving the vehicle on the school grounds or on a hoist, both of which carry severe risks. Attempt this task only with full permission from your supervisor/instructor and follow all the guidelines exactly.
- Caution: If you are working in an area where there could be "brake dust" present (may contain asbestos, which has been determined to cause cancer when inhaled or ingested), ensure that you wear and use all OSHA-approved asbestos protective/removal equipment.
- Lifting equipment such as vehicle jacks and stands, vehicle hoists, and engine hoists are important tools that increase productivity and make the job easier. However, they can also cause severe injury or death if used improperly. Make sure you follow the manufacturer's operation procedures. Also make sure you have your supervisor's/instructor's permission to use any particular type of lifting equipment.
- Comply with personal and environmental safety practices associated with clothing; eye protection; hand tools; power equipment; proper ventilation; and the handling, storage, and disposal of chemicals/materials in accordance with federal, state, and local regulations.
- Always wear the correct protective eyewear and clothing, and use the appropriate safety equipment, as well as fender covers, seat protectors, and floor mat protectors.
- Make sure you understand and observe all legislative and personal safety procedures when carrying out practical assignments. If you are unsure of what these are, ask your supervisor/instructor.

Performance Standard

0—No exposure: No information or practice provided during the program; complete training required

1—Exposure only: General information provided with no practice time; close supervision needed; additional training required

2—Limited practice: Has practiced job during training program; additional training required to develop skill

3—Moderately skilled: Has performed job independently during training program; limited additional training may be required

4—Skilled: Can perform job independently with no additional training

Student/intern information:

Name_____ Date_____ Class_____

Vehicle used for this activity:

Year_____ Make_____ Model_____

Odometer_____ VIN _____

NATEF 4A2.4

Time off_____
Time on_____
Total time_____

CDX Tasksheet Number: H234

1. Reference the appropriate manufacturer's service information for the correct procedure to perform power steering system pressure, temperature, and flow tests.
    a. List the steps involved to perform power steering system pressure, temperature, and flow tests:

    _____
    _____
    _____
    _____

    Note: This is a high pressure system. Be mindful of all safety requirements when working with hydraulics.

2. Discuss the steps involved to perform power steering system pressure, temperature, and flow tests with your instructor.

3. Following all procedures and safety requirements, perform power steering system pressure, temperature, and flow tests:
    a. System pressure: _____
    b. Max pressure: _____
    c. Max flow: _____
    d. Operating temperature: _____
    e. Within manufacturer's specifications: Yes: _____ No: _____
    f. If no, list the necessary actions or corrections:

    _____
    _____
    _____

4. Discuss the findings with instructor.

Performance Rating

CDX Tasksheet Number: H234

☐   ☐   ☐   ☐   ☐
0   1   2   3   4

Supervisor/instructor signature _____ Date_____

Student/intern information:

Name_____ Date_____ Class_____

Vehicle used for this activity:

Year_____ Make_____ Model_____

Odometer_____ VIN _____

▶ TASK Inspect, service, or replace power steering reservoir including filter, seals, and gaskets.

NATEF 4A2.5

Time off_____

Time on_____

Total time_____

CDX Tasksheet Number: H235

1. Reference the appropriate manufacturer's service information for the steps involved in inspecting, servicing, or replacing the power steering reservoir including filter, seals, and gaskets.
   a. List the steps involved in inspecting, servicing, or replacing the power steering reservoir including filter, seals, and gaskets.

   _____
   _____
   _____
   _____

2. Following all procedures and safety requirements, carry out this process:
   a. List your observations:

   _____
   _____
   _____
   _____

   b. Within manufacturer's specifications: Yes: _____ No: _____
   c. If no, list the necessary actions or corrections:

   _____
   _____

3. Discuss the findings with instructor.

Performance Rating

CDX Tasksheet Number: H235

☐	☐	☐	☐	☐
0	1	2	3	4

Supervisor/instructor signature _____ Date_____

Student/intern information:

Name_____ Date_____ Class_____

Vehicle used for this activity:

Year_____ Make_____ Model_____

Odometer_____ VIN _____

▶ TASK Inspect, power steering pump drive gear and coupling; replace as needed. NATEF 4A2.6

CDX Tasksheet Number: H236

1. Reference the appropriate manufacturer's service information for the steps involved in inspecting, removing, and replacing the power steering pump drive gear and coupling.
   a. List the steps involved in inspecting the power steering pump drive gear and coupling:

   _____
   _____
   _____
   _____

2. If directed by your instructor and following the procedures outlined, remove the power steering pump drive gear and coupling.

3. Inspect the steering pump drive gear and coupling. List your observations:

   _____
   _____
   _____

4. Have your instructor verify removal and your answers.
   Supervisor/instructor's initials: _____

5. Following the specified procedure, reinstall the power steering pump drive gear and coupling. List your observations:

   _____
   _____
   _____

6. Readjust the power steering drive belts, if equipped:
   a. Manufacturer's specifications: _____ ft-lb (Nm)
   b. Final tension setting: _____ ft-lb (Nm)

7. Have your instructor inspect and assess your workmanship.
   a. Meets manufacturer's specifications: Yes: _____ No: _____

8. Discuss the findings with instructor.

Performance Rating

CDX Tasksheet Number: H236

☐ 0   ☐ 1   ☐ 2   ☐ 3   ☐ 4

Supervisor/instructor signature _____ Date_____

Time off_____

Time on_____

Total time_____

© 2017 Jones & Bartlett Learning, LLC, an Ascend Learning Company

Truck Steering-Suspension Systems   31

Name_____ Date_____ Class_____

Vehicle used for this activity:

Year_____ Make_____ Model_____

Odometer_____ VIN _____

▶ TASK Inspect, adjust, or replace power steering pump, mountings, and brackets.

NATEF 4A2.7

Time off_____

Time on_____

Total time_____

CDX Tasksheet Number: H237

1. Reference the appropriate manufacturer's service information for the correct procedure to inspect the power steering pump, mountings, and brackets.
   a. List the steps involved to perform inspection of the power steering pump, mountings, and brackets:

   _____
   _____
   _____
   _____

2. Following all procedures and safety requirements, perform an inspection of the power steering pump:
   a. List your observations:

   _____
   _____
   _____

   b. Within manufacturer's specifications: Yes: _____ No: _____
   c. If no, list the necessary actions or corrections:

   _____

3. Following all procedures and safety requirements, perform an inspection of the power steering pump mountings and brackets:
   a. List your observations:

   _____
   _____
   _____

   b. Within manufacturer's specifications: Yes: _____ No: _____
   c. If no, list the necessary actions or corrections:

   _____

4. Discuss the findings with instructor.

Performance Rating

CDX Tasksheet Number: H237

☐   ☐   ☐   ☐   ☐

0   1   2   3   4

Supervisor/instructor signature _____ Date_____

Truck Steering-Suspension Systems: Steering Units 3

Student/intern information:

Name_____ Date_____ Class_____

Vehicle used for this activity:

Year_____ Make_____ Model_____

Odometer_____ VIN _____

Learning Objective / Task	CDX Tasksheet Number	2014 NATEF Priority Level	2014 NATEF Reference Number
• Inspect and replace power steering system cooler, lines, hoses, clamps/mountings, hose routings, and fittings.	H238	P-2	4A2.8
• Inspect, adjust, repair, or replace integral type power steering gear(s) (single and/or dual) and mountings.	H239	P-2	4A2.9

Time off_____

Time on_____

Total time_____

Materials Required

- Vehicle with possible steering concern
- Vehicle manufacturer's service information
- Manufacturer-specific tools depending on the concern
- Vehicle-lifting equipment, if applicable

Some Safety Issues to Consider

- Diagnosis of this fault may require test driving the vehicle on the school grounds or on a hoist, both of which carry severe risks. Attempt this task only with full permission from your supervisor/instructor and follow all the guidelines exactly.
- Caution: If you are working in an area where there could be "brake dust" present (may contain asbestos, which has been determined to cause cancer when inhaled or ingested), ensure that you wear and use all OSHA-approved asbestos protective/removal equipment.
- Lifting equipment such as vehicle jacks and stands, vehicle hoists, and engine hoists are important tools that increase productivity and make the job easier. However, they can also cause severe injury or death if used improperly. Make sure you follow the manufacturer's operation procedures. Also make sure you have your supervisor's/instructor's permission to use any particular type of lifting equipment.
- Comply with personal and environmental safety practices associated with clothing; eye protection; hand tools; power equipment; proper ventilation; and the handling, storage, and disposal of chemicals/materials in accordance with federal, state, and local regulations.
- Always wear the correct protective eyewear and clothing, and use the appropriate safety equipment, as well as fender covers, seat protectors, and floor mat protectors.
- Make sure you understand and observe all legislative and personal safety procedures when carrying out practical assignments. If you are unsure of what these are, ask your supervisor/instructor.

Performance Standard

0—No exposure: No information or practice provided during the program; complete training required

1—Exposure only: General information provided with no practice time; close supervision needed; additional training required

2—Limited practice: Has practiced job during training program; additional training required to develop skill

3—Moderately skilled: Has performed job independently during training program; limited additional training may be required

4—Skilled: Can perform job independently with no additional training

Student/intern information:

Name_____ Date_____ Class_____

Vehicle used for this activity:

Year_____ Make_____ Model_____

Odometer_____ VIN _____

▶ **TASK** Inspect and replace power steering system cooler, lines, hoses, clamps/mountings, hose routings, and fittings.   NATEF 4A2.8

Time off_____

Time on_____

Total time_____

CDX Tasksheet Number: H238

1. Reference the appropriate manufacturer's service information for the steps involved in inspecting and replacing the power steering system cooler, lines, hoses, clamps/mountings, hose routings, and fittings.
   a. List the steps involved in inspecting, servicing, and replacing the power steering system cooler, lines, hoses, clamps/mountings, hose routings, and fittings.

   _____
   _____
   _____
   _____

2. Following all procedures and safety requirements, carry out the inspection of the power steering system cooler:
   a. List your observations:

   _____
   _____
   _____

   b. Within manufacturer's specifications: Yes: _____ No: _____
   c. If no, list the necessary actions or corrections:

   _____
   _____
   _____

3. Following all procedures and safety requirements, carry out the replacement of the power steering system cooler:
   a. Drain the power steering reservoir oil and dispose of the waste in accordance with environmental legislation.
      i. Waste oil disposed of in accordance with environmental legislation: Yes: _____ No: _____
   b. Disconnect cooler lines and collect any leaking oil.
   c. Remove all mounting bolts; remove power steering oil cooler, and inspect.
      i. List your observations:

   _____
   _____
   _____

      ii. Within manufacturer's specifications: Yes: _____ No: _____
      iii. If no, replace the cooler.
      iv. Have instructor verify removal of the power steering oil cooler and your answers. Supervisor/instructor's initials: _____

© 2017 Jones & Bartlett Learning, LLC, an Ascend Learning Company

      d. Bolt new cooler in position and tension the mounting bolts in accordance with manufacturer's specification.
          i. Manufacturer's specifications for power steering cooler mounting bolts: _____ ft-lb (Nm)
          ii. Final tension setting: _____ ft-lb (Nm)

4. Check cooler hose condition:
    a. List your observations:

    _____
    _____
    _____

    b. Within manufacturer's specifications: Yes: _____ No: _____
    c. If no, replace the cooler hose(s) and clamps.

5. Check cooler hose routing:
    a. List your observations:

    _____
    _____
    _____

    b. Within manufacturer's specifications: Yes: _____ No: _____
    c. If no, replace the cooler hose(s) or re-route.

6. Discuss the findings with instructor.

Performance Rating

CDX Tasksheet Number: H238

☐   ☐   ☐   ☐   ☐
0   1   2   3   4

Supervisor/instructor signature _____ Date_____

Name_____ Date_____ Class_____

Vehicle used for this activity:

Year_____ Make_____ Model_____

Odometer_____ VIN _____

▶ **TASK** Inspect, adjust, repair, or replace integral type power steering gear(s) (single and/or dual) and mountings. NATEF 4A2.9

Time off_____

Time on_____

Total time_____

CDX Tasksheet Number: H239

1. Identify the make and model of the instructor designated integral type power steering linkage fitted to the vehicle being assigned to you.

2. Inspect integral type power steering gear for:
    a. Leaks
        i. List your observations:

        _____
        _____
        _____

        ii. If leaks are present, research all information necessary to repair the steering gear or replace it. List any necessary actions:

        _____
        _____

3. Check for proper alignment of pump and belts, if mounted.
    a. List your observations:

        _____
        _____
        _____

    b. Check to see that the pump mounting bolts are secure and the pulley is not wobbling or bent.
    c. Are mounting bolts tight and is the pulley in satisfactory shape? Yes: _____ No: _____
    d. If no, research all information necessary to repair, align and replace the pump belts to factory specifications. List the procedure:

        _____
        _____
        _____

4. Check all pump brackets for tightness and proper components.
    a. Are the components tight and are the proper components used? Yes: _____ No: _____
    b. If no, research all information including parts manuals for the correct mounting parts and proper torque specifications. List your observations:

        _____
        _____
        _____

5. Check for proper mounting of the steering pump to the block, if gear driven.
    a. List your observations:

    _____
    _____
    _____

    b. Check the steering pump for proper mounting of the gear flange to the block. List your observations:

    _____
    _____
    _____

    c. If replacing the pump, ensure that a new gasket is installed between the pump flange and the block.
    d. Check mounting bolts for tightness and record torque necessary to attach the pump to the block.
        i. Bolt torque required _____ft-lb (Nm)

6. Discuss the findings with instructor.

Performance Rating

CDX Tasksheet Number: H239

☐   ☐   ☐   ☐   ☐

0   1   2   3   4

Supervisor/instructor signature _____ Date_____

Truck Steering-Suspension Systems: Steering Linkage

Student/intern information:

Name_____ Date_____ Class_____

Vehicle used for this activity:

Year_____ Make_____ Model_____

Odometer_____ VIN _____

Time off_____

Time on_____

Total time_____

Learning Objective / Task	CDX Tasksheet Number	2014 NATEF Priority Level	2014 NATEF Reference Number
• Inspect and align pitman arm; replace as needed.	H240	P-1	4A3.1
• Check and adjust steering (wheel) stops; verify relief pressures.	H241	P-1	4A3.2
• Inspect and lubricate steering components.	H242	P-1	4A3.3

Materials Required

- Vehicle with possible steering/suspension concern
- Vehicle manufacturer's service information
- Manufacturer-specific tools depending on the concern
- Vehicle-lifting equipment, if applicable

Some Safety Issues to Consider

- Diagnosis of this fault may require test driving the vehicle on the school grounds or on a hoist, both of which carry severe risks. Attempt this task only with full permission from your supervisor/instructor and follow all the guidelines exactly.
- Caution: If you are working in an area where there could be "brake dust" present (may contain asbestos, which has been determined to cause cancer when inhaled or ingested), ensure that you wear and use all OSHA-approved asbestos protective/removal equipment.
- Lifting equipment such as vehicle jacks and stands, vehicle hoists, and engine hoists are important tools that increase productivity and make the job easier. However, they can also cause severe injury or death if used improperly. Make sure you follow the manufacturer's operation procedures. Also make sure you have your supervisor's/instructor's permission to use any particular type of lifting equipment.
- Comply with personal and environmental safety practices associated with clothing; eye protection; hand tools; power equipment; proper ventilation; and the handling, storage, and disposal of chemicals/materials in accordance with federal, state, and local regulations.
- Always wear the correct protective eyewear and clothing, and use the appropriate safety equipment, as well as fender covers, seat protectors, and floor mat protectors.
- Make sure you understand and observe all legislative and personal safety procedures when carrying out practical assignments. If you are unsure of what these are, ask your supervisor/instructor.

Performance Standard

0—No exposure: No information or practice provided during the program; complete training required

1—Exposure only: General information provided with no practice time; close supervision needed; additional training required

2—Limited practice: Has practiced job during training program; additional training required to develop skill

3—Moderately skilled: Has performed job independently during training program; limited additional training may be required

4—Skilled: Can perform job independently with no additional training

▶ **TASK** Inspect and align pitman arm; replace as needed.   NATEF 4A3.1

CDX Tasksheet Number: H240

1. Reference the appropriate manufacturer's service information for the correct procedure to inspect, align, and replace the pitman arm. List the steps:

    _____
    _____
    _____

2. Following all procedures and safety requirements, carry out the inspection and alignment of the pitman arm.
    a. List your observations:

        _____
        _____
        _____

    b. Within manufacturer's specifications: Yes: _____ No: _____
    c. If no, list the necessary actions or corrections:

        _____
        _____
        _____

3. Following all procedures and safety requirements, remove the worn pitman arm.
    a. List your observations:

        _____
        _____
        _____

4. Have your instructor verify removal of the pitman arm.
    Supervisor/instructor's initials: _____

5. Following the specified procedure, replace the pitman arm and correctly torque the pitman arm nut.
    a. List your observations:

        _____
        _____
        _____

b. Manufacturer's specifications: _____ ft-lb (Nm)

c. Final tension setting: _____ ft-lb (Nm)

6. Discuss the findings with instructor.

Performance Rating

CDX Tasksheet Number: H240

☐   ☐   ☐   ☐   ☐

0   1   2   3   4

Supervisor/instructor signature _____ Date_____

Student/intern information:

Name_____ Date_____ Class_____

Vehicle used for this activity:

Year_____ Make_____ Model_____

Odometer_____ VIN _____

▶ **TASK** Check and adjust steering (wheel) stops; verify relief pressures._____ NATEF 4A3.2

CDX Tasksheet Number: H241

Time off_____

Time on_____

Total time_____

1. Reference the appropriate manufacturer's service information for the correct procedure for adjustment of the vehicle's wheel stops.
   a. Manufacturer's recommended adjustment procedure:

   _____
   _____
   _____
   _____

2. Check and adjust wheel stops.
   a. Actual measurement: _____
   b. Within manufacturer's specifications: Yes: _____ No: _____
   c. If no, adjust the wheel stops to the manufacturer's specifications.
   d. Final measurement(s): Left side: _____ Right side: _____

3. Reference the appropriate service information for the correct procedure to test the steering system relief pressure.
   a. Specified relief pressure: _____ psi (kPa)

4. Connect the appropriate pressure gauge and test the relief pressure.
   a. List the measured relief pressure: _____ psi (kPa)
   b. Does this meet specifications: Yes: _____ No: _____
   c. Determine any necessary actions:

   _____
   _____
   _____

5. Discuss the findings with your instructor.

Performance Rating

CDX Tasksheet Number: H241

☐ 0   ☐ 1   ☐ 2   ☐ 3   ☐ 4

Supervisor/instructor signature _____ Date_____

Student/intern information:

Name_____ Date_____ Class_____

Vehicle used for this activity:

Year_____ Make_____ Model_____

Odometer_____ VIN _____

▶ **TASK** Inspect and lubricate steering components. NATEF 4A3.3

Time off_____

Time on_____

Total time_____

CDX Tasksheet Number: H242

1. Research manufacturer's procedures for lubrication of all steering components and types of lubricants to be used.
   a. Lubricant type:

   _____
   _____
   _____

   Note: Follow manufacturer's guidelines for lubrication intervals.

   b. Intervals recommended:

   _____
   _____
   _____

2. Inspect the steering components. List your observations:

   _____
   _____
   _____
   _____

3. Lubricate the steering components. List each component you lubricated:

   _____
   _____
   _____
   _____

4. Discuss your findings with the instructor.

Performance Rating

CDX Tasksheet Number: H242

☐ 0   ☐ 1   ☐ 2   ☐ 3   ☐ 4

Supervisor/instructor signature _____ Date_____

Truck Steering-Suspension Systems:
Suspension Systems 1

Student/intern information:

Name_____ Date_____ Class_____

Vehicle used for this activity:

Year_____ Make_____ Model_____

Odometer_____ VIN _____

Learning Objective / Task	CDX Tasksheet Number	2014 NATEF Priority Level	2014 NATEF Reference Number
• Inspect front axles and attaching hardware; determine needed action.	H243	P-1	4B1
• Inspect and service kingpins, steering knuckle bushings, locks, bearings, seals, and covers; determine needed action.	H244	P-1	4B2
• Inspect shock absorbers, bushings, brackets, and mounts; replace as needed.	H245	P-1	4B3
• Inspect leaf springs, center bolts, clips, pins and bushings, shackles, Ubolts, insulators, brackets, and mounts; determine needed action.	H246	P-1	4B4

Time off_____

Time on_____

Total time_____

Materials Required

- Vehicle with possible steering/suspension concern
- Vehicle manufacturer's service information
- Manufacturer-specific tools depending on the concern
- Vehicle-lifting equipment, if applicable

Some Safety Issues to Consider

- Diagnosis of this fault may require test driving the vehicle on the school grounds or on a hoist, both of which carry severe risks. Attempt this task only with full permission from your supervisor/instructor and follow all the guidelines exactly.
- Caution: If you are working in an area where there could be "brake dust" present (may contain asbestos, which has been determined to cause cancer when inhaled or ingested), ensure that you wear and use all OSHA-approved asbestos protective/removal equipment.
- Lifting equipment such as vehicle jacks and stands, vehicle hoists, and engine hoists are important tools that increase productivity and make the job easier. However, they can also cause severe injury or death if used improperly. Make sure you follow the manufacturer's operation procedures. Also make sure you have your supervisor's/instructor's permission to use any particular type of lifting equipment.
- Comply with personal and environmental safety practices associated with clothing; eye protection; hand tools; power equipment; proper ventilation; and the handling, storage, and disposal of chemicals/materials in accordance with federal, state, and local regulations.
- Always wear the correct protective eyewear and clothing, and use the appropriate safety equipment, as well as fender covers, seat protectors, and floor mat protectors.
- Make sure you understand and observe all legislative and personal safety procedures when carrying out practical assignments. If you are unsure of what these are, ask your supervisor/instructor.

Performance Standard

0–No exposure: No information or practice provided during the program; complete training required

1–Exposure only: General information provided with no practice time; close supervision needed; additional training required

2–Limited practice: Has practiced job during training program; additional training required to develop skill

3–Moderately skilled: Has performed job independently during training program; limited additional training may be required

4–Skilled: Can perform job independently with no additional training

Student/intern information:

Name_____ Date_____ Class_____

Vehicle used for this activity:

Year_____ Make_____ Model_____

Odometer_____ VIN _____

▶ **TASK** Inspect front axles and attaching hardware; determine needed action.　　NATEF 4B1

Time off_____

Time on_____

Total time_____

CDX Tasksheet Number: H243

1. Reference the appropriate manufacturer's service information for the correct procedure to inspect front axles, and hardware; list the main steps:

   _____
   _____
   _____

   Note: Some states have strict guidelines about the tolerances of front end components. Consult the state guidelines for proper specifications.

2. Following all procedures and safety requirements, carry out the inspection of axles and attaching hardware
   a. List your observations:

   _____
   _____
   _____
   _____

   b. Within manufacturer's specifications: Yes: _____ No: _____
   c. If no, list the necessary actions or corrections:

   _____
   _____
   _____

3. Discuss the findings with instructor.

Performance Rating

CDX Tasksheet Number: H243

☐　　　　☐　　　　☐　　　　☐　　　　☐
0　　　　1　　　　2　　　　3　　　　4

Supervisor/instructor signature _____ Date_____

© 2017 Jones & Bartlett Learning, LLC, an Ascend Learning Company

Student/intern information:

Name_____ Date_____ Class_____

Vehicle used for this activity:

Year_____ Make_____ Model_____

Odometer_____ VIN _____

▶ TASK Inspect and service kingpins, steering knuckle bushings, locks, bearings, seals, and covers; determine needed action.

NATEF 4B2

Time off_____

Time on_____

Total time_____

CDX Tasksheet Number: H244

1. Reference the appropriate manufacturer's service information for the correct procedure to inspect and service the kingpin, steering knuckle bushings, locks, bearings, seals, and covers; list any specifications:

   _____
   _____
   _____

2. Following all procedures and safety requirements, carry out the inspection of the kingpin, steering knuckle bushings, locks, bearings, seals, and covers:
   a. Prepare the vehicle; chock the rear wheels.
   b. As specified by the manufacturer, place the jack under the vehicle in the position to check the driver's side kingpin functionality.
   c. Test the kingpin for wear.
      i. Actual amount of movement present: _____ thousands/inches
   d. Within manufacturer's specifications: Yes: _____ No: _____
   e. If no, list the necessary actions or corrections:

      _____
      _____
      _____

   f. As specified by the manufacturer, place the jack under the vehicle in the position to check the passenger's side kingpin functionality.
   g. Test the kingpin for wear.
      i. Actual amount of movement present: _____ thousands/inches
   h. Within manufacturer's specifications: Yes: _____ No: _____
   i. If no, list the necessary actions or corrections:

      _____
      _____
      _____

3. If instructed by your instructor, follow the specified procedure to disassemble the kingpin assembly on one side of the vehicle.
    a. Inspect the components and list your observations:

    _____
    _____
    _____
    _____

    b. Determine any necessary actions:

    _____
    _____
    _____

    c. Have your instructor verify disassembly and your answers.
        Supervisor/instructor's initials: _____

4. Following the specified procedure, reassemble the kingpin assembly.
    a. List any difficulties you encountered in performing this task:

    _____
    _____
    _____

5. Discuss the findings with instructor.

Performance Rating

CDX Tasksheet Number: H244

☐ 0   ☐ 1   ☐ 2   ☐ 3   ☐ 4

Supervisor/instructor signature _____ Date_____

Student/intern information:

Name_____ Date_____ Class_____

Vehicle used for this activity:

Year_____ Make_____ Model_____

Odometer_____ VIN _____

▶ TASK Inspect shock absorbers, bushings, brackets, and mounts; replace as needed.

NATEF 4B3

Time off_____

Time on_____

Total time_____

CDX Tasksheet Number: H245

1. Reference the appropriate manufacturer's service information for the correct procedure to inspect the shock absorbers, bushings, brackets, and mounts; list any specifications:

   _____
   _____
   _____

2. Following all procedures and safety requirements, inspect the shock absorbers, bushings, brackets, and mounts.
   a. Driver's side shock absorbers, bushings, brackets, and mounts:
      i. List your observations:

      _____
      _____
      _____

      ii. Within manufacturer's specifications: Yes: _____ No: _____
      iii. If no, list the necessary actions or corrections:

      _____
      _____
      _____

   b. Passenger's side shock absorbers, bushings, brackets, and mounts:
      i. List your observations:

      _____
      _____
      _____

      ii. Within manufacturer's specifications: Yes: _____ No: _____
      iii. If no, list the necessary actions or corrections:

      _____
      _____
      _____

3. If instructed by your instructor, remove a shock absorber and bushings following the specified procedure. List your observations:

_____

_____

    a. Have your instructor verify removal and your answers.
       Supervisor/instructor's initials: _____

4. Following the specified procedure, replace the shock absorber and bushings. List your observations:

_____

_____

5. Discuss the findings with instructor.

Performance Rating

CDX Tasksheet Number: H245

☐   ☐   ☐   ☐   ☐

0   1   2   3   4

Supervisor/instructor signature _____ Date_____

Name_____ Date_____ Class_____

Vehicle used for this activity:

Year_____ Make_____ Model_____

Odometer_____ VIN _____

▶ **TASK** Inspect leaf springs, center bolts, clips, pins and bushings, shackles, u-bolts, insulators, brackets, and mounts; determine needed action. _____ NATEF 4B4

Time off_____

Time on_____

Total time_____

CDX Tasksheet Number: H246

1. Reference the appropriate manufacturer's service information for the correct procedure to inspect the leaf springs, center bolts, clips, eye bolts and bushings, shackles, slippers, insulators, brackets, and mounts; list any specifications:

    _____
    _____
    _____

2. Following all procedures and safety requirements, carry out the inspection of the leaf springs.
    a. Prepare the vehicle; chock the rear wheels.
    b. Inspect the spring packs. Identify the condition in table below:

Driver's Side Spring Pack		Passenger's Side Spring Pack	
Number the spring leaves from top to bottom:			
Leaf spring number	Serviceable (S) Non-serviceable (NS)	Leaf spring number	Serviceable (S) Non-serviceable (NS)
1			
2			
3			
4			
5			
6			
7			
8			
9			
10			

    c. Within manufacturer's specifications: Yes: _____ No: _____
    d. If no, list the necessary actions or corrections:

    _____
    _____
    _____

3. Following all procedures and safety requirements, carry out the inspection of the center bolts.
    a. Prepare the vehicle; chock the rear wheels.
    b. Inspect the center bolts:
        i. List your observations:

        _____
        _____

ii. Within manufacturer's specifications: Yes: _____ No: _____

iii. If no, list the necessary actions or corrections:

_____

_____

_____

4. Following all procedures and safety requirements, carry out the inspection of the clips.
   a. Prepare the vehicle; chock the rear wheels.
   b. Inspect the clips:
      i. List your observations:

_____

_____

      ii. Within manufacturer's specifications: Yes: _____ No: _____

      iii. If no, list the necessary actions or corrections:

_____

_____

_____

5. Following all procedures and safety requirements, carry out the inspection of the pins and bushings.
   a. Prepare the vehicle; chock the rear wheels.
   b. Inspect the spring pins and bushings:
      i. List your observations:

_____

_____

      ii. Within manufacturer's specifications: Yes: _____ No: _____

      iii. If no, list the necessary actions or corrections:

_____

_____

_____

6. Following all procedures and safety requirements, carry out the inspection of the shackles, u-bolts, insulators, brackets, and mounts.
   a. Prepare the vehicle; chock the rear wheels.
   b. Inspect the spring shackles, u-bolts, insulators, brackets, and mounts:
      i. List your observations:

_____

_____

      ii. Within manufacturer's specifications: Yes: _____ No: _____

      iii. If no, list the necessary actions or corrections:

_____

_____

_____

7. Discuss the findings with instructor.

Performance Rating

CDX Tasksheet Number: H246

☐   ☐   ☐   ☐   ☐

0   1   2   3   4

Supervisor/instructor signature _____ Date_____

Truck Steering-Suspension Systems: Suspension Systems 2

Student/intern information:

Name_____ Date_____ Class_____

Vehicle used for this activity:

Year_____ Make_____ Model_____

Odometer_____ VIN _____

Learning Objective / Task	CDX Tasksheet Number	2014 NATEF Priority Level	2014 NATEF Reference Number
• Inspect axle aligning devices such as radius rods, track bars, stabilizer bars, torque arms, related bushings, mounts, shims, and cams; determine needed action.	H247	P-1	4B5
• Inspect tandem suspension equalizer components; determine needed action.	H248	P-3	4B6
• Inspect and test air suspension pressure regulator and height control valves, lines, hoses, dump valves, and fittings; adjust, repair or replace as needed.	H249	P-1	4B7

Time off_____

Time on_____

Total time_____

Materials Required

- Vehicle with possible steering/suspension concern
- Vehicle manufacturer's service information
- Manufacturer-specific tools depending on the concern
- Vehicle-lifting equipment, if applicable

Some Safety Issues to Consider

- Diagnosis of this fault may require test driving the vehicle on the school grounds or on a hoist, both of which carry severe risks. Attempt this task only with full permission from your supervisor/instructor and follow all the guidelines exactly.
- Caution: If you are working in an area where there could be "brake dust" present (may contain asbestos, which has been determined to cause cancer when inhaled or ingested), ensure that you wear and use all OSHA-approved asbestos protective/removal equipment.
- Lifting equipment such as vehicle jacks and stands, vehicle hoists, and engine hoists are important tools that increase productivity and make the job easier. However, they can also cause severe injury or death if used improperly. Make sure you follow the manufacturer's operation procedures. Also make sure you have your supervisor's/instructor's permission to use any particular type of lifting equipment.
- Comply with personal and environmental safety practices associated with clothing; eye protection; hand tools; power equipment; proper ventilation; and the handling, storage, and disposal of chemicals/materials in accordance with federal, state, and local regulations.
- Always wear the correct protective eyewear and clothing, and use the appropriate safety equipment, as well as fender covers, seat protectors, and floor mat protectors.
- Make sure you understand and observe all legislative and personal safety procedures when carrying out practical assignments. If you are unsure of what these are, ask your supervisor/instructor.

Performance Standard

0—No exposure: No information or practice provided during the program; complete training required

1—Exposure only: General information provided with no practice time; close supervision needed; additional training required

2—Limited practice: Has practiced job during training program; additional training required to develop skill

3—Moderately skilled: Has performed job independently during training program; limited additional training may be required

4—Skilled: Can perform job independently with no additional training

Student/intern information:

Name_____ Date_____ Class_____

Vehicle used for this activity:

Year_____ Make_____ Model_____

Odometer_____ VIN _____

© 2017 Jones & Bartlett Learning, LLC, an Ascend Learning Company

▶ TASK Inspect axle-aligning devices such as radius rods, track bars, stabilizer bars, torque arms, related bushings, mounts, shims, and cams; determine needed action.   NATEF 4B5

Time off_____

Time on_____

Total time_____

CDX Tasksheet Number: H247

1. Reference the appropriate manufacturer's service information for the correct procedure to inspect axle-aligning devices such as radius rods, track bars, stabilizer bars, torque arms, and related bushings, mounts, shims, and cams; list any specifications:

   _____

   _____

   _____

   _____

2. Following all procedures and safety requirements, carry out the inspection of the axle-aligning devices such as radius rods, track bars, stabilizer bars, and related bushings, mounts, shims, and cams.

   a. Radius rod(s):
      Serviceable: _____ Unserviceable: _____ Not applicable: _____

   b. Track bar(s):
      Serviceable: _____ Unserviceable: _____ Not applicable: _____

   c. Stabilizer bar(s):
      Serviceable: _____ Unserviceable: _____ Not applicable: _____

   d. Bushings, mounts, shims, and cams:
      Serviceable: _____ Unserviceable: _____ Not applicable: _____

   e. Torque arms:
      Serviceable: _____ Unserviceable: _____ Not applicable: _____

   f. Torque arm bushing(s):
      Serviceable: _____ Unserviceable: _____ Not applicable: _____

   g. Torque arm mounting(s):
      Serviceable: _____ Unserviceable: _____ Not applicable: _____

   h. Overall condition of radius rods, track bars, stabilizer bars, torque arms, and related bushings, mounts, shims, and cams:
      i. Within manufacturer's specifications: Yes: _____ No: _____
      ii. If no, list the necessary actions or corrections:

      _____

      _____

      _____

3. Discuss the findings with instructor.

Performance Rating

CDX Tasksheet Number: H247

☐ 0   ☐ 1   ☐ 2   ☐ 3   ☐ 4

Supervisor/instructor signature _____ Date_____

Student/intern information:

Name_____ Date_____ Class_____

Vehicle used for this activity:

Year_____ Make_____ Model_____

Odometer_____ VIN _____

▶ TASK Inspect tandem suspension equalizer components; determine needed action.

NATEF 4B6

Time off_____

Time on_____

Total time_____

CDX Tasksheet Number: H248

Note: These come in two different types, aluminum and cast iron.

1. Check equalizer beams for condition, including twisting or cracks.
    a. Condition: Good: _____ Bad: _____
    b. Comments:

    _____

2. Check bushings for conditions such as missing, broken, and/or dry rotted rubber.
    a. Condition: Good: _____ Bad: _____
    b. Comments:

    _____

3. Check the cross tubes for play in the ends where they contact the center bushings.
    a. Play present: Yes: _____ No: _____
    b. Comments:

    _____

4. Check saddle mounts for looseness and main cap bolt torque.
    a. Manufacturer's torque specification: _____ ft-lb (Nm)

5. Check equalizer beam ends for condition of bushings and mounting hardware.
    a. Condition: Good: _____ Bad: _____
    b. Comments:

    _____

6. If any of these conditions are not within specification, consult and record the procedure necessary to correct them to manufacturer's specification.

    _____

    _____

    _____

7. Discuss the findings with the instructor.

Performance Rating

CDX Tasksheet Number: H248

☐	☐	☐	☐	☐
0	1	2	3	4

Supervisor/instructor signature _____ Date_____

Student/intern information:

Name_____ Date_____ Class_____

Vehicle used for this activity:

Year_____ Make_____ Model_____

Odometer_____ VIN _____

▶ TASK Inspect and test air suspension pressure regulator and height control valves, lines, hoses, dump valves, and fittings; adjust, repair, or replace as needed.　　NATEF 4B7

Time off_____

Time on_____

Total time_____

CDX Tasksheet Number: H249

1.　Inspect and test air suspension pressure regulator and height control valves, lines, hoses, dump valves, and fittings; adjust, repair, or replace as needed.
　　a.　Identify the make and model of the vehicle's air suspension:
　　　　i.　Vehicle make: _____
　　　　ii.　Air suspension make: _____
　　　　iii.　Air suspension model: _____

2.　Reference the appropriate manufacturer's service information for the correct procedure to inspect and test the air suspension pressure regulator and height control valves, lines, hoses, dump valves, and fittings; list any specifications:

_____
_____
_____

3.　Following all procedures and safety requirements, carry out an inspection and test the air suspension pressure regulator and height control valves, lines, hoses, dump valves, and fittings.
　　a.　Inspect pressure regulation and height control valve:
　　　　Serviceable: _____　Unserviceable: _____
　　　　i.　Comments:

　　　　_____

　　b.　Referring to the service information for the correct procedure, test air suspension pressure regulation:
　　　　i.　Manufacturer's specified air pressure: _____ psi (kPa)
　　　　ii.　Actual air pressure reading: _____ psi (kPa)

　　c.　Referring to the service information for the correct procedure, test air suspension height control valve(s):
　　　　i.　Manufacturer's specified air pressure: _____ psi (kPa)
　　　　ii.　Actual air pressure reading: _____ psi (kPa)

　　d.　Dump valve(s): Serviceable: _____　Unserviceable: _____
　　　　i.　Comments:

　　　　_____

　　e.　Lines, hoses, and fittings: Serviceable: _____　Unserviceable: _____
　　　　i.　Comments:

　　　　_____

f. Overall condition of the air suspension pressure regulator and height control valves, lines, hoses, dump valves, and fittings:
   i. Within manufacturer's specifications: Yes: _____ No: _____
   ii. If no, list the necessary actions or corrections:

   _____

   _____

4. Discuss the findings with instructor.

Performance Rating

CDX Tasksheet Number: H249

☐ 0   ☐ 1   ☐ 2   ☐ 3   ☐ 4

Supervisor/instructor signature _____ Date_____

Truck Steering-Suspension Systems:
Suspension Systems 3

Student/intern information:

Name_____ Date_____ Class_____

Vehicle used for this activity:

Year_____ Make_____ Model_____

Odometer_____ VIN _____

Learning Objective / Task	CDX Tasksheet Number	2014 NATEF Priority Level	2014 NATEF Reference Number
• Inspect air springs, mounting plates, springs, suspension arms, and bushings; replace as needed.	H250	P-1	4B8
• Measure and adjust ride height; determine needed action.	H251	P-1	4B9
• Identify rough ride problems; determine needed action.	H252	P-3	4B10

Time off_____

Time on_____

Total time_____

Materials Required
- Vehicle with possible steering/suspension concern
- Vehicle manufacturer's service information
- Manufacturer-specific tools depending on the concern
- Vehicle-lifting equipment, if applicable

Some Safety Issues to Consider
- Diagnosis of this fault may require test driving the vehicle on the school grounds or on a hoist, both of which carry severe risks. Attempt this task only with full permission from your supervisor/instructor and follow all the guidelines exactly.
- Caution: If you are working in an area where there could be "brake dust" present (may contain asbestos, which has been determined to cause cancer when inhaled or ingested), ensure that you wear and use all OSHA-approved asbestos protective/removal equipment.
- Lifting equipment such as vehicle jacks and stands, vehicle hoists, and engine hoists are important tools that increase productivity and make the job easier. However, they can also cause severe injury or death if used improperly. Make sure you follow the manufacturer's operation procedures. Also make sure you have your supervisor's/instructor's permission to use any particular type of lifting equipment.
- Comply with personal and environmental safety practices associated with clothing; eye protection; hand tools; power equipment; proper ventilation; and the handling, storage, and disposal of chemicals/materials in accordance with federal, state, and local regulations.
- Always wear the correct protective eyewear and clothing, and use the appropriate safety equipment, as well as fender covers, seat protectors, and floor mat protectors.
- Make sure you understand and observe all legislative and personal safety procedures when carrying out practical assignments. If you are unsure of what these are, ask your supervisor/instructor.

Performance Standard

0—No exposure: No information or practice provided during the program; complete training required

1—Exposure only: General information provided with no practice time; close supervision needed; additional training required

2—Limited practice: Has practiced job during training program; additional training required to develop skill

3—Moderately skilled: Has performed job independently during training program; limited additional training may be required

4—Skilled: Can perform job independently with no additional training

Student/intern information:

Name_____ Date_____ Class_____

Vehicle used for this activity:

Year_____ Make_____ Model_____

Odometer_____ VIN _____

▶ **TASK** Inspect air springs, mounting plates, springs, suspension arms, and bushings; replace as needed.

NATEF 4B8

Time off_____

Time on_____

Total time_____

CDX Tasksheet Number: H250

1. Reference the appropriate manufacturer's service information for the correct procedure to inspect and test air springs, mounting plates, springs, suspension arms, and bushings; list any specifications: _____
_____
_____

2. Following all procedures and safety requirements, carry out an inspection and test air springs, mounting plates, springs, suspension arms, and bushings; replace as needed.
   a. Inspect air spring: Serviceable: _____ Unserviceable: _____
      i. Comments: _____

   b. Referring to the service information for the correct procedure, test the air suspension height control valve(s):
      i. Manufacturer's specified air pressure: _____ psi (kPa)
      ii. Actual air pressure reading: _____ psi (kPa)

   d. Mounting plate(s): Serviceable: _____ Unserviceable: _____
      i. Comments: _____

   e. Springs: Serviceable: _____ Unserviceable: _____

   f. Suspension arms and bushings: Serviceable: _____ Unserviceable: _____
      i. Comments: _____

g. Overall condition of the air suspension pressure regulator and height control valves, lines, hoses, dump valves, and fittings:
   i. Within manufacturer's specifications: Yes: _____ No: _____
   ii. If no, list the necessary actions or corrections:

   _____

   _____

   _____

4. Discuss the findings with instructor.

Performance Rating

CDX Tasksheet Number: H250

☐   ☐   ☐   ☐   ☐
0   1   2   3   4

Supervisor/instructor signature _____ Date_____

Student/intern information:

Name_____ Date_____ Class_____

Vehicle used for this activity:

Year_____ Make_____ Model_____

Odometer_____ VIN _____

▶ **TASK** Measure and adjust ride height; determine needed action.   NATEF 4B9

Time off_____

Time on_____

Total time_____

CDX Tasksheet Number: H251

1. Reference the appropriate manufacturer's service information for the correct procedure to measure the vehicle frame angle (ride height).
   a. Specified ride height: _____

2. Position the vehicle on a level surface. Lock the brakes.

3. Following all procedures and safety requirements, measure the vehicle frame angle (ride height).
   a. Actual ride height measurement: _____ in/mm

   b. Overall frame height:
      i. Within manufacturer's specifications: Yes: _____ No: _____

   c. List any necessary actions to correct any faults:
      _____
      _____
      _____

4. Discuss the findings with instructor.

Performance Rating

CDX Tasksheet Number: H251

☐	☐	☐	☐	☐
0	1	2	3	4

Supervisor/instructor signature _____ Date_____

Student/intern information:

Name_____ Date_____ Class_____

Vehicle used for this activity:

Year_____ Make_____ Model_____

Odometer_____ VIN _____

▶ **TASK** Identify rough ride problems; determine needed action.   NATEF 4B10

Time off_____

Time on_____

Total time_____

CDX Tasksheet Number: H252

1. Reference the appropriate manufacturer's service information to correctly diagnose rough ride problems; determine needed action.
   a. List all the potential areas that can cause a rough ride problem:
      i. _____
      ii. _____
      iii. _____
      iv. _____
      v. _____
      vi. _____
      vii. _____
      viii. _____
      ix. _____
      x. _____

2. Following all procedures and safety requirements, carry out the diagnostics of the rough ride problems.
   a. List your tests and observations:
      _____
      _____
      _____

   b. Within manufacturer's specifications: Yes: _____ No: _____
   c. If no, list the necessary actions or corrections:
      _____
      _____
      _____

3. Discuss the findings with instructor.

Performance Rating   **CDX Tasksheet Number: H252**

☐	☐	☐	☐	☐
0	1	2	3	4

Supervisor/instructor signature _____ Date_____

Truck Steering-Suspension Systems:
Wheel Alignment Diagnosis, Adjustment, and Repair

Student/intern information:

Name_____ Date_____ Class_____

Vehicle used for this activity:

Year_____ Make_____ Model_____

Odometer_____ VIN _____

Time off_____

Time on_____

Total time_____

Learning Objective / Task	CDX Tasksheet Number	2014 NATEF Priority Level	2014 NATEF Reference Number
• Identify causes of vehicle wandering, pulling, shimmy, hard steering, and off-center steering wheel problems; adjust or repair as needed.	H253	P-1	4C1
• Check camber; determine needed action.	H254	P-2	4C2
• Check caster; adjust as needed.	H255	P-2	4C3
• Check and adjust toe settings.	H256	P-1	4C4
• Check rear axle(s) alignment (thrustline/centerline) and tracking; adjust or repair as needed.	H257	P-2	4C5
• Identify turning/Ackermann angle (toe-out-on-turns) problems; determine needed action.	H258	P-3	4C6
• Check front axle alignment (centerline); adjust or repair as needed.	H259	P-2	4C7

Materials Required

- Vehicle with possible wheel alignment concern
- Vehicle manufacturer's service information
- Manufacturer-specific tools depending on the concern
- Vehicle-lifting equipment, if applicable

Some Safety Issues to Consider

- Diagnosis of this fault may require test driving the vehicle on the school grounds or on a hoist, both of which carry severe risks. Attempt this task only with full permission from your supervisor/instructor and follow all the guidelines exactly.
- Caution: If you are working in an area where there could be "brake dust" present (may contain asbestos, which has been determined to cause cancer when inhaled or ingested), ensure that you wear and use all OSHA-approved asbestos protective/removal equipment.
- Lifting equipment such as vehicle jacks and stands, vehicle hoists, and engine hoists are important tools that increase productivity and make the job easier. However, they can also cause severe injury or death if used improperly. Make sure you follow the manufacturer's operation procedures. Also make sure you have your supervisor's/instructor's permission to use any particular type of lifting equipment.
- Comply with personal and environmental safety practices associated with clothing; eye protection; hand tools; power equipment; proper ventilation; and the handling, storage, and disposal of chemicals/materials in accordance with federal, state, and local regulations.
- Always wear the correct protective eyewear and clothing, and use the appropriate safety equipment, as well as fender covers, seat protectors, and floor mat protectors.
- Make sure you understand and observe all legislative and personal safety procedures when carrying out practical assignments. If you are unsure of what these are, ask your supervisor/instructor.

Performance Standard

0—No exposure: No information or practice provided during the program; complete training required

1—Exposure only: General information provided with no practice time; close supervision needed; additional training required

2—Limited practice: Has practiced job during training program; additional training required to develop skill

3—Moderately skilled: Has performed job independently during training program; limited additional training may be required

4—Skilled: Can perform job independently with no additional training

Student/intern information:

Name_____ Date_____ Class_____

Vehicle used for this activity:

Year_____ Make_____ Model_____

Odometer_____ VIN _____

NATEF 4C1

CDX Tasksheet Number: H253

1. Reference the appropriate manufacturer's service information to correctly identify causes of vehicle wandering, pulling, shimmy, hard steering, and off center steering wheel problem(s).

2. List all the potential areas that can cause a vehicle's wandering, pulling, shimmy, hard steering, and off-center steering wheel problem(s).

   a. _____
   b. _____
   c. _____
   d. _____
   e. _____
   f. _____
   g. _____
   h. _____
   i. _____
   j. _____

3. Following all procedures and safety requirements, carry out a diagnosis of vehicle wandering, pulling, shimmy, hard steering and off-center steering wheel problems.

   a. Inspect the tires:
      i. Manufacturer's recommended tire sizes and construction:
         • Make: _____
         • Size: _____
         • Construction type: _____

      ii. Are the tires the same make, type, and size? Yes: _____ No: _____

      iii. Actual tire sizes and construction:
         • Make: _____
         • Size: _____
         • Construction type: _____

   b. Check tire pressure and tread depth:
      i. Recommended tire pressure: _____ psi (kPa)
      ii. Recommended tread depth: _____ in/mm
      iii. Record the actual tire pressures and tread depths in the chart below.

Left	Right
Steer Axle	
Pressure: _____ psi (kPa)	Pressure: _____ psi (kPa)
Depth: _____ in/mm	Depth: _____ in/mm

Left	Right
1st Rear Axle	
Pressure: _____ psi (kPa)	Pressure: _____ psi (kPa)
Depth: _____ in/mm	Depth: _____ in/mm
Pressure: _____ psi (kPa)	Pressure: _____ psi (kPa)
Depth: _____ in/mm	Depth: _____ in/mm
2nd Rear Axle	
Pressure: _____ psi (kPa)	Pressure: _____ psi (kPa)
Depth: _____ in/mm	Depth: _____ in/mm
Pressure: _____ psi (kPa)	Pressure: _____ psi (kPa)
Depth: _____ in/mm	Depth: _____ in/mm

      iv. Serviceable: _____ Unserviceable: _____

      v. If tire pressures are not within the specific pressure range, adjust as necessary.

      vi. If the tread depths are not within the recommended range, list the necessary actions or corrections:

      _____

      _____

      _____

4. Referring to the service information for the correct procedure, inspect and diagnose possible causes for pulling characteristics.

    a. Check front brake adjustments:

      i. Serviceable: _____ Unserviceable: _____

        a. Comments:

        _____

      ii. If brake adjustments are not within the manufacturer's specification, correct as necessary.

    b. Inspect the tire treads for abnormal wear patterns:

      i. Serviceable: _____ Unserviceable: _____

        a. Comments:

        _____

      ii. Within manufacturer's specifications: Yes: _____ No: _____

      iii. If no, list the necessary actions or corrections:

      _____

      _____

      _____

5. Referring to the service information for the correct procedure, carry out a wheel balance on the front wheels:

    a. Chock the vehicle's rear wheels.

    b. Reference the wheel balancer's service information.

    c. Referencing the service information, carry out the wheel balancing of the steer wheels. How much weight was added to each wheel? _____

6. Referring to the service information for the correct procedure, inspect and diagnose possible causes for hard steering problem(s).
   a. Conduct an inspection and diagnosis for the hard steering complaint.
      i. List your tests and observations:

      _____
      _____
      _____
      _____

      ii. Within manufacturer's specifications: Yes: _____ No: _____
      iii. If no, list the necessary actions or corrections:

      _____
      _____
      _____

7. Discuss the findings with instructor.

Performance Rating

CDX Tasksheet Number: H253

☐ 0   ☐ 1   ☐ 2   ☐ 3   ☐ 4

Supervisor/instructor signature _____ Date_____

Student/intern information:

Name_____ Date_____ Class_____

Vehicle used for this activity:

Year_____ Make_____ Model_____

Odometer_____ VIN _____

© 2017 Jones & Bartlett Learning, LLC, an Ascend Learning Company

▶ **TASK** Check camber; determine needed action.　　　　　NATEF 4C2

Time off_____

Time on_____

Total time_____

CDX Tasksheet Number: H254

1. Reference the appropriate manufacturer's service information to check camber.
    a. List the specified camber angle: _____
    b. How is camber adjusted?
    _____
    _____

2. Referencing the appropriate service information, prepare the vehicle to be connected to the wheel alignment machine.

3. Check camber angles:
    a. Record the camber reading for both sides: R/F: _____　　L/F: _____
    b. Within manufacturer's specifications: Yes: _____ No: _____
    c. If no, list the necessary actions or corrections:
    _____
    _____
    _____
    _____

4. Discuss the findings with instructor.

Performance Rating

CDX Tasksheet Number: H254

☐　　　☐　　　☐　　　☐　　　☐
0　　　　1　　　　2　　　　3　　　　4

Supervisor/instructor signature _____ Date_____

Student/intern information:

Name_____ Date_____ Class_____

Vehicle used for this activity:

Year_____ Make_____ Model_____

Odometer_____ VIN _____

▶ **TASK** Check caster; adjust as needed.   NATEF 4C3

Time off_____

Time on_____

Total time_____

CDX Tasksheet Number: H255

1. Reference the appropriate manufacturer's service information to check caster.
   a. List the specified caster angle: _____
   b. How is caster adjusted?

      _____
      _____

2. Check caster angles:
   a. Record the caster reading for both sides: R/F: _____ L/F: _____
   b. Within manufacturer's specifications: Yes: _____ No: _____
   c. If no, list the necessary actions or corrections:

      _____
      _____
      _____

   d. If caster readings are not within the manufacturer's specification, adjust as necessary.
   e. Record the adjusted caster reading for both sides: R/F: _____ L/F: _____

3. Discuss the findings with instructor.

Performance Rating

CDX Tasksheet Number: H255

☐	☐	☐	☐	☐
0	1	2	3	4

Supervisor/instructor signature _____ Date_____

Student/intern information:

Name_____ Date_____ Class_____

Vehicle used for this activity:

Year_____ Make_____ Model_____

Odometer_____ VIN _____

▶ TASK Check and adjust toe settings. NATEF 4C4

Time off_____

Time on_____

Total time_____

CDX Tasksheet Number: H256

1. Reference the appropriate manufacturer's service information to check toe.
   a. List the specified toe angle: _____
   b. How is toe adjusted?
   _____
   _____

2. Check toe reading:
   a. Record the toe reading: Toe reading: _____
   b. Within manufacturer's specifications: Yes: _____ No: _____
   c. If no, list the necessary actions or corrections:
   _____
   _____
   _____
   _____

   d. If toe readings are not within the manufacturer's specification, adjust as necessary.
   e. Record the adjusted toe reading: Toe reading: _____

3. Discuss the findings with instructor.

Performance Rating

CDX Tasksheet Number: H256

☐ ☐ ☐ ☐ ☐
0 1 2 3 4

Supervisor/instructor signature _____ Date_____

Student/intern information:

Name_____ Date_____ Class_____

Vehicle used for this activity:

Year_____ Make_____ Model_____

Odometer_____ VIN _____

▶ **TASK** Check rear axle(s) alignment (thrustline/centerline) and tracking; adjust or repair as needed. NATEF 4C5

Time off_____

Time on_____

Total time_____

CDX Tasksheet Number: H257

1. Reference the appropriate manufacturer's service information to check rear axle(s) alignment (thrust line/centerline) and tracking; list any specifications:

   _____
   _____
   _____

2. Check rear axle(s) alignment (thrust line/centerline) and tracking:
   a. List your observations:

   _____
   _____
   _____

   b. Within manufacturer's specifications: Yes: _____ No: _____

   c. If no, list the necessary actions or corrections:

   _____
   _____
   _____

3. Discuss the findings with instructor.

Performance Rating

CDX Tasksheet Number: H257

☐	☐	☐	☐	☐
0	1	2	3	4

Supervisor/instructor signature _____ Date_____

Student/intern information:

Name_____ Date_____ Class_____

Vehicle used for this activity:

Year_____ Make_____ Model_____

Odometer_____ VIN _____

▶ TASK Identify turning/Ackerman angle (toe-out-on-turns) problems; determine needed action.

Time on_____

CDX Tasksheet Number: H258

Total time_____

1. Reference the appropriate manufacturer's service information to check toe-out on turns; list any specifications:

   _____
   _____
   _____
   _____

2. Check toe-out on turns reading:
   a. Record the toe-out on turns reading: _____
   b. Within manufacturer's specifications: Yes: _____ No: _____
   c. If no, list the necessary actions or corrections:

      _____
      _____
      _____
      _____

   d. If toe out on turns is not within manufacturer's specifications, there are bent or damaged components. All damaged parts need to be replaced and aligned. List components that you replaced/repaired:

      _____
      _____
      _____

   e. Record the adjusted toe-out on turns reading: _____

3. Discuss the findings with instructor.

Performance Rating

CDX Tasksheet Number: H258

☐   ☐   ☐   ☐   ☐

0   1   2   3   4

Supervisor/instructor signature _____ Date_____

© 2017 Jones & Bartlett Learning, LLC, an Ascend Learning Company

Truck Steering-Suspension Systems   **89**

Student/intern information:

Name_____ Date_____ Class_____

Vehicle used for this activity:

Year_____ Make_____ Model_____

Odometer_____ VIN _____

▶ TASK Check front axle alignment (centerline); adjust or repair as needed. _____ NATEF 4C7

Time off_____

Time on_____

Total time_____

CDX Tasksheet Number: H259

1. Reference the appropriate manufacturer's service information to check front axle alignment centerline.

2. Complete the total front axle alignment (centerline):

Reading	Specification	Adjusted Readings	Initial Readings
Camber – R/F			
Camber – L/F			
Caster – R/F			
Caster – L /F			
Total Toe			
Toe-Out on Turns			
R/F			
L/F			
KPI/SAI – R/F			
KPI/SAI – L/F			
Centerline/ thrust angle			

3. Discuss the findings with instructor.

Performance Rating

CDX Tasksheet Number: H259

☐ 0   ☐ 1   ☐ 2   ☐ 3   ☐ 4

Supervisor/instructor signature _____ Date_____

Truck Steering-Suspension Systems: Wheels and Tires 1

Student/intern information:

Name_____ Date_____ Class_____

Vehicle used for this activity:

Year_____ Make_____ Model_____

Odometer_____ VIN _____

Learning Objective / Task	CDX Tasksheet Number	2014 NATEF Priority Level	2014 NATEF Reference Number
• Identify tire wear patterns; check tread depth and pressure; determine needed action.	H260	P-1	4D1
• Identify wheel/tire vibration, shimmy, pounding, hop (tramp) problems; determine needed action.	H261	P-2	4D2

Time off_____

Time on_____

Total time_____

Materials Required

- Vehicle with possible tire/wheel alignment concern
- Vehicle manufacturer's service information
- Manufacturer-specific tools depending on the concern
- Vehicle-lifting equipment, if applicable

Some Safety Issues to Consider

- Diagnosis of this fault may require test driving the vehicle on the school grounds or on a hoist, both of which carry severe risks. Attempt this task only with full permission from your supervisor/instructor and follow all the guidelines exactly.
- Caution: If you are working in an area where there could be "brake dust" present (may contain asbestos, which has been determined to cause cancer when inhaled or ingested), ensure that you wear and use all OSHA-approved asbestos protective/removal equipment.
- Lifting equipment such as vehicle jacks and stands, vehicle hoists, and engine hoists are important tools that increase productivity and make the job easier. However, they can also cause severe injury or death if used improperly. Make sure you follow the manufacturer's operation procedures. Also make sure you have your supervisor's/instructor's permission to use any particular type of lifting equipment.
- Comply with personal and environmental safety practices associated with clothing; eye protection; hand tools; power equipment; proper ventilation; and the handling, storage, and disposal of chemicals/materials in accordance with federal, state, and local regulations.
- Always wear the correct protective eyewear and clothing, and use the appropriate safety equipment, as well as fender covers, seat protectors, and floor mat protectors.
- Make sure you understand and observe all legislative and personal safety procedures when carrying out practical assignments. If you are unsure of what these are, ask your supervisor/instructor.

Performance Standard

0—No exposure: No information or practice provided during the program; complete training required

1—Exposure only: General information provided with no practice time; close supervision needed; additional training required

2—Limited practice: Has practiced job during training program; additional training required to develop skill

3—Moderately skilled: Has performed job independently during training program; limited additional training may be required

4—Skilled: Can perform job independently with no additional training

© 2017 Jones & Bartlett Learning, LLC, an Ascend Learning Company

Student/intern information:

Name_____ Date_____ Class_____

Vehicle used for this activity:

Year_____ Make_____ Model_____

Odometer_____ VIN _____

▶ **TASK** Identify tire wear patterns; check tread depth and pressure; determine needed action.

NATEF 4D1

CDX Tasksheet Number: H260

1. Reference the appropriate manufacturer's service information to correctly identify tire wear patterns; check tread depth and pressure; determine needed action.

2. List all the potential areas that can cause unusual tire wear patterns:
   a. _____
   b. _____
   c. _____
   d. _____
   e. _____

3. Following all procedures and safety requirements, carry out a diagnosis of unusual tire wear patterns.

   Note: Tire sizes must be the same on all axles. New tires must be on front axle and recaps are allowed on following axles.
   a. Inspect the tires:
      i. Manufacturer's recommended tire sizes and construction:
         • Make: _____
         • Size: _____
         • Construction type: _____

      ii. Are the tires the same make, type, and size? Yes: _____ No: _____
      iii. Actual tire sizes and construction:
         • Make: _____
         • Size: _____
         • Construction type: _____

   b. Check tire pressure and tread depth:
      i. Specified tire pressure: _____ psi (kPa)
      ii. Specified tread depth: _____ in/mm
      iii. Record the actual tire pressures and tread depths in the chart below.

Left	Right
Steer Axle	
Pressure: _____ psi (kPa)	Pressure: _____ psi (kPa)
Depth: _____ in/mm	Depth: _____ in/mm

Left	Right
1st Rear Axle	
Pressure: _____ psi (kPa)	Pressure: _____ psi (kPa)
Depth: _____ in/mm	Depth: _____ in/mm
Pressure: _____ psi (kPa)	Pressure: _____ psi (kPa)
Depth: _____ in/mm	Depth: _____ in/mm
2nd Rear Axle	
Pressure: _____ psi (kPa)	Pressure: _____ psi (kPa)
Depth: _____ in/mm	Depth: _____ in/mm
Pressure: _____ psi (kPa)	Pressure: _____ psi (kPa)
Depth: _____ in/mm	Depth: _____ in/mm

iv. Serviceable: _____ Unserviceable: _____

    a. Comments:

    _____

v. If tire pressures are not within the specific pressure range, adjust as necessary.

c. Inspect the tire treads for unusual tire wear patterns:

    i. Serviceable: _____ Unserviceable: _____

       a. Comments:

       _____

    ii. Within manufacturer's specifications: Yes: _____ No: _____

    iii. If no, list the necessary actions or corrections:

    _____
    _____
    _____

    iv. If the treads are showing signs of abnormal wear patterns, list the probable cause(s):

    _____
    _____
    _____

4. Check tread design matches:

    a. Within manufacturer's specifications: Yes: _____ No: _____

    b. If no, list the necessary actions or corrections:

    _____
    _____
    _____

5. Discuss the findings with instructor.

Performance Rating

CDX Tasksheet Number: H260

☐   ☐   ☐   ☐   ☐

0   1   2   3   4

Supervisor/instructor signature _____ Date_____

Student/intern information:

Name_____ Date_____ Class_____

Vehicle used for this activity:

Year_____ Make_____ Model_____

Odometer_____ VIN _____

▶ **TASK** Identify wheel/tire vibration, shimmy, pounding, hop (tramp) problems; determine needed action.

NATEF 4D2

Time off_____

Time on_____

Total time_____

CDX Tasksheet Number: H261

1. Reference the appropriate manufacturer's service information to correctly identify wheel/tire vibration, shimmy, pounding, hop (tramp) problems; determine needed action.

2. List all the potential areas that can cause wheel/tire vibration, shimmy, pounding, hop (tramp):
   a. _____
   b. _____
   c. _____
   d. _____
   e. _____
   f. _____
   g. _____
   h. _____
   i. _____
   j. _____

3. Following all procedures and safety requirements, carry out procedures to determine the cause(s) for any wheel/tire vibration, shimmy, pounding, hop (tramp):
   a. Within manufacturer's specifications: Yes: _____ No: _____
   b. If no, list the necessary actions or corrections:
   _____
   _____
   _____

4. Discuss the findings with instructor.

Performance Rating

CDX Tasksheet Number: H261

☐   ☐   ☐   ☐   ☐
0   1   2   3   4

Supervisor/instructor signature _____ Date_____

Truck Steering-Suspension Systems: Wheels and Tires 2

Student/intern information:

Name_____ Date_____ Class_____

Vehicle used for this activity:

Year_____ Make_____ Model_____

Odometer_____ VIN _____

Learning Objective / Task	CDX Tasksheet Number	2014 NATEF Priority Level	2014 NATEF Reference Number
• Remove and install steering and drive axle wheel/hub assemblies; torque mounting hardware to specifications with torque wrench.	H262	P-1	4D3
• Inspect tire for proper application, (size, load range, position, and tread design); determine needed action.	H263	P-2	4D4
• Inspect wheel/rims for proper application, hand hole alignment, load range, size, and design; determine needed action.	H264	P-2	4D5
• Check operation of tire pressure monitoring system (TPMS); determine needed action if applicable.	H265	P-3	4D6

Time off_____

Time on_____

Total time_____

Materials Required

- Vehicle with possible tire/wheel alignment concern
- Vehicle manufacturer's service information
- Manufacturer-specific tools depending on the concern
- Vehicle lifting equipment if applicable

Some Safety Issues to Consider

- Diagnosis of this fault may require test driving the vehicle on the school grounds or on a hoist, both of which carry severe risks. Attempt this task only with full permission from your supervisor/instructor and follow all the guidelines exactly.
- Caution: If you are working in an area where there could be brake dust present (may contain asbestos, which has been determined to cause cancer when inhaled or ingested), ensure you wear and use all OSHA-approved asbestos protective/removal equipment.
- Lifting equipment such as vehicle jacks and stands, vehicle hoists, and engine hoists are important tools that increase productivity and make the job easier. However, they can also cause severe injury or death if used improperly. Make sure you follow the manufacturer's operation procedures. Also make sure you have your supervisor/instructor's permission to use any particular type of lifting equipment.
- Comply with personal and environmental safety practices associated with clothing; eye protection; hand tools; power equipment; proper ventilation; and the handling, storage, and disposal of chemicals/materials in accordance with federal, state, and local regulations.
- Always wear the correct protective eyewear and clothing and use the appropriate safety equipment, as well as fender covers, seat protectors, and floor mat protectors.
- Make sure you understand and observe all legislative and personal safety procedures when carrying out practical assignments. If you are unsure of what these are, ask your supervisor/instructor.

Performance Standard

0—No exposure: No information or practice provided during the program; complete training required

1—Exposure only: General information provided with no practice time; close supervision needed; additional training required

2—Limited practice: Has practiced job during training program; additional training required to develop skill

3—Moderately skilled: Has performed job independently during training program; limited additional training may be required

4—Skilled: Can perform job independently with no additional training

Student/intern information:

Name_____ Date_____ Class_____

Vehicle used for this activity:

Year_____ Make_____ Model_____

Odometer_____ VIN _____

▶ **TASK** Remove and install steering and drive axle wheel/hub assemblies; torque mounting hardware to specifications with torque wrench. NATEF 4D3

Time off_____

Time on_____

Total time_____

CDX Tasksheet Number: H262

1. Reference the appropriate manufacturer's service information to correctly remove and install steering axle wheel/tire assemblies.

2. List all the safety procedures that must be adhered to while removing and installing steering axle wheel/hub assemblies:
   a. _____
   b. _____
   c. _____
   d. _____
   e. _____

3. Referring to the service information, remove and install steering axle wheel/hub assemblies:
   a. Chock the vehicle's rear wheels.
   b. Jack the vehicle up until the wheels are off the ground.
   c. Install the appropriate size wheel safety stand under the vehicle. Slowly release the pressure of the jack while observing that the stands are in the correct location.
   d. Remove the dust/grease cap from the hub assembly. If oil filled hubs, ensure you collect the oil from the hub and dispose of in the appropriate manner taking into account all relevant environmental protection legislation.
   e. Remove the locking device from the retaining nut.
   f. Before removing retaining nut, check the preload or tension on the nut following the procedure outlined in the service information.
      i. Within manufacturer's specifications: Yes: _____ No: _____
      ii. If no, list the tension or preload obtained:

      _____
      _____
      _____

   g. Remove the locking nut and set aside.
   h. Using the recommended lift device, remove the wheel bearings and place on clean surface and cover.
   i. Following the procedure in the service information, remove the steering axle wheel/hub assemblies.
   j. Inspect the assembly.
      i. Brake drum or disc brake rotor condition:
         Serviceable: _____ Requires Servicing: _____
      ii. Inspect the hub seal:
         Serviceable: _____ Requires Servicing: _____

k. Inspect the tires for serviceability.
   i. Within manufacturer's specifications: Yes: _____ No: _____
   ii. If no, list the reason(s):

   _____
   _____
   _____

l. Determine what needs to be done to correct any faults and discuss these with your instructor.
m. If directed by your instructors, carry out any corrections and re-assembly of the wheel assembly as per the manufacturer's service information.
n. List the manufacturer's specifications for tightening and torque of the wheel assembly.

   _____
   _____
   _____
   _____

o. Final torque required: _____ft-lb (Nm)
p. After your instructor has examined your work in restoring the wheel steering axle assembly, jack up and remove the safety stands. Lower the vehicle to the ground.

4. Reference the appropriate manufacturer's service information to correctly remove and install drive axle wheel/hub assemblies; determine needed action.

5. List all the safety procedures that must be adhered to while removing and installing drive axle wheel/hub assemblies:
   a. _____
   b. _____
   c. _____
   d. _____
   e. _____

6. Referring to service information, remove and install drive axle wheel/hub assemblies:
   a. Chock the vehicle's front wheels.
   b. Jack the vehicle up until the wheels are off the ground.
   c. Install the appropriate size wheel safety stand under the vehicle. Slowly release the pressure of the jack while observing that the stands are in the correct location.
   d. Remove the dust/grease cap from the hub assembly. If oil filled hubs, ensure you collect the oil from the hub and dispose of in the appropriate manner taking into account all relevant environmental protection legislation.
   e. Remove the locking device from the retaining nut.
   f. Before removing retaining nut, check the preload or tension on the nut following the procedure outlined in the service information.
      i. Within manufacturer's specifications: Yes: _____ No: _____
      ii. If no, list the tension or preload obtained:

      _____
      _____
      _____

© 2017 Jones & Bartlett Learning, LLC, an Ascend Learning Company

g. Remove the locking nut and set aside.

h. Using the recommended lift device, remove the wheel bearings and place on clean surface and cover.

i. Following the procedure in the service information, remove the steering axle wheel/ hub assemblies.

j. Inspect the assembly.

    i. Brake drum or disc brake rotor condition:
       Serviceable: _____ Requires Servicing: _____

    ii. Inspect the hub seal:
       Serviceable: _____ Requires Servicing: _____

k. Inspect the tires for serviceability.

    i. Within manufacturer's specifications: Yes: _____ No: _____

    ii. If no, list the reason(s):

       _____
       _____
       _____

l. Determine what needs to be done to correct any faults and discuss these with your instructor.

m. If directed by your instructor, carry out any corrections and re-assembly of the wheel assembly as per the manufacturer's service information.

n. List the manufacturer's specifications for tightening and torque of the wheel assembly.

       _____
       _____
       _____
       _____

o. Final torque required: _____ft-lb (Nm)

p. After your instructor has examined your work in restoring the drive axle assembly, jack up and remove the safety stands. Lower the vehicle to the ground.

7. Discuss the findings with instructor.

Performance Rating

CDX Tasksheet Number: H262

☐ 0 ☐ 1 ☐ 2 ☐ 3 ☐ 4

Supervisor/instructor signature _____ Date_____

Student/intern information:

Name_____ Date_____ Class_____

Vehicle used for this activity:

Year_____ Make_____ Model_____

Odometer_____ VIN _____

▶ **TASK** Inspect tire for proper application, (size, load range, position, and tread design); determine needed action.   NATEF 4D4

Time off_____

Time on_____

Total time_____

CDX Tasksheet Number: H263

1. Research the following specifications found on the vehicle's tire placard or in the service information:
    a. Tire size (steering): _____
        i. Construction type: _____
        ii. Load range: _____
        iii. Pressure: _____ psi (kPa)
        iv. Minimum tread depth: _____ in/mm

    b. Tire size (rear): _____
        i. Construction type: _____
        ii. Load range: _____
        iii. Pressure: _____ psi (kPa)
        iv. Minimum tread depth: _____ in/mm

2. List the following information from the sidewall of each tire:
    a. Left steering tire:
        i. Tire size: _____
        ii. Tire construction type: _____
        iii. Load range: _____
        iv. Pressure: _____ psi (kPa)
        v. Tread design: _____
        vi. New tire: Yes: _____ No: _____   Retread tire: Yes: _____ No: _____

    b. Right steering tire:
        i. Tire size: _____
        ii. Tire construction type: _____
        iii. Load range: _____
        iv. Pressure: _____ psi (kPa)
        v. Tread design: _____
        vi. New tire: Yes: _____ No: _____   Retread tire: Yes: _____ No: _____
        vii. Do both steering tires match? Yes: _____ No: _____
        viii. Do both steering tires meet the requirements for this vehicle?
              Yes: _____ No: _____

    c. Left Rear Tire#1:
        i. Tire size: _____
        ii. Tire construction type: _____
        iii. Load range: _____
        iv. Maximum pressure: _____ psi (kPa)
        v. Tread design: _____
        vi. New tire: Yes: _____ No: _____   Retread tire: Yes: _____ No: _____

    d. Left Rear Tire#2:

        i. Tire size: _____

        ii. Tire construction type: _____

        iii. Load range: _____

        iv. Maximum pressure: _____ psi (kPa)

        v. Tread design: _____

        vi. New tire: Yes: _____   No: _____   Retread tire: Yes: _____   No: _____

    e. Right Rear Tire#3:

        i. Tire size: _____

        ii. Tire construction type: _____

        iii. Load range: _____

        iv. Maximum pressure: _____ psi (kPa)

        v. Tread design: _____

        vi. New tire: Yes: _____   No: _____   Retread tire: Yes: _____   No: _____

    f. Right Rear Tire#4:

        i. Tire size: _____

        ii. Tire construction type: _____

        iii. Load range: _____

        iv. Maximum pressure: _____ psi (kPa)

        v. Tread design: _____

        vi. New tire: Yes: _____   No: _____   Retread tire: Yes: _____   No: _____

        vii. Do all rear tires match?   Yes: _____   No: _____

        viii. Do all rear tires meet the requirements of this vehicle?   Yes: _____   No: _____

3.   Record the pressure, rim design, tread depth, and wear pattern for each tire listed:

Left	Right
Steer Axle	
Pressure: _____ psi (kPa)	Pressure: _____ psi (kPa)
Rim Design: _____	Rim Design: _____
Tread Depth: _____	Tread Depth: _____
Wear Pattern: _____	Wear Pattern: _____
1st Rear Axle	
Pressure: _____ psi (kPa)	Pressure: _____ psi (kPa)
Rim Design: _____	Rim Design: _____
Tread Depth: _____	Tread Depth: _____
Wear Pattern: _____	Wear Pattern: _____
Pressure: _____ psi (kPa)	Pressure: _____ psi (kPa)
Rim Design: _____	Rim Design: _____
Tread Depth: _____	Tread Depth: _____
Wear Pattern: _____	Wear Pattern: _____

Left	Right
2nd Rear Axle	
Pressure: _____ psi (kPa)	Pressure: _____ psi (kPa)
Rim Design: _____	Rim Design: _____
Tread Depth: _____	Tread Depth: _____
Wear Pattern: _____	Wear Pattern: _____
Pressure: _____ psi (kPa)	Pressure: _____ psi (kPa)
Rim Design: _____	Rim Design: _____
Tread Depth: _____	Tread Depth: _____
Wear Pattern: _____	Wear Pattern: _____

4. If tire pressures are not within the specific pressure range, adjust as necessary.

5. If the treads are showing signs of abnormal wear patterns; list the probable cause(s):

    _____

    _____

    _____

    _____

6. Based on the inspection of the tires, determine any necessary actions:

    _____

    _____

    _____

    _____

7. Discuss the findings with your instructor.

Performance Rating

CDX Tasksheet Number: H263

☐ 0   ☐ 1   ☐ 2   ☐ 3   ☐ 4

Supervisor/instructor signature _____ Date_____

© 2017 Jones & Bartlett Learning, LLC, an Ascend Learning Company

▶ **TASK** Inspect wheel/rims for proper application, hand hole alignment, load range, size, and design; determine needed action.

NATEF 4D5

Time off_____

Time on_____

Total time_____

CDX Tasksheet Number: H264

1. Check for proper application, hand hole alignment, load range, size, and design of each wheel/rim in the chart below.

Left	Right
Steer Axle	
Acceptable: _____	Acceptable: _____
Fault Found: _____ _____ _____	Fault Found: _____ _____ _____
1st Rear Axle	
Acceptable: _____	Acceptable: _____
Fault Found: _____ _____ _____	Fault Found: _____ _____ _____
Acceptable: _____	Acceptable: _____
Fault Found: _____ _____ _____	Fault Found: _____ _____ _____
2nd Rear Axle	
Acceptable: _____	Acceptable: _____
Fault Found: _____ _____ _____	Fault Found: _____ _____ _____
Acceptable: _____	Acceptable: _____
Fault Found: _____ _____ _____	Fault Found: _____ _____ _____

a. Overall condition and suitability: Acceptable: _____ Not Acceptable: _____

b. If not in an acceptable condition, determine any necessary actions:

_____

_____

_____

2. Discuss the findings with instructor.

Performance Rating

CDX Tasksheet Number: H264

☐   ☐   ☐   ☐   ☐

0   1   2   3   4

Supervisor/instructor signature _____ Date_____

Student/intern information:

Name_____ Date_____ Class_____

Vehicle used for this activity:

Year_____ Make_____ Model_____

Odometer_____ VIN _____

▶ TASK Check operation of tire pressure monitoring system (TPMS); determine needed action if
applicable.   NATEF 4D6

Time off_____

Time on_____

Total time_____

CDX Tasksheet Number: H265

1. Research the TPMS system in the appropriate service information.
   a. Choose the type of TMPS system: Indirect: _____ Direct: _____
   b. List or print off and attach to this sheet the process for calibrating the TPMS system:

   _____
   _____
   _____
   _____

   c. List how the instrument panel warning lamps should behave if the system is operating
   normally:

   _____
   _____
   _____

   d. List how the instrument panel warning lamps should behave if the system is NOT
   operating normally:

   _____
   _____
   _____

2. Describe how an indirect TPMS system detects a tire with low tire pressure:

   _____
   _____
   _____

3. Describe how a direct TPMS system detects a tire with low tire pressure:

   _____
   _____
   _____

4. Check the operation of the TPMS warning lamp and list your observations:

   _____
   _____
   _____

5. Swap the two front-wheel assemblies and calibrate the TPMS system in accordance with the manufacturer's instructions. List your steps and observations here:

_____

_____

_____

_____

6. Discuss the findings with your instructor.

Performance Rating

CDX Tasksheet Number: H265

☐	☐	☐	☐	☐
0	1	2	3	4

Supervisor/instructor signature _____ Date _____

Truck Steering-Suspension Systems: Frame and Coupling Devices

Student/intern information:

Name_____ Date_____ Class_____

Vehicle used for this activity:

Year_____ Make_____ Model_____

Odometer_____ VIN _____

Time off_____

Time on_____

Total time_____

Learning Objective / Task	CDX Tasksheet Number	2014 NATEF Priority Level	2014 NATEF Reference Number
• Inspect, service, and/or adjust fifth wheel, pivot pins, bushings, locking mechanisms, and mounting hardware.	H266	P-1	4E1
• Inspect and service sliding fifth wheel, tracks, stops, locking systems, air cylinders, springs, lines, hoses, and controls.	H267	P-2	4E2
• Inspect frame and frame members for cracks, breaks, corrosion, distortion, elongated holes, looseness, and damage; determine needed repairs.	H268	P-1	4E3
• Inspect, install, or repair frame hangers, brackets, and cross members in accordance with manufacturers' recommended procedures.	H269	P-3	4E4
• Inspect, repair, or replace pintle hooks and draw bars, if applicable.	H270	P-2	4E5

Materials Required

- Vehicle with possible tire/wheel alignment concern
- Vehicle manufacturer's service information
- Manufacturer-specific tools depending on the concern
- Vehicle-lifting equipment, if applicable

Some Safety Issues to Consider

- Diagnosis of this fault may require test driving the vehicle on the school grounds or on a hoist, both of which carry severe risks. Attempt this task only with full permission from your supervisor/instructor and follow all the guidelines exactly.
- Caution: If you are working in an area where there could be "brake dust" present (may contain asbestos, which has been determined to cause cancer when inhaled or ingested), ensure that you wear and use all OSHA-approved asbestos protective/removal equipment.
- Lifting equipment such as vehicle jacks and stands, vehicle hoists, and engine hoists are important tools that increase productivity and make the job easier. However, they can also cause severe injury or death if used improperly. Make sure you follow the manufacturer's operation procedures. Also make sure you have your supervisor's/instructor's permission to use any particular type of lifting equipment.
- Comply with personal and environmental safety practices associated with clothing; eye protection; hand tools; power equipment; proper ventilation; and the handling, storage, and disposal of chemicals/materials in accordance with federal, state, and local regulations.
- Always wear the correct protective eyewear and clothing, and use the appropriate safety equipment, as well as fender covers, seat protectors, and floor mat protectors.
- Make sure you understand and observe all legislative and personal safety procedures when carrying out practical assignments. If you are unsure of what these are, ask your supervisor/instructor.

Performance Standard

0—No exposure: No information or practice provided during the program; complete training required

1—Exposure only: General information provided with no practice time; close supervision needed; additional training required

2—Limited practice: Has practiced job during training program; additional training required to develop skill

3—Moderately skilled: Has performed job independently during training program; limited additional training may be required

4—Skilled: Can perform job independently with no additional training

Student/intern information:

Name_____ Date_____ Class_____

Vehicle used for this activity:

Year_____ Make_____ Model_____

Odometer_____ VIN _____

▶ **TASK** Inspect, service, and/or adjust fifth wheel, pivot pins, bushings, locking mechanisms, and mounting hardware.

NATEF 4E1

Time off_____

Time on_____

Total time_____

CDX Tasksheet Number: H266

1. Reference the appropriate fifth wheel coupler manufacturer's service information for the correct procedure to inspect, service and/or adjust fifth wheel, pivot pins, bushings, locking mechanisms, and mounting hardware.

2. Following all procedures and safety requirements, carry out the inspection and any necessary adjustments of the fifth wheel unit (if applicable):

Component	Serviceable	Requires Servicing
Test the locking mechanisms		
Perform external examination of unit		
Inspect levers and handles		
Inspect for stress cracks/fractures		
Check the security of securing nuts and bolts		
Inspect and check bushings		
Inspect and check locking bar		
Inspect lever with bushings		
Inspect locking jaw		
Inspect locking jaw spring		
Other		

   a. Within manufacturer's specifications: Yes: _____ No: _____
   b. If no, list the necessary actions or corrections:

   _____

   _____

   _____

3. Discuss the findings with instructor.

Performance Rating

CDX Tasksheet Number: H266

☐   ☐   ☐   ☐   ☐

0   1   2   3   4

Supervisor/instructor signature _____ Date_____

Name_____ Date_____ Class_____

Vehicle used for this activity:

Year_____ Make_____ Model_____

Odometer_____ VIN _____

▶ TASK Inspect and service sliding fifth wheel, tracks, stops, locking systems, air cylinders, springs, lines, hoses, and controls.   NATEF 4E2

Time off_____

Time on_____

Total time_____

CDX Tasksheet Number: H267

1. Reference the appropriate fifth wheel coupler manufacturer's service information for the correct procedure to inspect sliding fifth wheel, tracks, stops, locking systems, air cylinders, springs, lines, hoses, and controls.

2. Following all procedures and safety requirements, carry out the inspection and any necessary adjustments of the fifth wheel unit (if applicable):

Component	Serviceable	Requires Servicing
Inspect sliding fifth wheel		
Inspect tracks		
Inspect and adjust, as necessary, stops		
Check and adjust, as necessary, locking systems		
Inspect and check air cylinders		
Check springs		
Check lines		
Check hoses		
Check all controls		
Other		
Other		

  a. Within manufacturer's specifications: Yes: _____ No: _____
  b. If no, list the necessary actions or corrections:

  _____
  _____
  _____

3. Discuss the findings with instructor.

Performance Rating

CDX Tasksheet Number: H267

☐ 0   ☐ 1   ☐ 2   ☐ 3   ☐ 4

Supervisor/instructor signature _____ Date_____

Name_____ Date_____ Class_____

Vehicle used for this activity:

Year_____ Make_____ Model_____

Odometer_____ VIN _____

▶ TASK Inspect frame and frame members for cracks, breaks, corrosion, distortion, elongated holes, looseness, and damage; determine needed repairs.   NATEF 4E3

CDX Tasksheet Number: H268

1. Reference the appropriate manufacturer's service information for the correct procedure to inspect frame and frame members for cracks, breaks, corrosion, distortion, elongated holes, looseness, and damage; determine needed repairs.

2. Following all procedures and safety requirements, carry out the inspection of the frame and frame members for cracks, breaks, corrosion, distortion, elongated holes, looseness, and damage, list your observations:

    _____
    _____
    _____
    _____

    a. Within manufacturer's specifications: Yes: _____ No: _____
    b. If no, list the necessary actions or corrections:

        _____
        _____
        _____

3. Discuss the findings with instructor.

Performance Rating

CDX Tasksheet Number: H268

☐ 0   ☐ 1   ☐ 2   ☐ 3   ☐ 4

Supervisor/instructor signature _____ Date_____

Name_____ Date_____ Class_____

Vehicle used for this activity:

Year_____ Make_____ Model_____

Odometer_____ VIN _____

▶ **TASK** Inspect, install, or repair frame hangers, brackets, and cross members in accordance with manufacturers' recommended procedures.   NATEF 4E4

Time off_____

Time on_____

Total time_____

CDX Tasksheet Number: H269

1. Reference the appropriate manufacturer's service information for the correct procedure to inspect, install, or repair frame hangers, brackets, and cross members in accordance with manufacturer's recommended procedures.

2. Following all procedures and safety requirements, inspect, install, or repair frame hangers, brackets, and cross members in accordance with manufacturer's recommended procedures, list your observations:

    _____
    _____
    _____
    _____
    _____

    a. Within manufacturer's specifications: Yes: _____ No: _____
    b. If no, list the necessary actions or corrections:

        _____
        _____
        _____

3. Discuss the findings with instructor.

Performance Rating

CDX Tasksheet Number: H269

☐ 0   ☐ 1   ☐ 2   ☐ 3   ☐ 4

Supervisor/instructor signature _____ Date_____

Student/intern information:

Name_____ Date_____ Class_____

Vehicle used for this activity:

Year_____ Make_____ Model_____

Odometer_____ VIN _____

▶ **TASK** Inspect, repair, or replace pintle hooks and draw bars, if applicable.   NATEF 4E5

Time off_____

Time on_____

Total time_____

CDX Tasksheet Number: H270

1. Reference the appropriate manufacturer's service information for the correct procedure to inspect, repair, or replace pintle hooks and draw bars.

2. Following all procedures and safety requirements, inspect, install, repair, or replace pintle hooks and draw bars.

Component	Serviceable	Requires Servicing
Check the pintle hook for cracks or breaks and excessive wear		
Inspect the locking mechanism for missing or broken parts		
Inspect the locking mechanism security		
Check for deformed or cracked fasteners including welds		
Check all mounting bolts, fasteners, or weld beads for advanced corrosion		
Inspect pin coupling or pintle hook welds for cracks		
Check that pin couplings or pintle hooks are not worn beyond the manufacturer's limits		
Other		

a. Within manufacturer's specifications: Yes: _____ No: _____
b. If no, list the necessary actions or corrections:

_____

_____

_____

3. Discuss the findings with instructor.

Performance Rating

CDX Tasksheet Number: H270

☐ 0   ☐ 1   ☐ 2   ☐ 3   ☐ 4

Supervisor/instructor signature _____ Date_____

Air & Hydraulic Brake Systems, DT107

CONTENTS

Air &
Hydraulic
Brake
Systems,
DT107

Air & Hydraulic Brake Systems:
Air Brakes 1: Air Supply and Service Systems

Student/intern information:

Name_____ Date_____ Class_____

Vehicle used for this activity:

Year_____ Make_____ Model_____

Odometer_____ VIN _____

Time off_____

Time on_____

Total time_____

Learning Objective / Task	CDX Tasksheet Number	2014 NATEF Priority Level	2014 NATEF Reference Number
• Identify poor stopping, air leaks, premature wear, pulling, grabbing, dragging, or balance problems caused by supply and service system malfunctions; determine needed action.	H171	P-1	3A1.1
• Check air system build-up time; determine needed action.	H172	P-1	3A1.2

Materials Required

- Vehicle with possible brake concern
- Vehicle manufacturer's service information
- Manufacturer-specific tools depending on the concern
- Vehicle lifting equipment if applicable

Some Safety Issues to Consider

- Diagnosis of this fault may require test driving the vehicle on the school grounds or on a hoist, both of which carry severe risks. Attempt this task only with full permission from your supervisor/instructor and follow all the guidelines exactly.
- Caution: If you are working in an area where there could be brake dust present (may contain asbestos, which has been determined to cause cancer when inhaled or ingested), ensure you wear and use all OSHA-approved asbestos protective/removal equipment.
- Lifting equipment such as vehicle jacks and stands, vehicle hoists, and engine hoists are important tools that increase productivity and make the job easier. However, they can also cause severe injury or death if used improperly. Make sure you follow the manufacturer's operation procedures. Also make sure you have your supervisor/instructor's permission to use any particular type of lifting equipment.
- Comply with personal and environmental safety practices associated with clothing; eye protection; hand tools; power equipment; proper ventilation; and the handling, storage, and disposal of chemicals/materials in accordance with federal, state, and local regulations.
- Always wear the correct protective eyewear and clothing and use the appropriate safety equipment, as well as fender covers, seat protectors, and floor mat protectors.
- Make sure you understand and observe all legislative and personal safety procedures when carrying out practical assignments. If you are unsure of what these are, ask your supervisor/instructor.

Performance Standard

0—No exposure: No information or practice provided during the program; complete training required

1—Exposure only: General information provided with no practice time; close supervision needed; additional training required

2—Limited practice: Has practiced job during training program; additional training required to develop skill

3—Moderately skilled: Has performed job independently during training program; limited additional training may be required

4—Skilled: Can perform job independently with no additional training

Student/intern information:

Name_____ Date_____ Class_____

Vehicle used for this activity:

Year_____ Make_____ Model_____

Odometer_____ VIN _____

▶ **TASK** Identify poor stopping, air leaks, premature wear, pulling, grabbing, dragging, or balance problems caused by supply and service system malfunctions; determine needed action.

NATEF 3A1.1

Time off_____

Time on_____

Total time_____

CDX Tasksheet Number: H171

- **Engine "OFF" pre-checks and checks**

    1. List all possible causes for poor stopping:

    _____
    _____
    _____
    _____
    _____

    2. Check for air leaks. Record any air leaks detected during your inspection:

    _____
    _____
    _____
    _____
    _____

    3. Check brake material for premature wear. List all areas of premature wear detected during your inspection:

    _____
    _____
    _____
    _____
    _____

    4. List all possible causes for pulling, grabbing, dragging, or balance problems:

    _____
    _____
    _____
    _____
    _____

    5. Check for any service system malfunctions. List any malfunctions detected during your inspection:

    _____
    _____
    _____
    _____
    _____

6. Determine the action required to correct any faults within the system:

_____

_____

_____

_____

_____

7. Discuss these findings with your instructor.

CDX Tasksheet Number: H171

Performance Rating

☐   ☐   ☐   ☐   ☐

0   1   2   3   4

Supervisor/instructor signature _____ Date_____

Name _____ Date_____ Class_____

Vehicle used for this activity:

Year_____ Make_____ Model_____

Odometer_____ VIN _____

Time off_____

Time on_____

Total time_____

▶ **TASK** Check air system build-up time; determine needed action.   **NATEF 3A1.2**

CDX Tasksheet Number: H172

- **Engine "Running" checks**

  Note: Ensure all OSHA precautions are observed at all times.

  Note: The air compressor is responsible for air pressure build up. If the system itself is leak free, any delay in build up may be a direct result of worn internal compressor parts.

  1. Reference the manufacturer's service information for the correct procedure for checking the air pressure build timing.
     a. List the pressure and time specifications for build pressures and low pressure warning devices:

     _____
     _____
     _____
     _____

  2. Block and/or hold the vehicle by means other than air brakes during these tests.

  3. Drain the vehicle reservoirs; ensure that a container(s) is placed under the drain cocks to collect any contaminants, then close the drain cocks.

  4. Pressure gauge reading: _____ psi (kPa)

  5. Start time of air build: _____ minutes _____ seconds

  6. Start the engine and build up system pressure.

  7. Record the pressure when the "low pressure warning device" goes out:
     a. Pressure gauge reading: _____ psi (kPa)
     b. Time to build up to shut off low pressure warning device:
        _____ minutes _____ seconds

  8. Record the pressure when the "governor cut-out" pressure is reached.
     a. Pressure gauge reading: _____ psi (kPa)
     b. Time to build up to the "governor cut-out" pressure:
        _____ minutes _____ seconds

  9. Record the total time from the start of pumping to reach the governor cut-out pressure:
     _____ minutes _____ seconds

10. Did the air pressure build-up time operate within specifications?
Yes: _____ No: _____
   a. If no, list the problem and your recommendation(s):

_____

_____

_____

11. Shut the engine down and discuss these findings with your instructor.

Performance Rating

CDX Tasksheet Number: H172

☐   ☐   ☐   ☐   ☐

0   1   2   3   4

Supervisor/instructor signature _____ Date_____

Air & Hydraulic Brake Systems:
Air Brakes 2: Air Supply and Service Systems

Student/intern information:

Name_____ Date_____ Class_____

Vehicle used for this activity:

Year_____ Make_____ Model_____

Odometer_____ VIN _____

Time off_____

Time on_____

Total time_____

Learning Objective / Task	CDX Tasksheet Number	2014 NATEF Priority Level	2014 NATEF Reference Number
• Drain air reservoir/tanks; check for oil, water, and foreign material; determine needed action.	H173	P-1	3A1.3
• Inspect air compressor drive gear, belts and coupling; adjust or replace as needed.	H174	P-3	3A1.4
• Inspect air compressor inlet; inspect oil supply and coolant lines, fittings, and mounting brackets; repair or replace as needed.	H175	P-1	3A1.5

Materials Required

- Vehicle with possible brake concern
- Vehicle manufacturer's service information
- Manufacturer-specific tools depending on the concern
- Vehicle lifting equipment if applicable

Some Safety Issues to Consider

- Diagnosis of this fault may require test driving the vehicle on the school grounds or on a hoist, both of which carry severe risks. Attempt this task only with full permission from your supervisor/instructor and follow all the guidelines exactly.
- Caution: If you are working in an area where there could be brake dust present (may contain asbestos, which has been determined to cause cancer when inhaled or ingested), ensure you wear and use all OSHA-approved asbestos protective/removal equipment.
- Lifting equipment such as vehicle jacks and stands, vehicle hoists, and engine hoists are important tools that increase productivity and make the job easier. However, they can also cause severe injury or death if used improperly. Make sure you follow the manufacturer's operation procedures. Also make sure you have your supervisor/instructor's permission to use any particular type of lifting equipment.
- Comply with personal and environmental safety practices associated with clothing; eye protection; hand tools; power equipment; proper ventilation; and the handling, storage, and disposal of chemicals/materials in accordance with federal, state, and local regulations.
- Always wear the correct protective eyewear and clothing and use the appropriate safety equipment, as well as fender covers, seat protectors, and floor mat protectors.
- Make sure you understand and observe all legislative and personal safety procedures when carrying out practical assignments. If you are unsure of what these are, ask your supervisor/instructor.

Performance Standard

0–No exposure: No information or practice provided during the program; complete training required

1–Exposure only: General information provided with no practice time; close supervision needed; additional training required

2–Limited practice: Has practiced job during training program; additional training required to develop skill

3–Moderately skilled: Has performed job independently during training program; limited additional training may be required

4–Skilled: Can perform job independently with no additional training

Student/intern information:

Name_____ Date_____ Class_____

Vehicle used for this activity:

Year_____ Make_____ Model_____

Odometer_____ VIN _____

▶ **TASK** Drain air reservoir/tanks; check for oil, water, and foreign material; determine needed action.
NATEF 3A1.3

Time off_____

Time on_____

Total time_____

CDX Tasksheet Number: H173

- **Engine "OFF" checks**

    1. Drain the air reservoir. Use an appropriate drain container to capture any discharged fluid.
        a. With the drain container under each air reservoir tank, open the drain cock, and collect all waste fluid.

    2. Check for any contamination:
        a. Is there any oil present in the reservoir residue?
           Yes: _____ No: _____ Comments: _____
        b. Is there any water present in the reservoir residue?
           Yes: _____ No: _____ Comments: _____
        c. Is there any foreign material present in the reservoir residue?
           Yes: _____ No: _____ Comments: _____

    3. Determine what action is required to correct any faults within the system.
        a. List all the actions that are required to identify the source of the contamination:

           _____
           _____
           _____
           _____

        b. List all the actions that are required to correct any identified fault(s):

           _____
           _____
           _____
           _____

    4. Discuss these findings with your instructor.

Performance Rating

CDX Tasksheet Number: H173

☐   ☐   ☐   ☐   ☐
0   1   2   3   4

Supervisor/instructor signature _____ Date_____

Student/intern information:

Name_____ Date_____ Class_____

Vehicle used for this activity:

Year_____ Make_____ Model_____

Odometer_____ VIN _____

▶ **TASK** Inspect air compressor drive gear, belts and coupling; adjust or replace as needed.

NATEF 3A1.4

Time off_____

Time on_____

Total time_____

CDX Tasksheet Number: H174

1. Inspect air compressor drive gear, belts and coupling; adjust or replace as needed.

   a. Condition of drive gear:
      Good: _____ Needs adjustment: _____ Needs replacing: _____

   b. Condition of coupling (if applicable):
      Good: _____ Needs adjustment: _____ Needs replacing: _____

   c. Condition and tightness of belt (if applicable):
      Good: _____ Needs replacing: _____

   d. List the faults indicated above:

      _____
      _____
      _____

   e. List adjustment procedures as per the manufacturer's service information:

      _____
      _____
      _____
      _____

2. Discuss these findings with your instructor.

3. If directed by your instructor, carry out any necessary repairs.

Performance Rating

CDX Tasksheet Number: H174

☐ 0   ☐ 1   ☐ 2   ☐ 3   ☐ 4

Supervisor/instructor signature _____ Date_____

Student/intern information:

Name_____ Date_____ Class_____

Vehicle used for this activity:

Year_____ Make_____ Model_____

Odometer_____ VIN _____

▶ TASK Inspect air compressor inlet; inspect oil supply and coolant lines, fittings, and mounting brackets; repair or replace as needed.   NATEF 3A1.5

CDX Tasksheet Number: H175

© 2017 Jones & Bartlett Learning, LLC, an Ascend Learning Company

Time off_____

Time on_____

Total time_____

1. Inspect the air compressor inlet connections and piping.

    a. Condition of inlet connectors: Good: _____ Needs replacing: _____

    b. Condition of air compressor piping from air compressor to reservoirs:
        Good: _____ Needs replacing: _____

    c. List the faults indicated above:

        _____
        _____
        _____

    d. List your recommendations to correct any problems uncovered:

        _____
        _____

2. Inspect the air compressor coolant lines and connections.

    a. Condition of coolant lines: Good: _____ Needs replacing: _____

    b. Condition of coolant connections at the air compressor and engine connections:
        Good: _____ Needs replacing: _____

    c. List the faults indicated above:

        _____
        _____
        _____

    d. List your recommendations to correct any problems uncovered:

        _____
        _____

3. Inspect the air compressor mounting bracket(s).

    a. Condition of bracket(s): Good: _____ Needs replacing: _____

    b. List the faults indicated above:

        _____
        _____
        _____

    c. List your recommendations to correct any problems uncovered:

        _____

4. If directed by your instructor, carry out any necessary repairs.

5. Discuss findings and completed work repairs with your instructor.

Performance Rating

☐   ☐   ☐   ☐   ☐

0   1   2   3   4

Supervisor/instructor signature _____ Date_____

Air & Hydraulic Brake Systems:
Air Brakes 3: Air Supply and Service Systems

Student/intern information:

Name_____ Date_____ Class_____

Vehicle used for this activity:

Year_____ Make_____ Model_____

Odometer_____ VIN _____

Time off_____

Time on_____

Total time_____

Learning Objective / Task	CDX Tasksheet Number	2014 NATEF Priority Level	2014 NATEF Reference Number
• Inspect and test air system pressure controls, governor, unloader assembly valves, filters, lines, hoses, and fittings; adjust or replace as needed.	H176	P-1	3A1.6
• Inspect air system lines, hoses, fittings, and couplings; repair or replace as needed.	H177	P-1	3A1.7
• Inspect and test air tank relief (safety) valves, one-way (single) check valves, two-way (double) check valves, manual and automatic drain valves; replace as needed.	H178	P-1	3A1.8
• Inspect and clean air drier systems, filters, valves, heaters, wiring, and connectors; repair or replace as needed.	H179	P-1	3A1.9
• Inspect and test brake application (foot/treadle) valve, fittings, and mounts; check pedal operation; replace as needed.	H180	P-1	3A1.10
• Inspect and test stop light circuit switches, wiring, and connectors; repair or replace as needed.	H181	P-1	3A1.11
• Inspect and test hand brake (trailer) control valve, lines, fittings, and mountings; repair or replace as needed.	H182	P-1	3A1.12
• Inspect and test brake relay valves; replace as needed.	H183	P-1	3A1.13
• Inspect and test quick release valves; replace as needed.	H184	P-1	3A1.14
• Inspect and test tractor protection valve; replace as needed.	H185	P-1	3A1.15
• Inspect and test emergency (spring) brake control/ modulator valve(s); replace as needed.	H186	P-1	3A1.16
• Inspect and test low pressure warning devices, wiring, and connectors; repair or replace as needed.	H187	P-1	3A1.17
• Inspect and test air pressure gauges, lines, and fittings; replace as needed.	H188	P-2	3A1.18

Materials Required

- Vehicle with possible brake concern
- Vehicle manufacturer's service information
- Manufacturer-specific tools depending on the concern
- Vehicle lifting equipment if applicable

Some Safety Issues to Consider

- Diagnosis of this fault may require test driving the vehicle on the school grounds or on a hoist, both of which carry severe risks. Attempt this task only with full permission from your supervisor/instructor and follow all the guidelines exactly.

- Caution: If you are working in an area where there could be brake dust present (may contain asbestos, which has been determined to cause cancer when inhaled or ingested), ensure you wear and use all OSHA-approved asbestos protective/removal equipment.

- Lifting equipment such as vehicle jacks and stands, vehicle hoists, and engine hoists are important tools that increase productivity and make the job easier. However, they can also cause severe injury or death if used improperly. Make sure you follow the manufacturer's operation procedures. Also make sure you have your supervisor/instructor's permission to use any particular type of lifting equipment.

- Comply with personal and environmental safety practices associated with clothing; eye protection; hand tools; power equipment; proper ventilation; and the handling, storage, and disposal of chemicals/materials in accordance with federal, state, and local regulations.

- Always wear the correct protective eyewear and clothing and use the appropriate safety equipment, as well as fender covers, seat protectors, and floor mat protectors.

- Make sure you understand and observe all legislative and personal safety procedures when carrying out practical assignments. If you are unsure of what these are, ask your supervisor/instructor.

Performance Standard

0–No exposure: No information or practice provided during the program; complete training required

1–Exposure only: General information provided with no practice time; close supervision needed; additional training required

2–Limited practice: Has practiced job during training program; additional training required to develop skill

3–Moderately skilled: Has performed job independently during training program; limited additional training may be required

4–Skilled: Can perform job independently with no additional training

Student/intern information:

Name______________________ Date__________ Class______________

Vehicle used for this activity:

Year__________ Make______________________ Model______________

Odometer__________________ VIN __________________________

▶ TASK Inspect and test air system pressure controls, governor, unloader assembly valves, filters, lines, hoses, and fittings; adjust or replace as needed. **NATEF 3A1.6**

Time off________

Time on________

Total time________

CDX Tasksheet Number: H176

- **Engine "OFF" checks**

1. With reference to the manufacturer's service information, inspect the governor and unloader valve for any signs of malfunction.
    a. List your observations:

    ____

    ____

    ____

2. Discuss any visible defects with your instructor before proceeding.

3. Carry out any corrections as authorized by your instructor.

4. Governor cut-out specifications.
    a. Reference the manufacturer's service information and record the recommended "governor cut-out pressure": Specification: ________ psi (kPa)

- **Engine "ON" checks**

5. Testing the governor operation.
    a. Block and/or hold the vehicle by means other than air brakes during these tests.
    b. Drain the vehicle reservoirs. Ensure that a container(s) is placed under the drain cocks to collect any contaminants, then close the drain cocks.
    c. Install a test pressure gauge in the unloader circuit at the air governor.
    d. Start the engine and build up system pressure.
    e. As pressure in the system builds up there should be no pressure reading on the test gauge. You will need to time this procedure.
    f. Record the air pressure when the compressor is cut out by the governor.
        i. Air gauge reading when the governor cut out: ________ psi (kPa)
        ii. Time taken: ________ minutes
        iii. Are these measurements within the manufacturer's specifications: Yes: _____ No: _____
        iv. If no, list the necessary actions or corrections:

        ____

        ____

        ____

        ____

        ____

6. Shut the engine down.

7. Discuss these findings with your instructor.

8. If directed by your instructor, carry out the necessary repairs.

Performance Rating

CDX Tasksheet Number: H176

☐	☐	☐	☐	☐
0	1	2	3	4

Supervisor/instructor signature _____ Date_____

Student/intern information:

Name_____ Date_____ Class_____

Vehicle used for this activity:

Year_____ Make_____ Model_____

Odometer_____ VIN _____

▶ **TASK** Inspect air system lines, hoses, fittings, and couplings; repair or replace as needed.

CDX Tasksheet Number: H177

1. Carry out a visual inspection of the air compressor air filter, lines, hoses, and fittings.
   a. With reference to the manufacturer's service information, inspect, clean, or replace the air cleaner filter.

      i. Filter required: Yes: _____ No: _____

      ii. Cleaning and refitting required: Yes: _____ No: _____

      iii. Replacment required: Yes: _____ No: _____

      iv. Replaced: Yes: _____ No: _____

2. Inspection of the system piping.
   a. With reference to the manufacturer's service information, inspect the vehicle's air system lines and hoses. Reusable: Yes: _____ No: _____

   b. Inspect all air system fittings and couplings. Reusable: Yes: _____ No: _____

3. Discuss these findings with your instructor.

4. If directed by your instructor, carry out the necessary repairs.

5. Discuss findings and completed work repairs with your instructor.

CDX Tasksheet Number: H177

☐	☐	☐	☐	☐
0	1	2	3	4

Supervisor/instructor signature _____ Date_____

Time on_____

Total time_____

Student/intern information:

Name_____ Date_____ Class_____

Vehicle used for this activity:

Year_____ Make_____ Model_____

Odometer_____ VIN _____

▶ TASK Inspect and test air tank relief (safety) valves, one-way (single) check valves, two-way (double) check valves, manual and automatic drain valves; replace as needed.

NATEF 3A1.8

Time off_____

Time on_____

Total time_____

CDX Tasksheet Number: H178

> **Note:** When working with the air system, always wear safety glasses as a rupture in the system could cause injury to the eyes.

1. Build air system up to manufacturer specifications. Manufacturer's specifications: _____ psi (kPa)

2. Check for air leaks at all connections by using a soap and water solution in a spray bottle. Leaks present: Yes: _____ No: _____ Comments: _____

3. Test the air tank relief valve by setting the governor air pressure above pop off limit. This can also be done utilizing shop air. When pop off limit is reached, the valve should open up and vent the excess air pressure to prevent air system damage. Some relief valves have a ring or cable to pull to manually make the valve work. Working condition: Good: _____ Bad: _____ Comments: _____

4. Test the one-way check valve by removing it and blowing air in the direction of flow through the supply port, then reverse air pressure to the delivery port. Air should flow through the supply port but not through the delivery port in the reverse direction. Working condition: Good: _____ Bad: _____ Comments: _____

5. Test the two-way double-check valve. The two-way double-check valve seals against the lowest inlet pressure in the event of primary or secondary air loss. It will protect the circuit without air loss from the circuit with air loss. The outlet is supplied with both primary and secondary air.

   Testing can be done by building the air pressure up in both air tanks to govenor cut pressure. Then, with the engine off, drain the primary air tank only and note the secondary air pressure gauge on the dash. The air pressure should not have dropped. If it matches the primary air tank pressure, then the double-check valve failed and needs to be replaced. Repeat the procedure with the secondary air tank and watch the primary gauge. Working condition: Good: _____ Bad: _____ Comments: _____

6. Manual and automatic drain valves are used for removing moisture from the system. Manual valves have a pull cord to manually activate the valve to manually remove the moisture. Automatic valves operate when the air dryer pops off when air pressure in the system is fully charged. Automatic valves can be tested by unseating the wire stem valve with a sideways motion utilizing a finger or a plastic probe. Working condition: Good: _____ Bad: _____ Comments: _____

7. If directed by your instructor, inspect and replace all air valves discussed in accordance with the specifications listed in the service information; record any difficulties you ran into during this task:

_____
_____
_____
_____
_____

8. Discuss these findings with your instructor.

Performance Rating

CDX Tasksheet Number: H178

☐   ☐   ☐   ☐   ☐

0   1   2   3   4

Supervisor/instructor signature _____ Date_____

Student/intern information:

Name_____ Date_____ Class_____

Vehicle used for this activity:

Year_____ Make_____ Model_____

Odometer_____ VIN _____

▶ TASK Inspect and clean air drier systems, filters, valves, heaters, wiring, and connectors; repair or replace as needed. NATEF 3A1.9

Time off_____

Time on_____

Total time_____

CDX Tasksheet Number: H179

Note: Most vehicles do not operate under the same types of conditions so maintenance intervals may vary.

1. Open drain valves to check for moisture or contaminants in the system and drain them.
   a. Moisture or contaminants present: Yes: _____ No: _____ Comments: _____
   Note: A small amount of oil is not uncommon in the system and is not a cause to replace the desiccant in the air dryer.

2. Test the outlet port check valve by building air pressure up to the system governor cut off specification.
   a. Record system cutoff pressure: _____
   b. Outlet check valve operation: Good: _____ Bad: _____ Comments: _____

3. Check all lines leading to the air dryer itself for any possible leakage by utilizing a spray bottle with a soap and water solution or equivalent.
   a. Leaks present: Yes: _____ No: _____ Comments: _____

4. In servicing of the air dryer (depending on the type) follow the manufacturer's service information's procedure to replace filters and desiccants.
   a. If service is required, list the procedure you used to service the air dryer:

   _____
   _____
   _____

5. Inspect and test the heater element by utilizing a DVOM (Digital Volt Ohm Meter) to check for the correct resistance at the connector.
   a. Record manufacturer specified resistance value: _____ ohms
   b. Record actual resistance value: _____ ohms
   c. Condition of heater: Good: _____ Bad: _____ Comments: _____

6. Inspect electrical supply to the heater by utilizing a DVOM or test light to check for the proper electrical voltage.
   a. Record manufacturer specified supply voltage: _____volts
   b. Record actual supply voltage at the connector: _____volts
   c. Is the correct voltage supplied? Yes: _____ No: _____ Comments: _____

7. If any of the electrical components in the system need to be replaced, consult the manufacturer's service information for proper procedure to do so. Record the steps you took:

_____

_____

_____

_____

8. If directed by your instructor, service and replace failed components in the air dryer. List the steps you took:

_____

_____

_____

_____

9. Discuss these findings with your instructor.

Performance Rating

CDX Tasksheet Number: H179

☐   ☐   ☐   ☐   ☐
0   1   2   3   4

Supervisor/instructor signature _____ Date_____

Student/intern information:

Name_____ Date_____ Class_____

Vehicle used for this activity:

Year_____ Make_____ Model_____

Odometer_____ VIN _____

▶ TASK Inspect and test brake application (foot/treadle) valve, fittings, and mounts; check pedal operation; replace as needed.   **NATEF 3A1.10**

CDX Tasksheet Number: H180

Note: In testing and inspecting the foot/treadle/dual circuit application valve, be sure to have a working knowledge of the normal operation of the component.

1. Visually inspect the foot valve for any damage to the pedal or mountings.
    a. Condition: Good: _____ Bad: _____ Comments: _____

2. Inspect the condition of all air lines connected to the valve for looseness, cracking, kinking or air leaks.
    a. Record the condition of the lines:

    _____
    _____
    _____

3. Clean the area around the foot valve pedal boot for dirt or debris that may be present.

4. Check pedal pivot pin for looseness. Sometimes the pin can corrode from moisture and create a sticking condition that may cause the brake pedal to lock up in the applied position.
    Note: Spray WD-40 or equivalent on the pivot pin and move the pedal up and down to ensure correct pedal movement.
    a. Condition of the pivot pin: Good: _____ Bad: _____ Comments: _____

5. Check the rubber plunger boot for cracking (this can allow dirt/debris to enter).
    a. Condition of the pedal boot: Good: _____ Bad: _____ Comments: _____

6. Lubricate the plunger with oil to ensure smooth operation of the foot valve. Follow manufacturer guidelines.

7. Depress the foot valve and hold for 10 seconds while listening for leaks coming from or around the pedal area and lines. Good: _____ Bad: _____ Comments: _____

8. If leakage is present, record the procedure to repair the leak.

    _____
    _____
    _____
    _____
    _____

9. To test for pedal operation, build maximum air pressure and make a brake application. Look at the primary and secondary gauges on the dash board.

Time off_____

Time on_____

Total time_____

© 2017 Jones & Bartlett Learning, LLC, an Ascend Learning Company

Air & Hydraulic Brake Systems 151

10. The primary side gauge should read 2 psi (14 kPa) more than the secondary side gauge when both tanks are completely full.

11. Maximum pressure drop should be 25 psi (172 kPa) or less.
    a. Maximum pressure drop from foot valve application: _____ psi (kPa)

12. If leakage is present, check all connections outside the vehicle first. If massive leakage is present, at the exhaust port or anywhere else on the valve, it should be recommended for replacement.

13. Replace foot valve according to the manufacturer's service information. Record the steps you took:

    _____
    _____
    _____
    _____
    _____

14. Discuss these findings with your instructor.

Performance Rating

CDX Tasksheet Number: H180

☐   ☐   ☐   ☐   ☐

0   1   2   3   4

Supervisor/instructor signature _____ Date_____

Student/intern information:

Name_____ Date_____ Class_____

Vehicle used for this activity:

Year_____ Make_____ Model_____

Odometer_____ VIN _____

▶ **TASK** Inspect and test stop light circuit switches, wiring, and connectors; repair or replace as needed.   **NATEF 3A1.11**

Time off_____

Time on_____

Total time_____

CDX Tasksheet Number: H181

1. The double check valve and stop light switch is a combination of a stop light switch and a double check valve used for the front and rear axle service brakes application.

2. Inspect the circuit for any exposed wiring due to fraying or damage.
   a. Condition of wiring: Good: _____ Bad: _____ Comments: _____

3. Inspect the switch for any loose connections, corroded terminals or cracked housing conditions.
   a. Condition of switch and terminal: Good: _____ Bad: _____ Comments: _____

4. Check for proper voltage to the switch with the brakes in the applied position.
   a. Manufacturer recommended voltage: _____ volts
   b. Actual voltage supplied: _____ volts

5. If voltage is present but the lights do not illuminate, check all wiring to the rear tail lights. List your observations:

   _____

   _____

6. Record the manufacturer procedure to replace the stop light switch in the event of a failure.

   _____

   _____

   _____

   _____

   _____

7. Discuss these findings with your instructor.

Performance Rating

CDX Tasksheet Number: H181

☐	☐	☐	☐	☐
0	1	2	3	4

Supervisor/instructor signature _____ Date_____

Student/intern information:

Name_____ Date_____ Class_____

Vehicle used for this activity:

Year_____ Make_____ Model_____

Odometer_____ VIN _____

▶ **TASK**   Inspect and test hand brake (trailer) control valve, lines, fittings, and mountings; repair
or replace as needed.   **NATEF 3A1.12**

Time off_____

Time on_____

Total time_____

CDX Tasksheet Number: H182

> **Note:** This valve operates the trailer service brakes only.

1. Inspect mounting of the hand brake or trailer control valve (sometimes referred to as a trolley brake). Test to see if the hand brake valve is securely mounted to the steering column or, in some cases, on the dashboard.
   a. Condition of mountings: Good: _____ Bad: _____ Comments: _____

2. Verify all service supply and discharge lines are tight. List your observations:
   _____
   _____

3. Apply hand brake. Pull down on the handle and listen for any types of air leaks.
   a. Leaks present: Yes: _____ No: _____
   b. If leaks are present, identify the location of the leak and record the procedure to repair it.
   _____
   _____
   _____
   _____
   _____

4. Discuss these findings with your instructor.

Performance Rating

CDX Tasksheet Number: H182

☐	☐	☐	☐	☐
0	1	2	3	4

Supervisor/instructor signature _____ Date_____

Student/intern information:

Name_____ Date_____ Class_____

Vehicle used for this activity:

Year_____ Make_____ Model_____

Odometer_____ VIN _____

▶ **TASK** Inspect and test brake relay valves; replace as needed.   NATEF 3A1.13

CDX Tasksheet Number: H183

Time off_____

Time on_____

Total time_____

1. Inspect the relay valve every 3 months or 25,000 miles.

2. Every 12 months or 100,000 miles relay valves should be performance tested.
   a. Signal pressures and output of application pressures need to be tested for accuracy.

3. Block the wheels and bring the air system up to a full charge.
   a. Record manufacturer recommended system pressure: _____ psi (kPa)
   b. Record actual vehicle maximum pressure: _____ psi (kPa)

4. Verify that all brakes are adjusted as per manufacturer procedures. List your observations:
   _____
   _____
   _____

5. Make a series of brake applications and check each wheel for proper application and release. Record your findings:
   a. Wheel #1: _____
   b. Wheel #2: _____
   c. Wheel #3: _____
   d. Wheel #4: _____
   e. Wheel #5: _____
   f. Wheel #6: _____

6. Check each exhaust port for oil seepage. Oil seepage may indicate compressor problems.
   a. Leakage present: Yes: _____ No: _____ Comments: _____

7. Check all o-rings and any covers for the valve pistons. Spray a soap and water solution and observe for leaks. A one-inch (25 mm) bubble over a period of three seconds is acceptable. List your observations:
   _____
   _____
   _____

8. If the valve is being used for spring brake release, make sure the parking brake is in the released position.

9. If the valve does not function correctly, recommendations for replacement should be considered. List your observations:

_____
_____
_____

Note: New and remanufactured units are available.

10. If troubleshooting is required, consult the manufacturer's service information for procedures. Record the tests you performed and their results:

_____
_____
_____
_____
_____

11. Discuss these findings with your instructor.

Performance Rating

CDX Tasksheet Number: H183

☐   ☐   ☐   ☐   ☐

0   1   2   3   4

Supervisor/instructor signature _____ Date _____

Student/intern information:

Name_____ Date_____ Class_____

Vehicle used for this activity:

Year_____ Make_____ Model_____

Odometer_____ VIN _____

▶ **TASK** Inspect and test quick release valves; replace as needed. **NATEF 3A1.14**

CDX Tasksheet Number: H184

Time off_____

Time on_____

Total time_____

1. Inspect the quick release valve mountings. Check for loose bolts and any physical damage from road conditions.
    a. Condition of valve: Good: _____ Bad: _____ Comments: _____

2. Inspect the fittings and lines for looseness or cracking.
    a. Condition of fittings and lines: Good: _____ Bad: _____ Comments: _____

3. Inspect the exhaust port for oil contamination or air leakage.
    a. Condition of exhaust port: Good: _____ Bad: _____ Comments: _____

4. Ask a colleague to hold the pedal in the applied position while you check for air leakage.
    a. Leakage present: Yes: _____ No: _____ Comments: _____

5. If leakage is present, consult the manufacturer's service information for the procedure to repair or replace the quick release valve. List the steps you took to correct the fault:

    _____
    _____
    _____
    _____
    _____

6. Discuss these findings with your instructor.

Performance Rating

CDX Tasksheet Number: H184

☐	☐	☐	☐	☐
0	1	2	3	4

Supervisor/instructor signature _____ Date_____

Student/intern information:

Name_____ Date_____ Class_____

Vehicle used for this activity:

Year_____ Make_____ Model_____

Odometer_____ VIN _____

▶ **TASK**   Inspect and test tractor protection valve; replace as needed.   **NATEF 3A1.15**

CDX Tasksheet Number: H185

Time off_____

Time on_____

Total time_____

Note: The purpose of the tractor protection valve is to protect the tractor in case of a trailer breakaway.

1. Inspect the tractor protection valve for cracks and/or physical damage.
   a. Condition of tractor protection valve: Good: _____ Bad: _____ Comments: _____

2. Inspect all lines and connections for looseness or defects such as kinking or cracking.
   a. Condition of lines and connections: Good: _____ Bad: _____ Comments: _____

3. Test the tractor protection valve by building up full air pressure with the trailer connector or the trailer emergency line blocked with a "dummy" glad hand and the trailer brakes released. Then, remove the trailer supply line. Air will rush out for a few seconds, then stop. The trailer push/pull valve should pop out almost immediately to a few seconds.
   a. Testing of the valve: Pass: _____ Fail: _____ Comments: _____

4. If the test failed, follow the specified procedure to repair or replace the tractor protection valve. List the steps you performed to correct the fault:
   _____
   _____
   _____
   _____
   _____

5. Discuss these findings with your instructor.

Performance Rating

CDX Tasksheet Number: H185

☐ 0   ☐ 1   ☐ 2   ☐ 3   ☐ 4

Supervisor/instructor signature _____ Date_____

Student/intern information:

Name_____ Date_____ Class_____

Vehicle used for this activity:

Year_____ Make_____ Model_____

Odometer_____ VIN _____

▶ **TASK** Inspect and test low pressure warning devices, wiring, and connectors; repair or replace as needed. **NATEF 3A1.17**

Time off_____

Time on_____

Total time_____

CDX Tasksheet Number: H187

> **Note:** The low pressure warning switch illuminates a light on the dash to warn the driver of a low air pressure system condition. The light must turn on at a minimum of 55 psi (379 kPa). The light should be off at slightly above 60 psi (414 kPa).

1. Located in the supply or wet tank, inspect the switch for any damage to the switch itself.
   a. Condition of switch: Good: _____ Bad: _____ Comments: _____

2. Inspect all wiring for fraying, loose connections and/or bad connectors.
   a. Condition of electrical wiring: Good: _____ Bad: _____ Comments: _____

3. Test the switch terminals for resistance: _____ Volts/Ohms
   Note: Resistance value varies by manufacturer.

4. Test switch operation by building up air pressure to maximum pressure.
   a. The light should be off.

5. Drain the air from the system and record the air pressure when the light illuminates.
   a. The light illuminates at: _____ psi (kPa)

6. If the light failed to come on, follow the specified procedure to repair or replace the low pressure warning switch. List the steps you performed to correct the fault:
   _____
   _____
   _____
   _____
   _____

7. Discuss these findings with your instructor.

Performance Rating

CDX Tasksheet Number: H187

☐ 0   ☐ 1   ☐ 2   ☐ 3   ☐ 4

Supervisor/instructor signature _____ Date_____

Student/intern information:

Name_____ Date_____ Class_____

Vehicle used for this activity:

Year_____ Make_____ Model_____

Odometer_____ VIN _____

▶ **TASK** Inspect and test air pressure gauges, lines, and fittings; replace as needed.

NATEF 3A1.18

Time off_____

Time on_____

Total time_____

CDX Tasksheet Number: H188

1. Inspect air pressure gauge for moisture or fogging of the gauge face.
    a. Condition of gauge: Good: _____ Bad: _____ Comments: _____

2. Inspect air pressure gauge needles for operation and condition.
    a. Condition of gauge needles: Pass: _____ Fail: _____ Comments: _____

3. Inspect air pressure gauge for cracking or missing glass face.
    a. Condition of gauge face: Good: _____ Bad: _____ Comments: _____

4. Inspect mounting of the gauges in the dashboard for looseness.

5. Inspect gauge air line connections for looseness or leaking.
    a. Leaks present: Yes: _____ No: _____ Comments: _____

6. Check condition or fittings and lines for cracking or kinking. Comments: _____

7. Test gauge accuracy by starting the vehicle and building the air pressure to maximum.
    Compare readings to a known good gauge set.
    a. Accuracy of gauge: Pass: _____ Fail: _____ Comments: _____

8. If the gauge fails or is inaccurate, follow the specified procedure to repair or replace the gauge.
    List the steps you performed to correct the fault:

    _____

    _____

    _____

    _____

9. Discuss these findings with your instructor.

Performance Rating

CDX Tasksheet Number: H188

☐ 0   ☐ 1   ☐ 2   ☐ 3   ☐ 4

Supervisor/instructor signature _____ Date_____

Air & Hydraulic Brake Systems:
Air Brakes 4: Mechanical and Foundation Brakes

Student/intern information:

Name_____ Date_____ Class_____

Vehicle used for this activity:

Year_____ Make_____ Model_____

Odometer_____ VIN _____

Time off_____

Time on_____

Total time_____

Learning Objective / Task	CDX Tasksheet Number	2014 NATEF Priority Level	2014 NATEF Reference Number
• Identify poor stopping, brake noise, premature wear, pulling, grabbing, or dragging problems caused by the foundation brake, slack adjuster, and brake chamber problems; determine needed action.	H189	P-1	3A2.1

Materials Required

- Vehicle with possible engine concern
- Vehicle manufacturer's service information
- Manufacturer-specific tools depending on the concern
- Vehicle lifting equipment if applicable

Some Safety Issues to Consider

- Diagnosis of this fault may require test driving the vehicle on the school grounds or on a hoist, both of which carry severe risks. Attempt this task only with full permission from your supervisor/instructor and follow all the guidelines exactly.
- Caution: If you are working in an area where there could be brake dust present (may contain asbestos, which has been determined to cause cancer when inhaled or ingested), ensure you wear and use all OSHA-approved asbestos protective/removal equipment.
- Lifting equipment such as vehicle jacks and stands, vehicle hoists, and engine hoists are important tools that increase productivity and make the job easier. However, they can also cause severe injury or death if used improperly. Make sure you follow the manufacturer's operation procedures. Also make sure you have your supervisor/instructor's permission to use any particular type of lifting equipment.
- Comply with personal and environmental safety practices associated with clothing; eye protection; hand tools; power equipment; proper ventilation; and the handling, storage, and disposal of chemicals/materials in accordance with federal, state, and local regulations.
- Always wear the correct protective eyewear and clothing and use the appropriate safety equipment, as well as fender covers, seat protectors, and floor mat protectors.
- Make sure you understand and observe all legislative and personal safety procedures when carrying out practical assignments. If you are unsure of what these are, ask your supervisor/instructor.

Performance Standard

0—No exposure: No information or practice provided during the program; complete training required

1—Exposure only: General information provided with no practice time; close supervision needed; additional training required

2—Limited practice: Has practiced job during training program; additional training required to develop skill

3—Moderately skilled: Has performed job independently during training program; limited additional training may be required

4—Skilled: Can perform job independently with no additional training

Student/intern information:

Name_____ Date_____ Class_____

Vehicle used for this activity:

Year_____ Make_____ Model_____

Odometer_____ VIN _____

▶ **TASK** Identify poor stopping, brake noise, premature wear, pulling, grabbing, or dragging problems caused by the foundation brake, slack adjuster, and brake chamber problems; determine needed action.   **NATEF 3A2.1**

CDX Tasksheet Number: H189

1. Obtain information about the circumstances surrounding the complaint.
   a. Obtain current vehicle trip maintenance reports.
   b. Are there any comments on braking issues? Yes: _____ No: _____
      i. If yes, summarize the driver's comments:

      _____
      _____
      _____

   c. If the driver's comments are unavailable, obtain as much information as possible on the complaint.

2. Test air pressure build-up time:
   a. Reference manufacturer's service information:
      i. Record recommended air pressure build-up time:
         Specification: _____ psi (kPa)   within _____ minutes
      ii. How long did it take for the air pressure to build up to the specified pressure?

      _____

      iii. Did the air pressure build-up time meet manufacturer's specifications?
         Yes: _____ No: _____
      iv. If no, list the necessary actions or corrections:

      _____
      _____
      _____

3. Check brake chambers and air lines for secure mounting and damage:
   a. Ensure all brake chambers, mountings, and air activation lines are operational and in serviceable conditions:
      i. Following the procedure from the manufacturer's service information, carry out visual inspection of air brake chambers, mounting, and air lines:
         Serviceable: _____ Need Repairs/Unserviceable: _____ Comments: _____
      ii. If no, list the necessary actions or corrections:

      _____
      _____
      _____

4. Check brake circuit for any signs of air leakage:
   a. Check air system for air leaks **(brakes released)**:
      i. Following the procedure from the manufacturer's service information, check the air brake system components for air leaks: No Leaks: _____ Leaks: _____
      ii. If leaks are detected, list the areas and the necessary actions or corrections:

      _____
      _____
      _____

b. Check air system for air leaks **(brakes applied)**:
   i. Following the procedure from manufacturer's service information, recheck the air brake system components for air leaks: No Leaks: _____ Leaks: _____
   ii. If leaks are detected, list the areas and the necessary actions or corrections:
   _____
   _____

5. Check operation of brake manual slack adjusters; adjust as needed (if applicable):
   a. Check serviceability of manual slack adjusters:
      i. Reference manufacturer's service information for the correct procedure for checking the manual slack adjusters operation. List the specified slack adjustment: _____
      ii. Inspect each manual slack adjuster for serviceability. List your observations:
      _____
      _____

      iii. List any necessary actions or corrections:
      _____
      _____

      iv. Apply the foundation brakes.
      v. With the brakes applied, check the pushrod travel:
         a. Specified pushrod travel: _____
         b. Actual pushrod travel: _____
         c. Within specifications: Yes: _____ No: _____
      vi. If no, adjust manual slack adjusters to come within vehicle manufacturer's specifications. List the steps you performed.
      _____
      _____

6. Check operation and adjustment of brake automatic slack adjusters:
   a. Check serviceability of automatic slack adjusters:
      i. Reference manufacturer's service information for the correct procedure for checking the automatic slack adjusters operation.
      ii. Inspect each automatic slack adjuster for serviceability: Within specifications: Yes: _____ No: _____
      iii. If no, list the necessary actions or corrections:
      _____
      _____
      _____

      iv. Apply the foundation brakes.
      v. With the brakes applied, check the pushrod travel:
         a. Specified pushrod travel: _____
         b. Actual pushrod travel: _____
         c. Within specifications: Yes: _____ No: _____
      vi. If no, list the necessary actions or corrections:
      _____
      _____
      _____

7. Discuss these findings with your instructor.

Performance Rating

CDX Tasksheet Number: H189

0	1	2	3	4
☐	☐	☐	☐	☐

Supervisor/instructor signature _____ Date _____

Air & Hydraulic Brake Systems:
Air Brakes 5: Mechanical and Foundation Brakes

Student/intern information:

Name_____ Date_____ Class_____

Vehicle used for this activity:

Year_____ Make_____ Model_____

Odometer_____ VIN _____

Learning Objective / Task	CDX Tasksheet Number	2014 NATEF Priority Level	2014 NATEF Reference Number
• Inspect and test service brake chambers, diaphragm, clamp, spring, pushrod, clevis, and mounting brackets; repair or replace as needed.	H190	P-1	3A2.2
• Identify type, inspect and service slack adjusters; perform needed action.	H191	P-1	3A2.3

Time off_____

Time on_____

Total time_____

Materials Required

- Vehicle with possible engine concern
- Vehicle manufacturer's service information
- Manufacturer-specific tools depending on the concern
- Vehicle lifting equipment if applicable

Some Safety Issues to Consider

- Diagnosis of this fault may require test driving the vehicle on the school grounds or on a hoist, both of which carry severe risks. Attempt this task only with full permission from your supervisor/instructor and follow all the guidelines exactly.
- Caution: If you are working in an area where there could be brake dust present (may contain asbestos, which has been determined to cause cancer when inhaled or ingested), ensure you wear and use all OSHA-approved asbestos protective/removal equipment.
- Lifting equipment such as vehicle jacks and stands, vehicle hoists, and engine hoists are important tools that increase productivity and make the job easier. However, they can also cause severe injury or death if used improperly. Make sure you follow the manufacturer's operation procedures. Also make sure you have your supervisor/instructor's permission to use any particular type of lifting equipment.
- Comply with personal and environmental safety practices associated with clothing; eye protection; hand tools; power equipment; proper ventilation; and the handling, storage, and disposal of chemicals/materials in accordance with federal, state, and local regulations.
- Always wear the correct protective eyewear and clothing and use the appropriate safety equipment, as well as fender covers, seat protectors, and floor mat protectors.
- Make sure you understand and observe all legislative and personal safety procedures when carrying out practical assignments. If you are unsure of what these are, ask your supervisor/instructor.

Performance Standard

0–No exposure: No information or practice provided during the program; complete training required

1–Exposure only: General information provided with no practice time; close supervision needed; additional training required

2–Limited practice: Has practiced job during training program; additional training required to develop skill

3–Moderately skilled: Has performed job independently during training program; limited additional training may be required

4–Skilled: Can perform job independently with no additional training

Student/intern information:

Name_____ Date_____ Class_____

Vehicle used for this activity:

Year_____ Make_____ Model_____

Odometer_____ VIN _____

Inspect and test service brake chambers, diaphragm, clamp, spring, pushrod, clevis, and mounting brackets; repair or replace as needed.   NATEF 3A2.2

Time off_____

Time on_____

CDX Tasksheet Number: H190

Total time_____

1. Reference the manufacturer's service information for the correct procedure for checking the service brake chamber(s), including internal components:
    a. List the procedure for servicing the service brake chamber, noting all safety precautions listed by the manufacturer.

    _____

    _____

    _____

    b. Discuss these findings with your instructor.
    c. If directed by your instructor, carry out this service procedure.

2. Remove and inspect service brake chamber.
    a. Referencing the manufacturer's service information, remove and dismantle the service brake chamber.

    Note: Read the safety precautions before releasing the chamber clamp retaining bolt assembly.

3. Inspect the serviceability of each component:
    a. Clevis Pin: Within specifications: Yes: _____ No: _____ Comments: _____
        i. If no, list the necessary actions or corrections:

        _____

        _____

        _____

    b. Visual inspection of brake chamber housing: Within specifications:
       Yes: _____ No: _____ Comments: _____
        i. If no, list the necessary actions or corrections:

        _____

        _____

        _____

    c. Brake chamber housing clamp and retainer: Within specifications:
       Yes: _____ No: _____ Comments: _____
        i. If no, list the necessary actions or corrections:

        _____

        _____

        _____

d. Brake chamber diaphragm: Within specifications:
   Yes: _____ No: _____ Comments: _____
      i. If no, list the necessary actions or corrections:

   _____
   _____
   _____

e. Brake chamber spring: Within specifications:
   Yes: _____ No: _____ Comments: _____
      i. If no, list the necessary actions or corrections:

   _____
   _____
   _____

4. Discuss these findings with your instructor.

5. If directed by your instructor, reassemble the service brake chamber in accordance with the manufacturer's procedure and reinstall on the vehicle.

Performance Rating

CDX Tasksheet Number: H190

☐
0

☐
1

☐
2

☐
3

☐
4

Supervisor/instructor signature _____ Date_____

Student/intern information:

Name_____ Date_____ Class_____

Vehicle used for this activity:

Year_____ Make_____ Model_____

Odometer_____ VIN _____

▶TASK Identify type, inspect and service slack adjusters; perform needed action.

NATEF 3A2.3

CDX Tasksheet Number: H191

1. Reference the manufacturer's service information for the correct procedure for checking and servicing the service brake slack adjuster(s):
   a. List the procedure for servicing the service brake slack adjuster, noting all safety precautions listed by the manufacturer:

   _____
   _____
   _____
   _____
   _____

   b. Discuss these findings with your instructor.
   c. If directed by your instructor, carry out this service procedure.

2. Remove and inspect service brake slack adjuster(s):
   a. Referencing the manufacturer's service information, remove and inspect the service brake slack adjuster.
      i. Remove the slack adjuster from the S-cam shaft and place on your work station
      ii. Inspect the serviceability of each component:
         a. Clevis Pin hole(s): Within specifications:
            Yes: _____ No: _____ Comments: _____
            i. If no, list the necessary actions or corrections:

            _____
            _____
            _____
            _____
            _____

         b. Visual inspection of slack adjuster housing for signs of cracking or damage: Within specifications:
            Yes: _____ No: _____ Comments: _____
            i. If no, list the necessary actions or corrections:

            _____
            _____
            _____
            _____
            _____

  c. Visual inspection of slack adjuster adjustment components for seizure, looseness, cracking, or damage: Within specifications:

   Yes: _____ No: _____ Comments: _____

    i. If no, list the necessary actions or corrections:

     _____

     _____

     _____

     _____

     _____

  b. Lubricate the slack adjuster as outlined in the manufacturer's service information.

  c. Discuss these findings with your instructor.

  d. If directed by your instructor, reassemble the service brake chamber in accordance with the manufacturer's procedure and reinstall on the vehicle.

3. Discuss these findings with your instructor.

Performance Rating

CDX Tasksheet Number: H191

☐	☐	☐	☐	☐
0	1	2	3	4

Supervisor/instructor signature _____ Date_____

© 2017 Jones & Bartlett Learning, LLC, an Ascend Learning Company

Air & Hydraulic Brake Systems:
Air Brakes 6: Mechanical and Foundation Brakes

Student/intern information:

Name_____ Date_____ Class_____

Vehicle used for this activity:

Year_____ Make_____ Model_____

Odometer_____ VIN _____

Time off_____

Time on_____

Total time_____

Learning Objective / Task	CDX Tasksheet Number	2014 NATEF Priority Level	2014 NATEF Reference Number
• Inspect camshafts, tubes, rollers, bushings, seals, spacers, retainers, brake spiders, shields, anchor pins, and springs; replace as needed.	H192	P-1	2A2.4
• Inspect, clean, and adjust air disc brake caliper assemblies; determine needed repairs.	H193	P-2	3A2.5
• Inspect and measure brake shoes or pads; perform needed action.	H194	P-1	3A2.6
• Inspect and measure brake drums or rotors; perform needed action.	H195	P-1	3A2.7

Materials Required
- Vehicle with possible engine concern
- Vehicle manufacturer's service information
- Manufacturer-specific tools depending on the concern
- Vehicle lifting equipment if applicable

Some Safety Issues to Consider
- Diagnosis of this fault may require test driving the vehicle on the school grounds or on a hoist, both of which carry severe risks. Attempt this task only with full permission from your supervisor/instructor and follow all the guidelines exactly.
- Caution: If you are working in an area where there could be brake dust present (may contain asbestos, which has been determined to cause cancer when inhaled or ingested), ensure you wear and use all OSHA-approved asbestos protective/removal equipment.
- Lifting equipment such as vehicle jacks and stands, vehicle hoists, and engine hoists are important tools that increase productivity and make the job easier. However, they can also cause severe injury or death if used improperly. Make sure you follow the manufacturer's operation procedures. Also make sure you have your supervisor/instructor's permission to use any particular type of lifting equipment.
- Comply with personal and environmental safety practices associated with clothing; eye protection; hand tools; power equipment; proper ventilation; and the handling, storage, and disposal of chemicals/materials in accordance with federal, state, and local regulations.
- Always wear the correct protective eyewear and clothing and use the appropriate safety equipment, as well as fender covers, seat protectors, and floor mat protectors.
- Make sure you understand and observe all legislative and personal safety procedures when carrying out practical assignments. If you are unsure of what these are, ask your supervisor/instructor.

Performance Standard

0–No exposure: No information or practice provided during the program; complete training required

1–Exposure only: General information provided with no practice time; close supervision needed; additional training required

2–Limited practice: Has practiced job during training program; additional training required to develop skill

3–Moderately skilled: Has performed job independently during training program; limited additional training may be required

4–Skilled: Can perform job independently with no additional training

Name_____ Date_____ Class_____

Vehicle used for this activity:

Year_____ Make_____ Model_____

Odometer_____ VIN _____

▶ **TASK** Inspect camshafts, tubes, rollers, bushings, seals, spacers, retainers, brake spiders, shields, anchor pins, and springs; replace as needed.   **NATEF 3A2.4**

Time off_____

Time on_____

CDX Tasksheet Number: H192

Total time_____

1. With reference to the vehicle manufacturer's service information, research the description and operation of the brake system for this vehicle including the drum brake inspection and servicing procedures plus wheel assembly and brake drum(s) removal/installation procedures:

    a. List the procedure for servicing the service brake assembly, noting all safety precautions listed by the manufacturer:

    _____
    _____
    _____
    _____
    _____

    b. Discuss these findings with your instructor.

2. If instructed by your instructor, carry out the inspection procedure.

    a. Referencing the manufacturer's service information, remove and disassemble the wheel and drum assembly.

    b. Inspect the serviceability of each component:

        i. Cam shaft: Within specifications:
            Yes: _____ No: _____ Comments: _____
            a. If no, list the necessary actions or corrections:

            _____
            _____
            _____
            _____
            _____

        ii. S-cam tubes: Within specifications:
            Yes: _____ No: _____ Comments: _____
            a. If no, list the necessary actions or corrections:

            _____
            _____
            _____

        iii. S Cam rollers: Within specifications:
            Yes: _____ No: _____ Comments: _____
            a. If no, list the necessary actions or corrections:

            _____
            _____
            _____

iv. Cam shaft bushings, seals spacers, and retainers: Within specifications:
   Yes: _____ No: _____ Comments: _____
   a. If no, list the necessary actions or corrections:
   _____
   _____
   _____

v. Brake spider(s): Within specifications:
   Yes: _____ No: _____ Comments: _____
   a. If no, list the necessary actions or corrections:
   _____
   _____
   _____

vi. Dust shield, anchor pins, and springs: Within specifications:
   Yes: _____ No: _____ Comments: _____
   a. If no, list the necessary actions or corrections:
   _____
   _____
   _____

3. Have your instructor verify disassembly and your answers.
   Supervisor/instructor's initials: _____

4. If directed by your instructor, reassemble the brake assembly. List any difficulties you encounter:
   _____
   _____
   _____

Performance Rating

CDX Tasksheet Number: H192

☐   ☐   ☐   ☐   ☐

0   1   2   3   4

Supervisor/instructor signature _____ Date_____

Student/intern information:

Name_____ Date_____ Class_____

Vehicle used for this activity:

Year_____ Make_____ Model_____

Odometer_____ VIN _____

Inspect, clean, and adjust air disc brake caliper assemblies (if applicable); determine needed repairs.   **NATEF 3A2.5**

Time off_____

Time on_____

Total time_____

CDX Tasksheet Number: H193

1. List the procedure for inspecting, cleaning, and adjusting the air disc brake caliper assemblies, noting all safety precautions listed by the manufacturer:

   _____
   _____
   _____
   _____
   _____

   a. Discuss these findings with your instructor.

2. Following the specified procedure, inspect the air disc brake caliper assemblies' components:
   a. List your observations:

   _____
   _____

   b. Within specifications: Yes: _____ No: _____
   c. Determine any necessary actions:

   _____
   _____

3. Following the specified procedure, clean and adjust the air disc brake caliper assembly.
   a. List your observations:

   _____
   _____
   _____

   b. Within specifications: Yes: _____ No: _____
   c. Determine any necessary actions:

   _____
   _____

4. Discuss these findings with your instructor.

Performance Rating

CDX Tasksheet Number: H193

☐	☐	☐	☐	☐
0	1	2	3	4

Supervisor/instructor signature _____ Date_____

Student/intern information:

Name_____ Date_____ Class_____

Vehicle used for this activity:

Year_____ Make_____ Model_____

Odometer_____ VIN _____

▶ **TASK** Inspect and measure brake shoes or pads; perform needed action.   NATEF 3A2.6

CDX Tasksheet Number: H194

1. With reference to the vehicle manufacturer's service information, research the description and operation of the brake system for this vehicle, including the researching of drum brake diagnostic procedures plus wheel assembly and brake drum(s) removal/installation procedures:
    a. Record the following specifications:
        i.   Maximum drum diameter: _____ in/mm
        ii. Maximum drum out-of-round: _____ in/mm
        iii. Minimum lining thickness (Primary): _____ in/mm
        iv. Minimum lining thickness (Secondary): _____ in/mm

2. Visually inspect the brake shoes. List your observations:
    _____
    _____

3. Measure each of the components and list their readings:
    a. Drum diameter: _____ in/mm
    b. Drum out-of-round: _____ in/mm
    c. Minimum lining thickness (Primary): _____ in/mm
    d. Minimum lining thickness (Secondary): _____ in/mm
    e. Are these measurements within specifications? Yes: _____ No: _____
    f. Determine any necessary actions or corrections:
        _____
        _____
        _____

4. Have your instructor verify disassembly and your answers.
    Supervisor/instructor's initials: _____

5. Reassemble the drum and wheel assembly in accordance with manufacturer's specifications.

6. Ensure the wheel lug nuts are torqued to manufacturer's specifications.

7. Discuss these findings with your instructor.

Time off_____

Time on_____

Total time_____

Performance Rating

CDX Tasksheet Number: H194

☐ 0   ☐ 1   ☐ 2   ☐ 3   ☐ 4

Supervisor/instructor signature _____ Date_____

© 2017 Jones & Bartlett Learning, LLC, an Ascend Learning Company

Name_____ Date_____ Class_____

Vehicle used for this activity:

Year_____ Make_____ Model_____

Odometer_____ VIN _____

▶ **TASK** Inspect and measure brake drums or rotors; perform needed action. **NATEF 3A2.7**

CDX Tasksheet Number: H195

Time off_____

Time on_____

Total time_____

1. Research the procedure to inspect and measure brake drums and rotors in the appropriate service information. List the following specifications:
   a. Maximum rotor diameter: _____ in/mm
   b. Maximum rotor out-of-round: _____ in/mm
   c. Maximum rotor thickness variation: _____ in/mm
   d. Minimum pad thickness: (Outer) _____ in/mm
   e. Minimum pad thickness (Inner) _____ in/mm

2. Following the specified procedure, remove the caliper and brake pads from one brake assembly.
   a. Visually inspect the brake pads and rotor for any damage and wear. List your observations:

   _____

   _____

   b. Perform the following measurements:
      i. Actual rotor diameter: _____ in/mm
      ii. Actual rotor out-of-round: _____ in/mm
      iii. Actual rotor thickness variation: _____ in/mm
      iv. Actual pad thickness: (Outer) _____ in/mm
      v. Actual pad thickness (Inner) _____ in/mm
   c. Are these measurements within specifications? Yes: _____ No: _____
   d. Determine any necessary actions or corrections:

   _____

   _____

3. Have your instructor verify disassembly and your answers.
   Supervisor/instructor's initials: _____

4. Reassemble the disc caliper/pad(s) and wheel assembly following the specified procedure.

5. Ensure the wheel lug nuts are torqued to manufacturer's specification and tightening sequence.

6. Wheel lug nut torque specification: _____ ft-lb (Nm)

7. Actual torque: _____ ft-lb (Nm)

8. Discuss these findings with your instructor.

Performance Rating

CDX Tasksheet Number: H195

☐	☐	☐	☐	☐
0	1	2	3	4

Supervisor/instructor signature _____ Date_____

Air & Hydraulic Brake Systems:
Air Brakes 7: Parking Brakes

Student/intern information:

Name_____ Date_____ Class_____

Vehicle used for this activity:

Year_____ Make_____ Model_____

Odometer_____ VIN _____

Learning Objective / Task	CDX Tasksheet Number	2014 NATEF Priority Level	2014 NATEF Reference Number
• Manually release (cage) and reset (uncage) parking (spring) brakes in accordance with manufacturers' recommendations.	H199	P-1	3A3.4
• Inspect and test parking (spring) brake chamber diaphragm and seals; replace parking (spring) brake chamber; dispose of removed chambers in accordance with local regulations.	H196	P-1	3A3.1
• Inspect and test parking (spring) brake check valves, lines, hoses, and fittings; replace as needed.	H197	P-1	3A3.2
• Inspect and test parking (spring) brake application and release valve; replace as needed.	H198	P-1	3A3.3
• Identify and test anti compounding brake function.	H200	P-1	3A3.5

Time off_____

Time on_____

Total time_____

Materials Required

- Vehicle with possible engine concern
- Vehicle manufacturer's service information
- Manufacturer-specific tools depending on the concern
- Vehicle lifting equipment if applicable

Some Safety Issues to Consider

- Diagnosis of this fault may require test driving the vehicle on the school grounds or on a hoist, both of which carry severe risks. Attempt this task only with full permission from your supervisor/instructor and follow all the guidelines exactly.
- Caution: If you are working in an area where there could be brake dust present (may contain asbestos, which has been determined to cause cancer when inhaled or ingested), ensure you wear and use all OSHA-approved asbestos protective/removal equipment.
- Lifting equipment such as vehicle jacks and stands, vehicle hoists, and engine hoists are important tools that increase productivity and make the job easier. However, they can also cause severe injury or death if used improperly. Make sure you follow the manufacturer's operation procedures. Also make sure you have your supervisor/instructor's permission to use any particular type of lifting equipment.
- Comply with personal and environmental safety practices associated with clothing; eye protection; hand tools; power equipment; proper ventilation; and the handling, storage, and disposal of chemicals/materials in accordance with federal, state, and local regulations.
- Always wear the correct protective eyewear and clothing and use the appropriate safety equipment, as well as fender covers, seat protectors, and floor mat protectors.
- Make sure you understand and observe all legislative and personal safety procedures when carrying out practical assignments. If you are unsure of what these are, ask your supervisor/instructor.

© 2017 Jones & Bartlett Learning, LLC, an Ascend Learning Company

Performance Standard

0—No exposure: No information or practice provided during the program; complete training required

1—Exposure only: General information provided with no practice time; close supervision needed; additional training required

2—Limited practice: Has practiced job during training program; additional training required to develop skill

3—Moderately skilled: Has performed job independently during training program; limited additional training may be required

4—Skilled: Can perform job independently with no additional training

Student/intern information:

Name_____ Date_____ Class_____

Vehicle used for this activity:

Year_____ Make_____ Model_____

Odometer_____ VIN _____

▶ **TASK** Manually release (cage) and reset (uncage) parking (spring) brakes in accordance with manufacturers' recommendations. **NATEF 3A3.4**

Time off_____

Time on_____

Total time_____

CDX Tasksheet Number: H199

Note: Most spring brake chamber manufacturers incorporate a spring brake caging bolt attached to the chamber housing on the outside.

1. In order to cage the spring brake chamber, remove the caging bolt nut from the caging bolt and remove the bolt from the side of the chamber housing.

2. Insert the caging bolt into the back side of the spring brake chamber and lock it into the slot provided in the chamber.

3. Turn the bolt one quarter of a turn in the chamber housing and thread the washer and the nut onto the end of the caging bolt.

4. Turn the nut clockwise until the brake assembly is released (compressing the large spring inside) and the tire and wheel assembly is free to turn.

    Note: This procedure would need to be done if servicing the brakes or brake chamber in the event of a brake or chamber failure.

    a. Check to see if the wheel is free to turn. Yes: _____ No: _____ Comments: _____

        Note: If a servicing of the spring brake chamber is required, always exercise extreme caution when removing the chamber diaphragm clamp. Follow all manufacturer recommended guidelines to perform this service. The spring brake chamber must be in the caged position in order to perform this service safely. If not done correctly, personal injury may result.

5. Inspect chamber for any physical damage or distortion of the housing.

    a. Condition of spring brake chamber: Good: _____ Bad: _____ Comments: _____

6. To uncage the spring brake chamber, simply rotate the caging bolt nut in the counter clockwise position until the bolt is free and can be removed safely.

7. Replace the bolt, nut and washer in the hole provided on the side of the spring brake chamber housing.

8. Discuss these findings with your instructor.

Performance Rating

CDX Tasksheet Number: H199

☐	☐	☐	☐	☐
0	1	2	3	4

Supervisor/instructor signature _____ Date_____

Student/intern information:

Name_____ Date_____ Class_____

Vehicle used for this activity:

Year_____ Make_____ Model_____

Odometer_____ VIN _____

▶ TASK Inspect and test parking (spring) brake chamber diaphragm and seals; replace parking (spring) brake chamber; dispose of removed chambers in accordance with local regulations.   NATEF 3A3.1

CDX Tasksheet Number: H196

Time off_____

Time on_____

Total time_____

1. Reference the manufacturer's service information for the correct procedure for checking the parking brake chamber(s), diaphragm and seals:
    a. Inspect and test parking brake operation:
        i. Ensure the air pressure has been completely built up; apply parking brake:
            Operational: _____ Require servicing: _____ Comments: _____
            a. If no, list the necessary actions or corrections:

            _____
            _____
            _____
            _____
            _____

        ii. Check to ensure all park brake chamber have applied:
            Yes: _____ No: _____ Comments: _____
            a. If no, list the necessary actions or corrections:

            _____
            _____
            _____
            _____
            _____

2. Replace parking (spring) brake chamber.
    a. Reference the manufacturer's service information for the correct procedure for replacing the parking brake chamber(s), including all safety precautions:
        i. List the procedure and all safety requirements when replacing a parking (spring) brake chamber assembly:

        _____
        _____
        _____
        _____
        _____

        ii. Discuss the procedure with your instructor.
        iii. Verify whether your instructor wants you to replace the parking brake chamber:
            Yes: _____ No: _____

© 2017 Jones & Bartlett Learning, LLC, an Ascend Learning Company

b. Replace parking (spring) brake chamber in accordance with the manufacturer's service information.

    i. Removal:

        a. As outlined in the manufacturer's service information, fit manual cage retaining bolt.

        b. Disconnect the air line hoses and seal hoses from the environment.

        c. Remove clevis pin.

        d. Remove mounting bolts and remove parking (spring) brake chamber.

        e. Check mounting bracket for any damage.
Condition: Good: _____ Needs replacing: _____ Comments: _____

        f. Check bracket mounting holes for elongation.
Condition: Good: _____ Needs replacing: _____ Comments: _____

        g. Determine any necessary actions or corrections:

_____

_____

        h. Have your instructor verify removal and your answers.
Supervisor/instructor's initials: _____

    ii. Replacement:

        a. Install new parking (spring) brake chamber and fit and torque mounting bolts.

        b. Adjust push rod to align with clevis pin and refit clevis pin and cotter pin.

        c. Remove protective covers from brake hoses and reconnect in the correct manner as outlined in the manufacturer's service information.

3. Referencing local, and where necessary, state/federal legislation/regulations for the correct procedure for disposing of a used parking (spring) brake chamber(s), determine the proper method of disposing of used parking (spring) brake chambers:

_____

_____

    a. Discuss these findings with your instructor.

    b. If directed by your instructor, dispose of the used spring brake chambers.

Performance Rating

CDX Tasksheet Number: H196

☐	☐	☐	☐	☐
0	1	2	3	4

Supervisor/instructor signature _____ Date_____

Student/intern information:

Name_____ Date_____ Class_____

Vehicle used for this activity:

Year_____ Make_____ Model_____

Odometer_____ VIN _____

▶ **TASK** Inspect and test parking (spring) brake check valves, lines, hoses, and fittings; replace as needed.

NATEF 3A3.2

CDX Tasksheet Number: H197

1. Consult the manufacturer's service information for the procedures to inspect and test parking (spring) brake check valves; replace as needed.
   a. List any precautions while performing this task:
   _____
   _____
   _____

2. Following the specified procedure, inspect and test parking (spring) brake check valves.
   a. List your tests and observations:
   _____
   _____
   _____

3. Following the specified procedure, inspect the parking (spring) brake lines, hoses, and fittings.
   a. List your tests and observations:
   _____
   _____
   _____

4. Determine any necessary actions or corrections:
   _____
   _____
   _____

5. Discuss these findings with your instructor.

Time off_____

Time on_____

Total time_____

Performance Rating

CDX Tasksheet Number: H197

☐ 0   ☐ 1   ☐ 2   ☐ 3   ☐ 4

Supervisor/instructor signature _____ Date_____

Student/intern information:

Name_____ Date_____ Class_____

Vehicle used for this activity:

Year_____ Make_____ Model_____

Odometer_____ VIN _____

▶ **TASK** Inspect and test parking (spring) brake application and release valve; replace as needed.

NATEF 3A3.3

Time off_____

Time on_____

Total time_____

CDX Tasksheet Number: H198

1. Inspect and test parking (spring) brake application and release valve:
   a. Check air system for air leaks (brakes released):
      i. Following the procedure from manufacturer's service information, check the air brake system components for air leaks: No Leaks: _____ Leaks: _____
         Comments: _____
      ii. Determine any necessary actions or corrections:
         _____
         _____

   b. Check air system for air leaks (brakes applied):
      i. Following the procedure from manufacturer's service information, recheck the air brake system components for air leaks:
         No Leaks: _____ Leaks: _____ Comments: _____
      ii. Determine any necessary actions or corrections:
         _____
         _____

   c. Check the serviceability of parking (spring) brake actuating valve:
      i. Are the components within specifications? Yes: _____ No: _____
         Comments: _____
      ii. Determine any necessary actions or corrections:
         _____
         _____

2. Discuss these findings with your instructor.

Performance Rating

CDX Tasksheet Number: H198

☐	☐	☐	☐	☐
0	1	2	3	4

Supervisor/instructor signature _____ Date_____

Student/intern information:

Name_____ Date_____ Class_____

Vehicle used for this activity:

Year_____ Make_____ Model_____

Odometer_____ VIN _____

▶ TASK Identify and test anti compounding brake function.   NATEF 3A3.5

CDX Tasksheet Number: H200

Time off_____

Time on_____

Total time_____

Note: The anti-compounding function in the air brake system is designed to prevent the parking brake and service brake from being applied at the same time, therefore saving the brake components from any undue stress that may cause a premature brake component failure.

1.   Identify the anti-compounding valve in the R-8 or R-14 relay valve by its exhaust cover and an air line connected to the balance/quick release exhaust port. See Figure 1.

2.   Check to make sure there are no air leaks at the exhaust cover by spraying the area with a soap and water solution; observe any air bubbles present.
        a. Air leaks at exhaust cover: Yes: _____ No: _____ Comments: _____

3.   Check for any leaks present at the air line connections to the valve.
        a. Leaks present at connections: Yes: _____ No: _____ Comments: _____

4.   Check for any cracks or kinks in the air lines.
        a. Condition of air lines: Good: _____ Bad: _____ Comments: _____

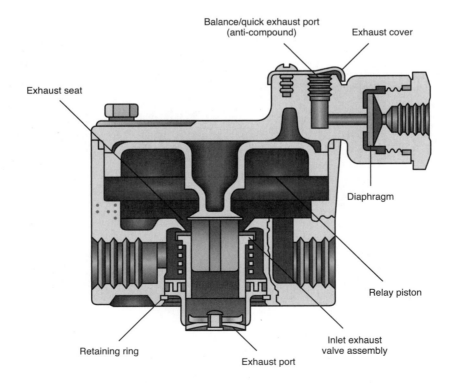

Figure 1

5. If any leaks are present, follow the manufacturer's service information and record the procedure to repair or replace the valve.

_____

_____

_____

_____

_____

6. To test the anti-compounding function:
   a. Park the vehicle but do not apply the parking brakes.
   b. Install an air pressure gauge in the delivery line of the R-8/R-14 valve or at the spring brake chamber.
   c. Make sure that maximum air pressure is available.
   d. Pull the PP-1 parking brake valve which will exhaust all air from the valve and apply the spring brakes.
   e. Make a service brake application by stepping on the foot valve.
   f. Observe and record the pressure on the gauge in the service line to the valve or brake chambers.
   g. Pressure reading: _____ psi (kPa)
   h. If reservoir pressure is present on the gauge, the function of the anti-compounding valve is operational.

7. If no pressure is available to the gauge, consult the manufacturer's service information and record the procedure to repair or replace the anti-compounding valve:

_____

_____

_____

_____

_____

8. Discuss these findings with your instructor.

Performance Rating

CDX Tasksheet Number: H200

☐	☐	☐	☐	☐
0	1	2	3	4

Supervisor/instructor signature _____ Date_____

Air & Hydraulic Brake Systems:
Hydraulic Brakes 1: Hydraulic System

Student/intern information:

Name_____ Date_____ Class_____

Vehicle used for this activity:

Year_____ Make_____ Model_____

Odometer_____ VIN _____

© 2017 Jones & Bartlett Learning, LLC, an Ascend Learning Company

Learning Objective / Task	CDX Tasksheet Number	2014 NATEF Priority Level	2014 NATEF Reference Number
• Identify poor stopping, premature wear, pulling, dragging, balance, or pedal feel problems caused by the hydraulic system; determine needed action.	H201	P-2	3B1.1
• Inspect/test brake fluid; bleed and/or flush system; determine needed action.	H207	P-1	3B1.7
• Inspect and test master cylinder for internal/external leaks and damage; replace as needed.	H202	P-1	3B1.2
• Inspect hydraulic system brake lines, flexible hoses, and fittings for leaks and damage; replace as needed.	H203	P-1	3B1.3

Time off_____

Time on_____

Total time_____

Materials Required

- Vehicle with possible engine concern
- Vehicle manufacturer's service information
- Manufacturer-specific tools depending on the concern
- Vehicle lifting equipment if applicable

Some Safety Issues to Consider

- Diagnosis of this fault may require test driving the vehicle on the school grounds or on a hoist, both of which carry severe risks. Attempt this task only with full permission from your supervisor/instructor and follow all the guidelines exactly.
- Caution: If you are working in an area where there could be brake dust present (may contain asbestos, which has been determined to cause cancer when inhaled or ingested), ensure you wear and use all OSHA-approved asbestos protective/removal equipment.
- Lifting equipment such as vehicle jacks and stands, vehicle hoists, and engine hoists are important tools that increase productivity and make the job easier. However, they can also cause severe injury or death if used improperly. Make sure you follow the manufacturer's operation procedures. Also make sure you have your supervisor/instructor's permission to use any particular type of lifting equipment.
- Comply with personal and environmental safety practices associated with clothing; eye protection; hand tools; power equipment; proper ventilation; and the handling, storage, and disposal of chemicals/materials in accordance with federal, state, and local regulations.
- Always wear the correct protective eyewear and clothing and use the appropriate safety equipment, as well as fender covers, seat protectors, and floor mat protectors.
- Make sure you understand and observe all legislative and personal safety procedures when carrying out practical assignments. If you are unsure of what these are, ask your supervisor/instructor.

Performance Standard

0—No exposure: No information or practice provided during the program; complete training required

1—Exposure only: General information provided with no practice time; close supervision needed; additional training required

2—Limited practice: Has practiced job during training program; additional training required to develop skill

3—Moderately skilled: Has performed job independently during training program; limited additional training may be required

4—Skilled: Can perform job independently with no additional training

Name_____ Date_____ Class_____

Vehicle used for this activity:

Year_____ Make_____ Model_____

Odometer_____ VIN _____

▶ **TASK** Identify poor stopping, premature wear, pulling, dragging, balance, or pedal feel problems caused by the hydraulic system; determine needed action.   **NATEF 3B1.1**

Time off_____

Time on_____

Total time_____

CDX Tasksheet Number: H201

1. List all possible causes for poor stopping:

    _____
    _____
    _____
    _____
    _____

    a. Check for any hydraulic leakage, and record any leaks detected during your inspection:

        _____
        _____
        _____
        _____
        _____

    b. Check for premature wear. List all the areas you are checking for premature wear, and record all premature wear detected during your inspection:

        _____
        _____
        _____
        _____
        _____

    c. List all possible causes for pulling, grabbing, or dragging problems:

        _____
        _____
        _____
        _____
        _____

2. Check for any service system malfunctions, and list any malfunctions detected during your inspection:

    _____
    _____
    _____
    _____
    _____

3. Determine what action is required to correct any faults within the system:

_____
_____
_____
_____
_____

4. Discuss these findings with your instructor.

Performance Rating

CDX Tasksheet Number: H201

☐   ☐   ☐   ☐   ☐

0   1   2   3   4

Supervisor/instructor signature _____ Date_____

Student/intern information:

Name_____ Date_____ Class_____

Vehicle used for this activity:

Year_____ Make_____ Model_____

Odometer_____ VIN _____

▶ **TASK** Inspect/test brake fluid; bleed and/or flush system; determine proper fluid type.

NATEF 3B1.7

Time off_____

Time on_____

Total time_____

CDX Tasksheet Number: H207

1. Check brake master cylinder fluid for correct quantity and test suitability.
   a. Locate brake master cylinder.
   b. Clean the top of the cylinder.
   c. Open master cylinder cap and check fluid level: At specified level:
      Yes: _____ Requires top up: _____
   d. Collect a sample of current brake fluid.
   e. Test the sample for contamination, etc. Results: Satisfactory: _____
      Requires changing: _____ Comments: _____
   f. Determine any necessary actions:

      _____
      _____

2. Reference the manufacturer's service information; list the recommended steps replace the brake fluid:

   _____
   _____
   _____

3. Following the procedures outlined in the manufacturer's service information, drain the old brake fluid and flush the braking system. Discard the old fluid in accordance with local, state, or federal legislation. List how you disposed of the old brake fluid:

   _____

4. Following the procedures outlined in the manufacturer's service information, refill braking circuit master cylinder.
   a. Determine proper fluid type and quantity:
      i. Proper fluid type: _____
   b. Fill the fluid system to capacity.
   c. Bleed the braking system until it is free from air bubbles.
   d. Discard the old fluid in accordance with local, state, or federal legislation.

5. Discuss these findings with your instructor.

Performance Rating

CDX Tasksheet Number: H207

☐ 0   ☐ 1   ☐ 2   ☐ 3   ☐ 4

Supervisor/instructor signature _____ Date_____

Student/intern information:

Name_____ Date_____ Class_____

Vehicle used for this activity:

Year_____ Make_____ Model_____

Odometer_____ VIN _____

▶ **TASK** Inspect and test master cylinder for internal/external leaks and damage; replace as needed.

NATEF 3B1.2

CDX Tasksheet Number: H2O2

1. Check the brake master cylinder fluid for correct quantity and test its suitability.
    a. Locate the brake master cylinder.
    b. Clean the top of the cylinder.
    c. Open the master cylinder cap and check the fluid level. At the specified level: _____ Requires top off: _____
    d. Collect a sample of the current brake fluid.
    e. Test the sample for contamination. Satisfactory: _____ Requires changing: _____
       Comments: _____
       i. Recommendations: _____
       _____
       _____

    f. Refill with correct fluid type. Specified fluid type: _____

2. Referencing the manufacturer's service information, list the recommended steps to check for internal and external leakage of the master cylinder:

    _____
    _____
    _____
    _____
    _____

3. Following the procedures outlined in the manufacturer's service information, check for any signs of internal or external leakage of the master cylinder.
    a. Meets manufacturer's specifications: Yes: _____ No: _____ Comments: _____
    b. If no, list the necessary actions or corrections:

       _____
       _____

4. As directed by your instructor, carry out any repairs as authorized.

5. Discuss these findings with your instructor.

Performance Rating

CDX Tasksheet Number: H2O2

☐ 0 ☐ 1 ☐ 2 ☐ 3 ☐ 4

Supervisor/instructor signature _____ Date_____

Student/intern information:

Name_____ Date_____ Class_____

Vehicle used for this activity:

Year_____ Make_____ Model_____

Odometer_____ VIN _____

▶ TASK Inspect hydraulic system brake lines, flexible hoses, and fittings for leaks and damage; replace as needed.   NATEF 3B1.3

CDX Tasksheet Number: H203

Time off_____

Time on_____

Total time_____

1. Inspect the brake lines, fittings, flexible hoses, and valves for leaks and damage.
    a. Inspect the condition and security of all brake lines, both solid and flexible.
        i. Meets manufacturer's specifications: Yes: _____ Requires maintenance: _____
            Comments: _____

        ii. If they require maintenance, list the necessary actions or corrections:
            _____
            _____
            _____

    b. Inspect the brake valves for signs of external leakage.
        i. Meets manufacturer's specifications: Yes: _____ Requires maintenance: _____
            Comments: _____

        ii. If they require maintenance, list the necessary actions or corrections:
            _____
            _____
            _____

    c. Replace damaged or faulty parts as required.

2. Discuss these findings with your instructor.

Performance Rating

CDX Tasksheet Number: H203

☐	☐	☐	☐	☐
0	1	2	3	4

Supervisor/instructor signature _____ Date_____

Air & Hydraulic Brake Systems:
Hydraulic Brakes 2: Hydraulic System

Student/intern information:

Name_____ Date_____ Class_____

Vehicle used for this activity:

Year_____ Make_____ Model_____

Odometer_____ VIN _____

Time off_____

Time on_____

Total time_____

Learning Objective / Task	CDX Tasksheet Number	2014 NATEF Priority Level	2014 NATEF Reference Number
• Inspect and test metering (hold-off), load sensing/ proportioning, proportioning, and combination valves; replace as needed.	H204	P-3	3B1.4
• Inspect and test brake pressure differential valve and warning light circuit switch, bulbs/LEDs, wiring, and connectors; repair or replace as needed.	H205	P-2	3B1.5
• Inspect disc brake caliper assemblies; replace as needed.	H206	P-1	3B1.6

Materials Required

- Vehicle with possible engine concern
- Vehicle manufacturer's service information
- Manufacturer-specific tools depending on the concern
- Vehicle lifting equipment if applicable

Some Safety Issues to Consider

- Diagnosis of this fault may require test driving the vehicle on the school grounds or on a hoist, both of which carry severe risks. Attempt this task only with full permission from your supervisor/instructor and follow all the guidelines exactly.
- Caution: If you are working in an area where there could be brake dust present (may contain asbestos, which has been determined to cause cancer when inhaled or ingested), ensure you wear and use all OSHA-approved asbestos protective/removal equipment.
- Lifting equipment such as vehicle jacks and stands, vehicle hoists, and engine hoists are important tools that increase productivity and make the job easier. However, they can also cause severe injury or death if used improperly. Make sure you follow the manufacturer's operation procedures. Also make sure you have your supervisor/instructor's permission to use any particular type of lifting equipment.
- Comply with personal and environmental safety practices associated with clothing; eye protection; hand tools; power equipment; proper ventilation; and the handling, storage, and disposal of chemicals/materials in accordance with federal, state, and local regulations.
- Always wear the correct protective eyewear and clothing and use the appropriate safety equipment, as well as fender covers, seat protectors, and floor mat protectors.
- Make sure you understand and observe all legislative and personal safety procedures when carrying out practical assignments. If you are unsure of what these are, ask your supervisor/instructor.

Performance Standard

0—No exposure: No information or practice provided during the program; complete training required

1—Exposure only: General information provided with no practice time; close supervision needed; additional training required

2—Limited practice: Has practiced job during training program; additional training required to develop skill

3—Moderately skilled: Has performed job independently during training program; limited additional training may be required

4—Skilled: Can perform job independently with no additional training

Student/intern information:

Name_____ Date_____ Class_____

Vehicle used for this activity:

Year_____ Make_____ Model_____

Odometer_____ VIN _____

▶ **TASK** Inspect and test metering (hold-off), load sensing/proportioning, proportioning, and combination valves; replace as needed.   NATEF 3B1.4

CDX Tasksheet Number: H204

Time off_____

Time on_____

Total time_____

1. Following the procedures outlined in the manufacturer's service information, inspect and test metering (hold-off valves).
   a. List your observations:
   _____

   b. Meets manufacturer's specifications: Yes: _____ No: _____
   c. If no, list the necessary actions or corrections:
   _____
   _____

   d. If directed by your instructor, replace the faulty unit.

2. Following the procedures outlined in the manufacturer's service information, inspect and test load sensing/proportioning valves.
   a. List your observations:
   _____

   b. Meets manufacturer's specifications: Yes: _____ No: _____
   c. If no, list the necessary actions or corrections:
   _____
   _____

   d. If directed by your instructor, replace the faulty unit.

3. Following the procedures outlined in the manufacturer's service information, inspect and test proportioning and combination valves.
   a. List your observations:
   _____

   b. Meets manufacturer's specifications: Yes: _____ No: _____
   c. If no, list the necessary actions or corrections:
   _____
   _____

   d. If directed by your instructor, replace the faulty unit.

Performance Rating

CDX Tasksheet Number: H204

☐	☐	☐	☐	☐
0	1	2	3	4

Supervisor/instructor signature _____ Date_____

Student/intern information:

Name_____ Date_____ Class_____

Vehicle used for this activity:

Year_____ Make_____ Model_____

Odometer_____ VIN _____

▶ **TASK** Inspect and test brake pressure differential valve and warning light circuit switch, bulbs/ LEDs, wiring, and connectors; repair or replace as needed. **NATEF 3B1.5**

Time off_____

Time on_____

Total time_____

CDX Tasksheet Number: H205

1. Following the procedures outlined in the manufacturer's service information, inspect and test brake pressure differential valve.
   a. List your observations:

   _____

   b. Meets manufacturer's specifications: Yes: _____ No: _____ Comments: _____

   c. If no, list the necessary actions or corrections:

   _____
   _____

   d. If directed by your instructor, replace the faulty unit.

2. Following the procedures outlined in the manufacturer's service information, inspect and test warning light circuit switch, bulbs, wiring, and connectors.
   a. List your observations:

   _____

   b. Meets manufacturer's specifications: Yes: _____ No: _____ Comments: _____

   c. If no, list the necessary actions or corrections:

   _____
   _____

   d. If directed by your instructor, replace the faulty unit.

3. List any difficulties you experienced during this task:

   _____
   _____
   _____

4. Discuss your findings with your instructor.

Performance Rating

CDX Tasksheet Number: H205

☐ 0   ☐ 1   ☐ 2   ☐ 3   ☐ 4

Supervisor/instructor signature _____ Date_____

Student/intern information:

Name_____ Date_____ Class_____

Vehicle used for this activity:

Year_____ Make_____ Model_____

Odometer_____ VIN _____

© 2017 Jones & Bartlett Learning, LLC, an Ascend Learning Company

▶ **TASK** Inspect disc brake caliper assemblies; replace as needed.   NATEF 3B1.6

CDX Tasksheet Number: H206

Time off_____

Time on_____

Total time_____

1. Research the procedure and specifications for inspecting hydraulic brake disc brake assembly.
   a. List the procedure for servicing the disc brake caliper assemblies, noting all safety precautions listed by the manufacturer.

   _____
   _____
   _____
   _____
   _____

   b. Discuss these findings with your instructor.

2. If instructed by your instructor, carry out the inspection procedure.
   a. With reference to the manufacturer's service information for precautions and specifications, inspect the disc brake caliper assemblies component.
      i. List your observations:

      _____
      _____
      _____

      ii. Within specifications: Yes: _____ No: _____ Comments: _____

      iii. Determine any necessary actions or corrections:

      _____
      _____
      _____
      _____
      _____

3. Discuss these findings with your instructor.

Performance Rating

CDX Tasksheet Number: H206

☐   ☐   ☐   ☐   ☐
0   1   2   3   4

Supervisor/instructor signature _____ Date_____

Air & Hydraulic Brake Systems:
Hydraulic Brakes 3: Mechanical/Foundation Brakes

Student/intern information:

Name_____ Date_____ Class_____

Vehicle used for this activity:

Year_____ Make_____ Model_____

Odometer_____ VIN _____

© 2017 Jones & Bartlett Learning, LLC, an Ascend Learning Company

Learning Objective / Task	CDX Tasksheet Number	2014 NATEF Priority Level	2014 NATEF Reference Number
• Identify poor stopping, brake noise, premature wear, pulling, grabbing, dragging, or pedal feel problems caused by mechanical components; determine needed action.	H208	P-2	3B2.1
• Inspect and measure rotors; perform needed action.	H209	P-1	3B2.2
• Inspect and measure disc brake pads; inspect mounting hardware; perform needed action.	H210	P-1	3B2.3
• Check parking brake operation; inspect parking brake application and holding devices; adjust and replace as needed.	H211	P-2	3B2.4

Time off_____

Time on_____

Total time_____

Materials Required

- Vehicle with possible engine concern
- Vehicle manufacturer's service information
- Manufacturer-specific tools depending on the concern
- Vehicle lifting equipment if applicable

Some Safety Issues to Consider

- Diagnosis of this fault may require test driving the vehicle on the school grounds or on a hoist, both of which carry severe risks. Attempt this task only with full permission from your supervisor/instructor and follow all the guidelines exactly.
- Caution: If you are working in an area where there could be brake dust present (may contain asbestos, which has been determined to cause cancer when inhaled or ingested), ensure you wear and use all OSHA-approved asbestos protective/removal equipment.
- Lifting equipment such as vehicle jacks and stands, vehicle hoists, and engine hoists are important tools that increase productivity and make the job easier. However, they can also cause severe injury or death if used improperly. Make sure you follow the manufacturer's operation procedures. Also make sure you have your supervisor/instructor's permission to use any particular type of lifting equipment.
- Comply with personal and environmental safety practices associated with clothing; eye protection; hand tools; power equipment; proper ventilation; and the handling, storage, and disposal of chemicals/materials in accordance with federal, state, and local regulations.
- Always wear the correct protective eyewear and clothing and use the appropriate safety equipment, as well as fender covers, seat protectors, and floor mat protectors.
- Make sure you understand and observe all legislative and personal safety procedures when carrying out practical assignments. If you are unsure of what these are, ask your supervisor/instructor.

Performance Standard

0—No exposure: No information or practice provided during the program; complete training required

1—Exposure only: General information provided with no practice time; close supervision needed; additional training required

2—Limited practice: Has practiced job during training program; additional training required to develop skill

3—Moderately skilled: Has performed job independently during training program; limited additional training may be required

4—Skilled: Can perform job independently with no additional training

Student/intern information:

Name_____ Date_____ Class_____

Vehicle used for this activity:

Year_____ Make_____ Model_____

Odometer_____ VIN _____

© 2017 Jones & Bartlett Learning, LLC, an Ascend Learning Company

▶ **TASK** Identify poor stopping, brake noise, premature wear, pulling, grabbing, dragging, or pedal feel problems caused by mechanical components; determine needed action.

NATEF 3B2.1

Time off_____

Time on_____

Total time_____

CDX Tasksheet Number: H208

1. Obtain information about the circumstances surrounding the complaint.
    a. Obtain current vehicle trip maintenance reports.
    b. Are there any comments on braking issues: Yes: _____ No: _____
       If yes, summarize the driver's comments:

       _____
       _____
       _____
       _____
       _____

    c. If the driver's comments are unavailable, obtain as much information as possible on the complaint.

2. Identify poor stopping, premature wear, pulling, dragging, balance, or pedal feel problems caused by the hydraulics system.
    a. List all possible causes for poor stopping:

       _____
       _____
       _____
       _____
       _____

3. Check for any hydraulic leakage.
    a. Record any leaks detected during your inspection:

       _____
       _____
       _____
       _____
       _____

4. Check for premature wear.
    a. List the component you inspected and the results:

       _____
       _____
       _____
       _____
       _____
       _____

5. List all possible causes for pulling, grabbing or dragging problems:

_____
_____
_____
_____
_____

6. Check for any service system malfunctions.
   a. List any malfunctions detected during your inspection:

   _____
   _____
   _____
   _____
   _____

7. Determine what action is required to correct any faults within the system:

_____
_____
_____
_____
_____

8. Discuss these findings with your instructor.

Performance Rating

CDX Tasksheet Number: H208

☐	☐	☐	☐	☐
0	1	2	3	4

Supervisor/instructor signature _____ Date_____

Name_____ Date_____ Class_____

Vehicle used for this activity:

Year_____ Make_____ Model_____

Odometer_____ VIN _____

▶ TASK Inspect and measure rotors; perform needed action.   **NATEF 3B2.2**

CDX Tasksheet Number: H209

1. Research the procedure and specifications for inspecting and measuring disc brake rotor(s), noting all safety precautions listed by the manufacturer:

    _____
    _____
    _____
    _____

    a. Specifications:
        i.   Minimum disc thickness: _____ in/mm
        ii. Diameter of rotor: _____ in/mm
        iii. Maximum run-out of rotor: _____ in/mm
        iv. Maximum thickness variation: _____ in/mm

2. With reference to the manufacturer's service information, inspect and measure the disc brake rotor(s) assemblies component:
    a. Specifications:
        i.   Minimum disc thickness: _____ in/mm
        ii. Diameter of rotor: _____ in/mm
        iii. Maximum run-out of rotor: _____ in/mm
        iv. Maximum thickness variation: _____ in/mm
        v.   Within specifications: Yes: _____ No: _____ Comments: _____
            a. Determine any necessary actions or corrections:
                _____
                _____

3. Discuss these findings with your instructor.

Performance Rating   **CDX Tasksheet Number: H209**

☐	☐	☐	☐	☐
0	1	2	3	4

Supervisor/instructor signature _____ Date_____

Student/intern information:

Name_____ Date_____ Class_____

Vehicle used for this activity:

Year_____ Make_____ Model_____

Odometer_____ VIN _____

▶ **TASK** Inspect and measure disc brake pads; inspect mounting hardware; perform needed action.

NATEF 3B2.3

CDX Tasksheet Number: H210

Time off_____

Time on_____

Total time_____

1. Research the procedure and specifications for inspecting and measuring disc brake pads, noting all safety precautions listed by the manufacturer:

   _____
   _____
   _____
   _____

   a. Specifications:
      i. Minimum disc pad thickness: _____ in/mm
      ii. Maximum run-out of rotor: _____ in/mm
      iii. Maximum allowable movement in wheel bearing(s): _____ in/mm
      iv. Torque for calliper mounting bolts: _____ ft-lb (Nm)

2. With reference to the manufacturer's service information for precautions and specifications, inspect and measure the disc brake rotor(s) assemblies component:
   a. Actual measurements:
      i. Minimum disc pad thickness: _____ in/mm
      ii. Maximum run-out of rotor: _____ in/mm
      iii. Maximum thickness variation: _____ in/mm
      iv. Maximum allowable movement in wheel bearing(s): _____ in/mm
      v. Torque for calliper mounting bolts: _____ ft-lb (Nm)
      vi. Within specifications: Yes: _____ No: _____ Comments: _____
         a. Determine any necessary actions or corrections:
            _____
            _____
            _____

3. Discuss these findings with your instructor.

Performance Rating

CDX Tasksheet Number: H210

☐   ☐   ☐   ☐   ☐
0   1   2   3   4

Supervisor/instructor signature _____ Date_____

Student/intern information:

Name_____ Date_____ Class_____

Vehicle used for this activity:

Year_____ Make_____ Model_____

Odometer_____ VIN _____

▶ **TASK** Check parking brake operation; inspect parking brake application and holding devices; adjust and replace as needed.   **NATEF 3B2.4**

Time off_____

Time on_____

Total time_____

CDX Tasksheet Number: H211

1. Referencing the manufacturer's service information, list the procedure for inspecting and checking parking brake operation, inspecting parking brake application and holding device, and note all safety precautions listed by the manufacturer:

   _____
   _____
   _____
   _____
   _____

2. Following the procedures outlined in the manufacturer's service information, check parking brake operation and inspect parking brake application and holding device.
   a. List your observations:

   _____
   _____
   _____

   b. Meets manufacturer's specifications: Yes: _____ No: _____
      i. Determine any necessary actions or corrections:

      _____
      _____
      _____
      _____

3. Discuss these findings with your instructor.

Performance Rating

CDX Tasksheet Number: H211

☐	☐	☐	☐	☐
0	1	2	3	4

Supervisor/instructor signature _____ Date_____

Air & Hydraulic Brake Systems:
Hydraulic Brakes 4: Power Assist Units

Student/intern information:

Name_____ Date_____ Class_____

Vehicle used for this activity:

Year_____ Make_____ Model_____

Odometer_____ VIN _____

Time off_____

Time on_____

Total time_____

Learning Objective / Task	CDX Tasksheet Number	2014 NATEF Priority Level	2014 NATEF Reference Number
• Identify stopping problems caused by the brake assist (booster) system; determine needed action.	H212	P-3	3B3.1
• Inspect, test, repair, or replace hydraulic brake assist (booster), hoses, and control valves; determine proper fluid type.	H213	P-3	3B3.2
• Check emergency (back-up, reserve) brake assist system.	H214	P-3	3B3.3

Materials Required

- Vehicle with possible engine concern
- Vehicle manufacturer's service information
- Manufacturer-specific tools depending on the concern
- Vehicle lifting equipment if applicable

Some Safety Issues to Consider

- Diagnosis of this fault may require test driving the vehicle on the school grounds or on a hoist, both of which carry severe risks. Attempt this task only with full permission from your supervisor/instructor and follow all the guidelines exactly.
- Caution: If you are working in an area where there could be brake dust present (may contain asbestos, which has been determined to cause cancer when inhaled or ingested), ensure you wear and use all OSHA-approved asbestos protective/removal equipment.
- Lifting equipment such as vehicle jacks and stands, vehicle hoists, and engine hoists are important tools that increase productivity and make the job easier. However, they can also cause severe injury or death if used improperly. Make sure you follow the manufacturer's operation procedures. Also make sure you have your supervisor/instructor's permission to use any particular type of lifting equipment.
- Comply with personal and environmental safety practices associated with clothing; eye protection; hand tools; power equipment; proper ventilation; and the handling, storage, and disposal of chemicals/materials in accordance with federal, state, and local regulations.
- Always wear the correct protective eyewear and clothing and use the appropriate safety equipment, as well as fender covers, seat protectors, and floor mat protectors.
- Make sure you understand and observe all legislative and personal safety procedures when carrying out practical assignments. If you are unsure of what these are, ask your supervisor/instructor.

Performance Standard

0–No exposure: No information or practice provided during the program; complete training required

1–Exposure only: General information provided with no practice time; close supervision needed; additional training required

2–Limited practice: Has practiced job during training program; additional training required to develop skill

3–Moderately skilled: Has performed job independently during training program; limited additional training may be required

4–Skilled: Can perform job independently with no additional training

Student/intern information:

Name_____ Date_____ Class_____

Vehicle used for this activity:

Year_____ Make_____ Model_____

Odometer_____ VIN _____

▶ **TASK** Identify stopping problems caused by the brake assist (booster) system; determine needed action.

NATEF 3B3.1

Time off_____

Time on_____

Total time_____

CDX Tasksheet Number: H212

1. Obtain information about the circumstances surrounding the complaint, it available.
   a. Obtain current vehicle trip maintenance reports.
   b. Are there any comments on braking issues: Yes: _____ No: _____
      i. If yes, summarize the driver's comments:

      _____

      _____

      _____

      _____

2. Research the following procedures and specifications for the vehicle you are working on in the appropriate service information.
   a. Type of power brake booster: Vacuum: _____ Hydraulic: _____ Other (list):_____
   b. List all possible causes of poor stopping caused by the brake assist (booster) system:

      _____

      _____

      _____

      _____

   • Common Causes of Booster Failure (depending on vehicle's type of engine)
      • **Gasoline Engines:** Gas is the cause of a large number of booster failures. If gas gets into the booster, it softens the rubber diaphragm, which makes it susceptible to rupture. This can happen in two ways. First, if the check valve leaks, then air will be drawn into the booster when the engine is shut down. Second, if the vacuum line slopes down from the throttle body to the booster, gas can condense in the hose and enter the booster over time.
      • **Diesel Engines:** Diesel engines with vacuum pumps need a check valve in the vacuum line to prevent oil from being drawn into the booster when the engine is shut down. Oil will ruin the diaphragm causing the booster to fail.

3. Diagnose the customer concern. List your tests and their results:

   _____

   _____

   _____

   _____

4. Determine any necessary actions or corrections:

_____

_____

5. Discuss these findings with your instructor.

Performance Rating

☐   ☐   ☐   ☐   ☐

0   1   2   3   4

Supervisor/instructor signature _____ Date_____

Student/intern information:

Name_____ Date_____ Class_____

Vehicle used for this activity:

Year_____ Make_____ Model_____

Odometer_____ VIN _____

▶ TASK Inspect, test, repair, or replace hydraulic brake assist (booster), hoses, and control valves; determine proper fluid type.   **NATEF 3B3.2**

CDX Tasksheet Number: H213

1. Reference the manufacturer's service information to inspect, test, repair, or replace hydraulic brake assist (booster), hoses, and control valves; determine proper fluid type.

    a. Specified type of brake fluid: _____

    b. List any safety precautions when testing the hydraulic brake booster:

    _____

    _____

    _____

    c. Discuss with your instructor the recommended procedures and/or action(s) needed to correct the brake system.

2. Check the system for any hydraulic leakage.

    a. Record any leaks detected during your inspection:

    _____

    _____

    _____

    _____

3. Inspect and test the control valves and lines for proper operation, leaks, or damage.

    a. List your tests and observations:

    _____

    _____

    _____

    b. Meets manufacturer's specifications: Yes: _____ Requires maintenance: _____

    c. If requires maintenance, list the necessary actions or corrections:

    _____

    _____

4. Check master cylinder fluid level and condition.

    a. Check brake master cylinder fluid for correct quantity and test suitability.

        i.   Locate brake master cylinder.

        ii. Clean the top of the cylinder.

        iii. Open master cylinder cap and check fluid level. At specified level:
             Yes: _____ Requires top up: _____

        iv. Collect a sample of current brake fluid.

        v.   Test the sample for contamination.

             a. Results: Satisfactory: _____ Requires changing: _____
                 Comments: _____

Time off_____

Time on_____

Total time_____

vi. Determine any necessary actions or corrections:

_____

_____

_____

5. Discuss these findings with your instructor.

Performance Rating

CDX Tasksheet Number: H213

☐	☐	☐	☐	☐
0	1	2	3	4

Supervisor/instructor signature _____ Date_____

Student/intern information:

Name_____ Date_____ Class_____

Vehicle used for this activity:

Year_____ Make_____ Model_____

Odometer_____ VIN _____

CDX Tasksheet Number: H214

Time off_____

Time on_____

1. Reference the manufacturer's service information to check emergency (back-up, reserve) brake assist system.

    a. List the procedure for checking emergency (back-up, reserve) brake assist system as outlined by the manufacturer in its manufacturer's service information:

Total time_____

    _____
    _____
    _____
    _____

2. Carry out this procedure for checking the emergency (back-up, reserve) brake assist system.

    a. List your tests and their results:

    _____
    _____
    _____
    _____

    b. Meets manufacturer's specifications: Yes: _____ Requires maintenance: _____
        Comments: _____

    c. If requires maintenance, list the necessary actions or corrections:

    _____
    _____

3. Discuss these findings with your instructor.

Performance Rating

CDX Tasksheet Number: H214

☐	☐	☐	☐	☐
0	1	2	3	4

Supervisor/instructor signature _____ Date_____

Air & Hydraulic Brake Systems:
Air and Hydraulic Antilock Brake Systems (ABS) and Automatic Traction Control (ATC)

Student/intern information:

Name_____ Date_____ Class_____

Vehicle used for this activity:

Year_____ Make_____ Model_____

Odometer_____ VIN _____

Time off_____

Time on_____

Total time_____

Learning Objective / Task	CDX Tasksheet Number	2014 NATEF Priority Level	2014 NATEF Reference Number
• Observe antilock brake system (ABS) warning light operation (includes trailer and dash mounted trailer ABS warning light); determine needed action.	H215	P-1	3C1
• Diagnose antilock brake system (ABS) electronic control(s) and components using self-diagnosis and/or electronic service tools; determine needed action.	H216	P-1	3C2
• Identify poor stopping and wheel lock-up problems caused by failure of the antilock brake system (ABS); determine needed action.	H217	P-1	3C3
• Test and check operation of antilock brake system (ABS) air, hydraulic, electrical, and mechanical components; perform needed action.	H218	P-1	3C4
• Test antilock brake system (ABS) wheel speed sensors and circuits; adjust or replace as needed.	H219	P-1	3C5
• Bleed the ABS hydraulic circuits.	H220	P-2	3C6
• Observe automatic traction control (ATC) warning light operation; determine needed action.	H221	P-3	3C7
• Diagnose automatic traction control (ATC) electronic control(s) and components using self-diagnosis and/or specified test equipment (scan tool, PC computer); determine needed action.	H222	P-3	3C8
• Verify power line carrier (PLC) operations.	H223	P-2	3C9

Materials Required

- Vehicle with possible engine concern
- Vehicle manufacturer's service information
- Manufacturer-specific tools depending on the concern
- Vehicle lifting equipment if applicable

Some Safety Issues to Consider

- Diagnosis of this fault may require test driving the vehicle on the school grounds or on a hoist, both of which carry severe risks. Attempt this task only with full permission from your supervisor/instructor and follow all the guidelines exactly.
- Caution: If you are working in an area where there could be brake dust present (may contain asbestos, which has been determined to cause cancer when inhaled or ingested), ensure you wear and use all OSHA-approved asbestos protective/removal equipment.
- Lifting equipment such as vehicle jacks and stands, vehicle hoists, and engine hoists are important tools that increase productivity and make the job easier. However, they can also cause severe injury or death if used improperly. Make sure you follow the manufacturer's operation procedures. Also make sure you have your supervisor/instructor's permission to use any particular type of lifting equipment.
- Comply with personal and environmental safety practices associated with clothing; eye protection; hand tools; power equipment; proper ventilation; and the handling, storage, and disposal of chemicals/materials in accordance with federal, state, and local regulations.
- Always wear the correct protective eyewear and clothing and use the appropriate safety equipment, as well as fender covers, seat protectors, and floor mat protectors.
- Make sure you understand and observe all legislative and personal safety procedures when carrying out practical assignments. If you are unsure of what these are, ask your supervisor/instructor.

Performance Standard

0—No exposure: No information or practice provided during the program; complete training required

1—Exposure only: General information provided with no practice time; close supervision needed; additional training required

2—Limited practice: Has practiced job during training program; additional training required to develop skill

3—Moderately skilled: Has performed job independently during training program; limited additional training may be required

4—Skilled: Can perform job independently with no additional training

Name_____ Date_____ Class_____

Vehicle used for this activity:

Year_____ Make_____ Model_____

Odometer_____ VIN _____

▶ **TASK** Observe antilock brake system (ABS) warning light operation (includes trailer and dash mounted trailer ABS warning light); determine needed action. _____ **NATEF 3C1**

Time off_____

CDX Tasksheet Number: H215

Time on_____

1. Observe antilock brake system (ABS) warning light operation (includes dash mounted trailer ABS warning light).

    a. Turn the vehicle's ignition; allow it to go through its confirmation checks for the various circuits including the ABS.

        i. List the warning system reactions:

            _____

            _____

        ii. Meets manufacturer's specifications: Yes: _____ No: _____

        iii. If requires maintenance, list the necessary actions or corrections:

            _____

            _____

            _____

    b. Did the ABS warning lights for both tractor and trailer pass this test?
        Yes: _____ No: _____

        i. If no, list the necessary actions or corrections:

            _____

            _____

            _____

            _____

2. If directed by your instructor, carry-out corrections as outlined in the manufacturer's service information.

Total time_____

Performance Rating

CDX Tasksheet Number: H215

☐	☐	☐	☐	☐
0	1	2	3	4

Supervisor/instructor signature _____ Date_____

Student/intern information:

Name _____ Date _____ Class _____

Vehicle used for this activity:

Year _____ Make _____ Model _____

Odometer _____ VIN _____

▶ **TASK** Diagnose antilock brake system (ABS) electronic control(s) and components using self-diagnosis and/or electronic service tool(s); determine needed action. **NATEF 3C2**

Time off _____

Time on _____

Total time _____

CDX Tasksheet Number: H216

1. Referencing the manufacturer's service information and the electronic service tool's operating information to determine the correct method for using this tool.

   a. List the possible 'fault codes' for the ABS system:

   _____
   _____
   _____
   _____

2. Plug the scan tool or diagnostic equipment into the vehicle's diagnostic terminal. Following the specified procedure, retrieve any diagnostic trouble codes.

   a. List any ABS-related diagnostic codes and their descriptions:

   _____
   _____
   _____
   _____

   b. Meets manufacturer's specifications: Yes: _____ Requires diagnosis: _____

      i. If requires diagnosis, list the tests you performed and their results:

      _____
      _____
      _____
      _____

   c. Determine any necessary actions:

   _____
   _____

3. Discuss these findings with your instructor.

Performance Rating

CDX Tasksheet Number: H216

☐ 0   ☐ 1   ☐ 2   ☐ 3   ☐ 4

Supervisor/instructor signature _____ Date _____

© 2017 Jones & Bartlett Learning, LLC, an Ascend Learning Company

Air & Hydraulic Brake Systems 241

Student/intern information:

Name_____ Date_____ Class_____

Vehicle used for this activity:

Year_____ Make_____ Model_____

Odometer_____ VIN _____

▶ TASK Identify poor stopping and wheel lock-up problems caused by failure of the antilock brake system (ABS); determine needed action.   NATEF 3C3

Time off_____

Time on_____

CDX Tasksheet Number: H217

Total time_____

1. Reference manufacturer's service information to identify the possible causes for poor stopping and wheel lock-up problems in the advent of a failure of the antilock brake system (ABS):
    a. List the possible causes and corrections as outlined by the manufacturer in its service information:

    _____
    _____
    _____
    _____
    _____
    _____
    _____
    _____
    _____

2. Discuss the recommended procedures and/or action(s) needed to correct the brake system with your instructor. If directed by your instructor, carry out inspections and corrections. List the tests you performed and their results:

    _____
    _____
    _____
    _____
    _____

Performance Rating

CDX Tasksheet Number: H217

☐	☐	☐	☐	☐
0	1	2	3	4

Supervisor/instructor signature _____ Date_____

Student/intern information:

Name_____ Date_____ Class_____

Vehicle used for this activity:

Year_____ Make_____ Model_____

Odometer_____ VIN _____

CDX Tasksheet Number: H218

Time off_____

Time on_____

Total time_____

1. Carry out an inspection of the antilock brake system (ABS) hardware components as outlined and listed in the appropriate service information.
   a. List the tests you performed and their results:

   _____
   _____
   _____
   _____

   b. Meets manufacturer's specifications: Yes: _____ No: _____ Comments: _____
      i. Determine any necessary actions or corrections:

      _____
      _____
      _____
      _____

2. Carry out an inspection of the antilock brake system (ABS) electrical components as outlined and listed in the appropriate service information.
   a. List the tests you performed and their results:

   _____
   _____
   _____
   _____

   b. Meets manufacturer's specifications: Yes: _____ No: _____ Comments: _____
      i. Determine any necessary actions or corrections:

      _____
      _____

3. Discuss these findings with your instructor.

Performance Rating

CDX Tasksheet Number: H218

☐ 0   ☐ 1   ☐ 2   ☐ 3   ☐ 4

Supervisor/instructor signature _____ Date_____

Student/intern information:

Name_____ Date_____ Class_____

Vehicle used for this activity:

Year_____ Make_____ Model_____

Odometer_____ VIN _____

▶ **TASK** Test antilock brake system (ABS) wheel speed sensors and circuits; adjust or replace as needed.   **NATEF 3C5**

CDX Tasksheet Number: H219

1. Research the procedure and specifications for diagnosing the ABS wheel sensors and circuits. List the following specifications:
    a. Tractor wheel speed sensor resistance, if applicable: _____ Ohms
    b. Trailer wheel speed sensor resistance, if applicable: _____ Ohms
    c. List any precautions when testing wheel speed sensors:

    _____

    _____

2. Test the anti-lock brake system (ABS) wheel speed sensor(s) electrical components/circuits as outlined and listed in the appropriate service information.
    a. Measure the resistance values of the wheel sensors:
        i. Tractor
            a. Actual (identify which sensor): _____ _____ Ω
            b. Actual (identify which sensor): _____ _____ Ω
            c. Actual (identify which sensor): _____ _____ Ω
            d. Actual (identify which sensor): _____ _____ Ω
            e. Actual (identify which sensor): _____ _____ Ω
            f. Actual (identify which sensor): _____ _____ Ω

        ii. Trailer
            a. Actual (identify which sensor): _____ _____ Ω
            b. Actual (identify which sensor): _____ _____ Ω
            c. Actual (identify which sensor): _____ _____ Ω
            d. Actual (identify which sensor): _____ _____ Ω

        iii. Meets manufacturer's specifications: Yes: _____ Requires service: _____
            a. If requires service, determine any necessary actions or corrections:

            _____

            _____

3. As directed, carry out any adjustment and/or replacements of affected components.

Time off_____

Time on_____

Total time_____

4. List any difficulties you encountered during this task.

   _____

   _____

   _____

5. Discuss these findings with your instructor.

Performance Rating

☐	☐	☐	☐	☐
0	1	2	3	4

Supervisor/instructor signature _____ Date_____

Name_____ Date_____ Class_____

Vehicle used for this activity:

Year_____ Make_____ Model_____

Odometer_____ VIN _____

▶ **TASK** Bleed the ABS hydraulic circuits.   **NATEF 3C6**

CDX Tasksheet Number: H220

Time off_____

Time on_____

Total time_____

1. Reference the manufacturer's service information and list the following specifications and procedures:
   a. Specified type of brake fluid:
   _____

   b. Recommended steps for bleeding the ABS hydraulic circuits:
   _____
   _____
   _____
   _____
   _____

2. Following the procedures outlined in the manufacturer's service information, bleed the ABS hydraulic circuits. List any difficulties you experienced in performing this task:
   _____
   _____
   _____

3. Carry out a final inspection of the ABS circuit to ensure it is functioning correctly.
   a. Meets manufacturer's specifications: Yes: _____ No: _____ Comments: _____
      i. Determine any necessary actions or corrections:
      _____
      _____
      _____

4. Discuss these findings with your instructor.

Performance Rating

CDX Tasksheet Number: H220

☐   ☐   ☐   ☐   ☐

0   1   2   3   4

Supervisor/instructor signature _____ Date_____

Name_____ Date_____ Class_____

Vehicle used for this activity:

Year_____ Make_____ Model_____

Odometer_____ VIN _____

▶ **TASK** Observe automatic traction control (ATC) warning light operation; determine needed action.

NATEF 3C7

Time off_____

Time on_____

Total time_____

CDX Tasksheet Number: H221

1. Turn the vehicle's ignition and allow it to go through its confirmation checks for the various circuits including the ATC.
   a. List the response of the warning lights:

   _____
   _____
   _____
   _____

   b. Meets manufacturer's specifications: Yes: _____ Requires diagnosis: _____
      i. Determine any necessary actions or corrections:

      _____
      _____
      _____
      _____

2. If directed by your instructor, carry out corrections as outlined in the manufacturer's service information:
   a. List the tests you performed and their results:

   _____
   _____
   _____
   _____

   b. Meets manufacturer's specifications: Yes: _____ No: _____
      i. If no, list the necessary actions or corrections:

      _____
      _____
      _____
      _____

3. Discuss these findings with your instructor.

Performance Rating

CDX Tasksheet Number: H221

☐ 0   ☐ 1   ☐ 2   ☐ 3   ☐ 4

Supervisor/instructor signature _____ Date_____

Student/intern information:

Name_____ Date_____ Class_____

Vehicle used for this activity:

Year_____ Make_____ Model_____

Odometer_____ VIN _____

▶ TASK Diagnose automatic traction control (ATC) electronic control(s) and components using self-diagnosis and/or specified test equipment (scan tool, PC computer); determine needed action.   **NATEF 3C8**

Time off_____

Time on_____

CDX Tasksheet Number: H222

Total time_____

1. Referencing the manufacturer's service information and electronic diagnostic tool's operating information, determine the correct method for using this tool.
    a. List the possible 'fault codes' for the ATC system:

    _____
    _____
    _____
    _____
    _____
    _____

2. Plug the scan tool or diagnostic equipment into the vehicle's diagnostic terminal. Following the specified procedure, retrieve any diagnostic trouble codes.
    a. List any ABS-related diagnostic codes and their descriptions:

    _____
    _____
    _____
    _____

    b. Meets manufacturer's specifications: Yes: _____ Requires diagnosis: _____
        i. If requires diagnosis, list the tests you performed and their results:

        _____
        _____
        _____
        _____

    c. Determine any necessary actions:

        _____
        _____

3. Discuss these findings with your instructor.

Performance Rating

CDX Tasksheet Number: H222

☐　　　　☐　　　　☐　　　　☐　　　　☐
0　　　　1　　　　2　　　　3　　　　4

Supervisor/instructor signature _____ Date_____

Name_____ Date_____ Class_____

Vehicle used for this activity:

Year_____ Make_____ Model_____

Odometer_____ VIN _____

> **TASK** Verify power line carrier (PLC) operations.   NATEF 3C9

Time off_____

Time on_____

Total time_____

CDX Tasksheet Number: H223

Note: Power line carrier (PLC) is the method used to relay data by multiplexing information across a single wire used in the ABS electrical power. This is an Federal Motor Vehicle Safety Standards (FMVSS) 121 requirement that is used for alerting the driver by a warning light on the dashboard of a fault in the trailer ABS brake system.

1. Power Line Carrier (PLC) will only work if the tractor and trailer are equipped with the same PLC ABS versions.

2. Check cab mounted trailer ABS malfunction lamp.

3. Check to see if the lamp lights when the vehicle starts for a system check. List your observations:

    _____
    _____
    _____

4. If the light stays on after startup, check for any malfunction codes that may be present.
    a. Codes present:
        i.   Code: _____ Description: _____
        ii. Code: _____ Description: _____
        iii. Code: _____ Description: _____
        iv. Code: _____ Description: _____
        v.   Code: _____ Description: _____
        vi. Code: _____ Description: _____

5. Consult the manufacturer's service information for the procedure to diagnose and repair the PLC system; list the tests you performed and their results:

    _____
    _____
    _____
    _____

6. Discuss these findings with your instructor.

Performance Rating

CDX Tasksheet Number: H223

☐   ☐   ☐   ☐   ☐
0   1   2   3   4

Supervisor/instructor signature _____ Date_____

Air & Hydraulic Brake Systems:
Wheel Bearings

Student/intern information:

Name_____ Date_____ Class_____

Vehicle used for this activity:

Year_____ Make_____ Model_____

Odometer_____ VIN _____

Time off_____

Time on_____

Total time_____

Learning Objective / Task	CDX Tasksheet Number	2014 NATEF Priority Level	2014 NATEF Reference Number
• Clean, inspect, lubricate, and replace wheel bearings and races/cups; replace seals and wear rings; inspect spindle/tube; inspect and replace retaining hardware; adjust wheel bearings. Verify end play with dial indicator method.	H224	P-1	3D1
• Identify, inspect or replace unitized/preset hub bearing assemblies.	H225	P-2	3D2

Materials Required

- Vehicle with possible engine concern
- Vehicle manufacturer's service information
- Manufacturer-specific tools depending on the concern
- Vehicle lifting equipment if applicable

Some Safety Issues to Consider

- Diagnosis of this fault may require test driving the vehicle on the school grounds or on a hoist, both of which carry severe risks. Attempt this task only with full permission from your supervisor/instructor and follow all the guidelines exactly.
- Caution: If you are working in an area where there could be brake dust present (may contain asbestos, which has been determined to cause cancer when inhaled or ingested), ensure you wear and use all OSHA-approved asbestos protective/removal equipment.
- Lifting equipment such as vehicle jacks and stands, vehicle hoists, and engine hoists are important tools that increase productivity and make the job easier. However, they can also cause severe injury or death if used improperly. Make sure you follow the manufacturer's operation procedures. Also make sure you have your supervisor/instructor's permission to use any particular type of lifting equipment.
- Comply with personal and environmental safety practices associated with clothing; eye protection; hand tools; power equipment; proper ventilation; and the handling, storage, and disposal of chemicals/materials in accordance with federal, state, and local regulations.
- Always wear the correct protective eyewear and clothing and use the appropriate safety equipment, as well as fender covers, seat protectors, and floor mat protectors.
- Make sure you understand and observe all legislative and personal safety procedures when carrying out practical assignments. If you are unsure of what these are, ask your supervisor/instructor.

Performance Standard

0—No exposure: No information or practice provided during the program; complete training required

1—Exposure only: General information provided with no practice time; close supervision needed; additional training required

2—Limited practice: Has practiced job during training program; additional training required to develop skill

3—Moderately skilled: Has performed job independently during training program; limited additional training may be required

4—Skilled: Can perform job independently with no additional training

Student/intern information:

Name_____ Date_____ Class_____

Vehicle used for this activity:

Year_____ Make_____ Model_____

Odometer_____ VIN _____

▶ **TASK** Clean, inspect, lubricate, and replace wheel bearings and races/cups; replace seals and wear rings; inspect spindle/tube; inspect and replace retaining hardware; adjust wheel bearings. Verify end play with dial indicator method. **NATEF 3D1**

Time off_____

Time on_____

Total time_____

CDX Tasksheet Number: H224

1. Reference the manufacturer's service information and record the recommended steps and safety precautions to clean, inspect, lubricate, and replace wheel bearings and races/cups; replace seals and wear rings; inspect spindle/tube; inspect and replace retaining hardware; adjust wheel bearings:

   _____
   _____
   _____
   _____

2. Park the vehicle on a flat surface in the workshop.

3. Select the appropriate floor jack capable of lifting the vehicle's weight.

4. Select the appropriate vehicle safety stands capable of supporting the vehicle's weight.

5. Have a waste-oil retaining collector available.

6. Following all the safety requirements and procedures outlined and recorded in the manufacturer's service information, remove the wheel bearing assembly, collecting all waste oil from the housing.

   a. Jack up the vehicle and install the safety stands.
   b. Remove the road wheels.
   c. Undo the retaining nut and lock nut from the hub assembly.
   d. While correctly supporting the bearing hub assembly, remove the hub from the axle shaft.
   e. Place the removed hub on an appropriate work station ensuring it is secure.

7. Following the procedure outlined in the manufacturer's service information, remove the bearings, seals, and bearing cups.

8. Following all recommended servicing procedures, clean/dry (observing all OSHA requirements) then inspect all bearing and bearing cups.

   a. Inspect the wheel bearings and components. List your observations:

      _____
      _____
      _____

   b. After inspection, lubricate the bearing as recommended in the manufacturer's service information.
   c. Within specifications: Yes: _____ No: _____
      i. If no, replace with the manufacturer's specified replacement component.

9. Following the procedure outlined in the manufacturer's service information, replace seals and wear rings if directed by your instructor.

   a. Replaced: Yes: _____ No: _____ Comments: _____

10. Inspect the spindle/tube.
    a. Within specifications: Yes: _____ No: _____ Comments: _____
        i. If no, list the necessary actions or corrections:
        _____
        _____

11. Have your instructor verify disassembly and your answers.
    Supervisor/instructor's initials: _____

12. Inspect and replace the retaining hardware (if directed).
    a. List your observations:
    _____
    _____

    b. Within specifications: Yes: _____ No: _____
        i. If no, list the necessary actions or corrections:
        _____
        _____

13. Have your instructor verify disassembly and your answers.
    Supervisor/instructor's initials: _____

14. Reassemble the hub assembly and refit to the lubricated axle shaft.

15. Following all recommended servicing procedures, list the steps necessary to properly adjust the wheel bearings:
    _____
    _____
    _____
    _____
    _____

16. Discuss the process with your instructor.

17. Perform the wheel bearing adjustment procedure.

18. Have your instructor verify correct wheel bearing adjustment.
    Supervisor/instructor's initials: _____

Performance Rating

CDX Tasksheet Number: H224

☐ 0   ☐ 1   ☐ 2   ☐ 3   ☐ 4

Supervisor/instructor signature _____ Date_____

Student/intern information:

Name_____ Date_____ Class_____

Vehicle used for this activity:

Year_____ Make_____ Model_____

Odometer_____ VIN _____

Time off_____

Time on_____

Total time_____

▶ **TASK** Identify, inspect or replace unitized/preset hub bearing assemblies. **NATEF 3D2**

CDX Tasksheet Number: H225

1. Reference the appropriate manufacturer's service information and list the recommended steps and safety precautions to inspect or replace the extended service wheel bearing assemblies:

   _____

   _____

   _____

   _____

2. Discuss with your instructor.

3. If directed by your instructor, inspect or replace the extended service wheel bearing assemblies.
   a. List your observations:

      _____

      _____

      _____

   b. Within specifications: Yes: _____ No: _____
      i. Determine any necessary actions or corrections:

         _____

         _____

         _____

4. Discuss these findings with your instructor.

Performance Rating

CDX Tasksheet Number: H225

☐	☐	☐	☐	☐
0	1	2	3	4

Supervisor/instructor signature _____ Date_____

Welding & Hydraulics, DT109

CONTENTS

Welding & Hydraulics, DT109

Welding & Hydraulics:
Basic Cutting and Welding

Student/intern information:

Name_____ Date_____ Class_____

Vehicle used for this activity:

Year_____ Make_____ Model_____

Odometer_____ VIN _____

Learning Objective / Task	CDX Tasksheet Number	2014 NATEF Priority Level	2014 NATEF Reference Number
• Describe the type of protection that must be worn when welding and cutting.	MHT03	N/A	N/A
• Identify and demonstrate the basic types of weld joints, which are the butt, t-joint and lap joint.	MHT04	N/A	N/A
• Identify and explain the main features of a weld and the correct welding positions.	MHT05	N/A	N/A
• Demonstrate and explain how to set up and operate a MIG Welder.	MHT06	N/A	N/A
• Identify some common problems encountered in MIG welding and be able to solve them correctly.	MHT07	N/A	N/A
• Demonstrate simple metal cutting by using the oxyacetylene combination torch.	MHT08	N/A	N/A
• Weld rosettes or plugs in all welding positions.	MHT09	N/A	N/A

Time off_____

Time on_____

Total time_____

Materials Required
- Vehicle with possible hydraulic concern
- Vehicle manufacturer's service information
- Manufacturer-specific tools depending on the concern
- Vehicle lifting equipment if applicable

Some Safety Issues to Consider
- Diagnosis of this fault may require test driving the vehicle on the school grounds or on a hoist, both of which carry severe risks. Attempt this task only with full permission from your supervisor/instructor and follow all the guidelines exactly.
- Caution: If you are working in an area where there could be "brake dust" present (may contain asbestos, which has been determined to cause cancer when inhaled or ingested), ensure you wear and use all OSHA-approved asbestos protective/removal equipment.
- Lifting equipment such as vehicle jacks and stands, vehicle hoists, and engine hoists are important tools that increase productivity and make the job easier. However, they can also cause severe injury or death if used improperly. Make sure you follow the manufacturer's operation procedures. Also make sure you have your supervisor/instructor's permission to use any particular type of lifting equipment.
- Comply with personal and environmental safety practices associated with clothing; eye protection; hand tools; power equipment; proper ventilation; and the handling, storage, and disposal of chemicals/materials in accordance with federal, state, and local regulations.
- Always wear the correct protective eyewear and clothing and use the appropriate safety equipment, as well as fender covers, seat protectors, and floor mat protectors.
- Make sure you understand and observe all legislative and personal safety procedures when carrying out practical assignments. If you are unsure of what these are, ask your supervisor/instructor.

© 2017 Jones & Bartlett Learning, LLC, an Ascend Learning Company

Performance Standard

0—No exposure: No information or practice provided during the program; complete training required

1—Exposure only: General information provided with no practice time; close supervision needed; additional training required

2—Limited practice: Has practiced job during training program; additional training required to develop skill

3—Moderately skilled: Has performed job independently during training program; limited additional training may be required

4—Skilled: Can perform job independently with no additional training

Student/intern information:

Name_____ Date_____ Class_____

Vehicle used for this activity:

Year_____ Make_____ Model_____

Odometer_____ VIN _____

▶ **TASK** Describe the type of protection that must be worn when welding and cutting.

Non-NATEF

Time off_____

Time on_____

Total time_____

CDX Tasksheet Number: MHT03

1. Describe the type of protection that must be worn when welding and cutting.

   a. Head gear:

   _____
   _____
   _____

   b. Hand protection:

   _____
   _____
   _____

   c. Clothing:

   _____
   _____
   _____

   d. Footwear:

   _____
   _____
   _____

   e. Eye protection:

   _____
   _____
   _____

Performance Rating

CDX Tasksheet Number: MHT03

☐	☐	☐	☐	☐
0	1	2	3	4

Supervisor/instructor signature _____ Date_____

Student/intern information:

Name_____ Date_____ Class_____

Vehicle used for this activity:

Year_____ Make_____ Model_____

Odometer_____ VIN _____

▶ **TASK** Identify and demonstrate the basic types of weld joints, which are the butt, t-joint, and
lap joint. **Non-NATEF**

Time off_____

Time on_____

Total time_____

CDX Tasksheet Number: MHT04

> **Note:** Criteria for evaluation of welds:
> • Weld joint must not contain excessive or insufficient filler metal.
> • Weld joint must have proper joint penetration and be readily visible.
> • Weld joint must not contain: cracks, porosity, inclusions, undercut, or overlap.
> • Convexity (i.e. toe to face in line with root) of weld bead should not exceed 0.125" (3.175 mm).
> • Width (i.e. toe to toe) of weld bead should not exceed 0.375" (9.525 mm), or three times the material thickness.
> • Heat and travel speed must be consistent and appropriate for material thickness.

1. Weld t-joints.
   a. Prepare the base metal plates for welding.
   b. Weld a t-joint bead that is 1–1.5" (25.4–38.1 mm) long.
   c. Skip 1" (25 mm) on the joint and repeat.

2. Weld butt joints.
   a. Prepare the base metal plates for welding.
   b. Weld a butt joint bead that is 1–1.5" (25.4–38.1 mm) long.
   c. Skip 1" (25 mm) on the joint and repeat.

3. Weld lap joints.
   a. Prepare the base metal plates for welding.
   b. Weld a lap joint bead that is 1–1.5" (25.4–38.1 mm) long.
   c. Skip 1" (25 mm) on the joint and repeat.

Performance Rating

CDX Tasksheet Number: MHT04

☐	☐	☐	☐	☐
0	1	2	3	4

Supervisor/instructor signature _____ Date_____

© 2017 Jones & Bartlett Learning, LLC, an Ascend Learning Company

Student/intern information:

Name_____ Date_____ Class_____

Vehicle used for this activity:

Year_____ Make_____ Model_____

Odometer_____ VIN _____

▶ **TASK** Identify and explain the main features of a weld and the correct welding positions.

CDX Tasksheet Number: MHT05

Note: Criteria for evaluation of welds:
- Weld joint must not contain excessive or insufficient filler metal.
- Weld joint must have proper joint penetration and be readily visible.
- Weld joint must not contain: cracks, porosity, inclusions, undercut, or overlap.
- Convexity (i.e. toe to face in line with root) of weld bead should not exceed 0.125" (3.175 mm).
- Width (i.e. toe to toe) of weld bead should not exceed 0.375" (9.525 mm), or three times the material thickness.
- Heat and travel speed must be consistent and appropriate for material thickness.

1. Weld t-joints.
   a. Weld 1F t-joints.
      i. Prepare the base metal plates for welding.
      ii. Weld a t-joint bead that is 1–1.5" (25.4-38.1 mm) long.
   b. Weld 2F t-joints.
      i. Prepare the base metal plates for welding.
      ii. Weld a t-joint bead that is 1–1.5" (25.4-38.1 mm) long.
   c. Weld 3F t-joints.
      i. Prepare the base metal plates for welding.
      ii. Weld a t-joint bead that is 1–1.5" (25.4-38.1 mm) long.
   d. Weld 4F t-joints.
      i. Prepare the base metal plates for welding.
      ii. Weld a t-joint bead that is 1–1.5" (25.4-38.1 mm) long.
   e. Have your supervisor/instructor verify satisfactory completion of these procedures.
      Supervisor/instructor's initials: _____

2. Weld butt joints.
   a. Weld 1G butt joints.
      i. Prepare the base metal plates for welding.
      ii. Weld a butt joint bead that is 1–1.5" (25.4-38.1 mm) long.
   b. Weld 2G butt joints.
      i. Prepare the base metal plates for welding.
      ii. Weld a butt joint bead that is 1–1.5" (25.4-38.1 mm) long.
   c. Weld 3G butt joints.
      i. Prepare the base metal plates for welding.
      ii. Weld a butt joint bead that is 1–1.5" (25.4-38.1 mm) long.
   d. Weld 4G butt joints.
      i. Prepare the base metal plates for welding.
      ii. Weld a butt joint bead that is 1–1.5" (25.4-38.1 mm) long.
   e. Have your supervisor/instructor verify satisfactory completion of these procedures.
      Supervisor/instructor's initials: _____

3. Weld lap joints.
   a. Weld 1F lap joints.
      i. Prepare the base metal plates for welding.
      ii. Weld a lap joint bead that is 1–1.5" (25.4–38.1 mm) long.
   b. Weld 2F lap joints.
      i. Prepare the base metal plates for welding.
      ii. Weld a lap joint bead that is 1–1.5" (25.4–38.1 mm) long.
   c. Weld 3F lap joints.
      i. Prepare the base metal plates for welding.
      ii. Weld a lap joint bead that is 1–1.5" (25.4–38.1 mm) long.
   d. Weld 4F lap joints.
      i. Prepare the base metal plates for welding.
      ii. Weld a lap joint bead that is 1–1.5" (25.4–38.1 mm) long.
   e. Have your supervisor/instructor verify satisfactory completion of this procedure
      Supervisor/instructor's initials: _____

Performance Rating

CDX Tasksheet Number: MHT05

☐ 0   ☐ 1   ☐ 2   ☐ 3   ☐ 4

Supervisor/instructor signature _____ Date_____

Student/intern information:

Name_____ Date_____ Class_____

Vehicle used for this activity:

Year_____ Make_____ Model_____

Odometer_____ VIN _____

▶ **TASK** Demonstrate and explain how to set up and operate a MIG welder.

Time off_____

Time on_____

Total time_____

CDX Tasksheet Number: MHT06

1. Inspect the welding machine and work area for hazards. List your findings:

   _____
   _____
   _____
   _____

2. Inspect your personal protective equipment and verify that it is appropriate for the type of welding and in good condition. List your findings:

   _____
   _____
   _____
   _____

3. Prepare the machine for the material thickness and weld joint type specified by your instructor. List the settings you prepared:

   _____
   _____
   _____

4. Stop here and have your instructor approve your progress.

Performance Rating

CDX Tasksheet Number: MHT06

☐	☐	☐	☐	☐
0	1	2	3	4

Supervisor/instructor signature _____ Date_____

Student/intern information:

Name_____ Date_____ Class_____

Vehicle used for this activity:

Year_____ Make_____ Model_____

Odometer_____ VIN _____

Identify some common problems encountered in MIG welding and solve them correctly.

Non-NATEF

CDX Tasksheet Number: MHT07

1. Name at least four common weld flaws, their causes, and a way to correct each problem. Name the flaws in the numbered boxes on the left. Describe what causes that flaw in the center box of the same row. Describe how that flaw can be avoided in the box on the right in the same row.

	Weld Flaw	Cause	Correction
1			
2			
3			
4			

Performance Rating

CDX Tasksheet Number: MHT07

☐ 0   ☐ 1   ☐ 2   ☐ 3   ☐ 4

Supervisor/instructor signature _____ Date_____

Student/intern information:

Name_____ Date_____ Class_____

Vehicle used for this activity:

Year_____ Make_____ Model_____

Odometer_____ VIN _____

▶ **TASK** Demonstrate simple metal cutting using an oxyacetylene combination torch.

Non-NATEF

Time off_____

Time on_____

Total time_____

CDX Tasksheet Number: MHT08

1. Prepare to cut metal using an oxyacetylene torch.
   a. Inspect the oxyacetylene equipment for damage or hazards. Note your findings:
      _____
      _____
      _____

   b. Inspect the work area for hazards. List your findings:
      Kitten   salt ⬤
      _____
      _____

   c. Prepare the torch for cutting. List the regulator pressure and valve position settings:
      _____
      _____
      _____

   d. Prepare and cut one piece of flat stock, as specified by your instructor. Inspect the cut and list your observations:
      _____
      _____
      _____

   e. Prepare and cut one piece of angle stock, as specified by your instructor. Inspect the cut and list your observations:
      _____
      _____
      _____

   f. Stop work here and prepare your torch for storage. List your preparations below:
      _____
      _____
      _____

   g. Have your supervisor/instructor verify satisfactory completion of these procedures. Supervisor/instructor's initials: _____

2. Prepare to cut metal using a plasma cutter.
   a. Inspect your plasma cutter for damage or hazards. List your findings:
      _____
      _____
      _____

b. Inspect your work area for hazards. List your findings:

_____
_____
_____

c. Prepare your plasma cutter for operation. List your setting:

_____
_____
_____

d. Prepare and cut one piece of flat stock, as specified by your instructor. Inspect the cut and list your observations:

_____
_____
_____

e. Prepare and cut one piece of angle stock, as specified by your instructor. Inspect the cut and list your observations:

_____
_____
_____

f. Stop work here and prepare your plasma cutter for storage. List your preparations:

_____
_____
_____

g. Have your supervisor/instructor verify satisfactory completion of these procedures. Supervisor/instructor's initials: _____

Performance Rating

☐   ☐   ☐   ☐   ☐
0   1   2   3   4

Supervisor/instructor signature _____ Date_____

Student/intern information:

Name_____ Date_____ Class_____

Vehicle used for this activity:

Year_____ Make_____ Model_____

Odometer_____ VIN _____

© 2017 Jones & Bartlett Learning, LLC, an Ascend Learning Company

▶ TASK Identify and demonstrate the basic types of weld joints, which are the butt, t-joint, and lap joint. **Non-NATEF**

Time off_____

Time on_____

Total time_____

CDX Tasksheet Number: MHT09

Note: Criteria for evaluation of welds:
- Weld joint must not contain excessive or insufficient filler metal.
- Weld joint must have proper joint penetration and be readily visible.
- Weld joint must not contain: cracks, porosity, inclusions, undercut, or overlap.
- Convexity (i.e. toe to face in line with root) of weld bead should not exceed 0.125" (3.175 mm).
- Width (i.e. toe to toe) of weld bead should not exceed 0.375" (9.525 mm), or three times the material thickness.
- Heat and travel speed must be consistent and appropriate for material thickness.

1. Weld 1F rosette/plug.
    a. Prepare the base metal plates with one .500" (12.700 mm) hole for welding.
    b. Weld one rosette.
2. Weld 2F rosette/plug.
    a. Prepare the base metal plates with one .500" (12.700 mm) hole for welding.
    b. Weld one rosette.
3. Weld 3F rosette/plug.
    a. Prepare the base metal plates with one .500" (12.700 mm) hole for welding.
    b. Weld one rosette.
4. Weld 4F rosette/plug.
    a. Prepare the base metal plates with one .500" (12.700 mm) hole for welding.
    b. Weld one rosette.

Performance Rating

CDX Tasksheet Number: MHT09

☐	☐	☐	☐	☐
0	1	2	3	4

Supervisor/instructor signature _____ Date_____

Welding & Hydraulics:
General System Operation 1

Student/intern information:

Name_____ Date_____ Class_____

Vehicle used for this activity:

Year_____ Make_____ Model_____

Odometer_____ VIN _____

Learning Objective / Task	CDX Tasksheet Number	2014 NATEF Priority Level	2014 NATEF Reference Number
• Identify system type (closed and open) and verify proper operation.	H537	P-1	8A1
• Read and interpret system diagrams and schematics.	H538	P-1	8A2

Time off_____

Time on_____

Total time_____

Materials Required

- Vehicle with possible hydraulic concern
- Vehicle manufacturer's service information
- Manufacturer-specific tools depending on the concern
- Vehicle lifting equipment if applicable

Some Safety Issues to Consider

- Hydraulics systems operate under extremely high pressures! Injection of high-pressure hydraulic oil into human skin may require emergency surgery to stop the damage. Never use your hand to search for the source of a hydraulic leak. Wear appropriate safety equipment.
- Diagnosis of this fault may require test driving the vehicle on the school grounds or on a hoist, both of which carry severe risks. Attempt this task only with full permission from your supervisor/instructor and follow all the guidelines exactly.
- Caution: If you are working in an area where there could be "brake dust" present (may contain asbestos, which has been determined to cause cancer when inhaled or ingested), ensure you wear and use all OSHA-approved asbestos protective/removal equipment.
- Lifting equipment such as vehicle jacks and stands, vehicle hoists, and engine hoists are important tools that increase productivity and make the job easier. However, they can also cause severe injury or death if used improperly. Make sure you follow the manufacturer's operation procedures. Also make sure you have your supervisor/instructor's permission to use any particular type of lifting equipment.
- Comply with personal and environmental safety practices associated with clothing; eye protection; hand tools; power equipment; proper ventilation; and the handling, storage, and disposal of chemicals/materials in accordance with federal, state, and local regulations.
- Always wear the correct protective eyewear and clothing and use the appropriate safety equipment, as well as fender covers, seat protectors, and floor mat protectors.
- Make sure you understand and observe all legislative and personal safety procedures when carrying out practical assignments. If you are unsure of what these are, ask your supervisor/instructor.

© 2017 Jones & Bartlett Learning, LLC, an Ascend Learning Company

Performance Standard

0—No exposure: No information or practice provided during the program; complete training required

1—Exposure only: General information provided with no practice time; close supervision needed; additional training required

2—Limited practice: Has practiced job during training program; additional training required to develop skill

3—Moderately skilled: Has performed job independently during training program; limited additional training may be required

4—Skilled: Can perform job independently with no additional training

Name_____ Date_____ Class_____

Vehicle used for this activity:

Year_____ Make_____ Model_____

Odometer_____ VIN _____

▶ **TASK** Identify system type (closed and open) and verify proper operation.   NATEF 8A1

Time off_____

Time on_____

CDX Tasksheet Number: H537

Total time_____

1. Locate the hydraulic component on the vehicle.
   a. Record the component manufacturer's name: _____
   b. Record the component model and serial/part number:
      i. Model number: _____
      ii. Serial/part number: _____

2. Reference the appropriate component service information for the correct identification of the attached product component.
   a. Name of the identified component: _____
   b. Identify from the component service information that this component is a(n):
      i. Open circuit component: _____
      ii. Closed circuit component: _____

3. Reference the appropriate service information for the correct procedure to diagnose/verify the correct operation.
   a. List the procedure and all safety requirements when inspecting/verifying the correct operation of the hydraulic component:

      _____
      _____
      _____

4. Verify the correct/proper operation of the hydraulic component.
   a. Research the procedure and specifications for the correct operation of the hydraulic component in the appropriate service information.
   b. Within the manufacturer's specifications: Yes: _____ No: _____ Comments: _____
      _____

   c. Determine any necessary action(s):
      _____
      _____

5. Discuss the findings with your instructor.

Performance Rating

CDX Tasksheet Number: H537

☐   ☐   ☐   ☐   ☐

0   1   2   3   4

Supervisor/instructor signature _____ Date_____

Student/intern information:

Name_____ Date_____ Class_____

Vehicle used for this activity:

Year_____ Make_____ Model_____

Odometer_____ VIN _____

▶ **TASK** Read and interpret system diagrams and schematics. **NATEF 8A2**

Time off_____

Time on_____

Total time_____

CDX Tasksheet Number: H538

Background:
In any hydraulic system, access and the ability to read and interpret a circuit diagram is essential, especially when you are undertaking any identification for causes of hydraulic problems.

When troubleshooting problems within the hydraulic equipment you must find out whether there is an actual problem with the system or not. First, conduct a visual inspection of the hydraulic system, and research the warning signs that could cause the related problem. Second, study a circuit diagram of the hydraulic system.

In this exercise you may have to refer back to your earlier studies in basic hydraulic theory.
1. Research the specifications for the correct schematic layout for this vehicle's components in the appropriate service information.

2. Study this schematic diagram.

3. When you are familiar with this diagram, explain the circuit and symbols to your instructor. Explain the circuits and their power flow and the action of each actuator.

4. Discuss the findings with your instructor.

Performance Rating

CDX Tasksheet Number: H538

☐ 0   ☐ 1   ☐ 2   ☐ 3   ☐ 4

Supervisor/instructor signature _____ Date_____

© 2017 Jones & Bartlett Learning, LLC, an Ascend Learning Company

Welding & Hydraulics **285**

Welding & Hydraulics:
General System Operation 2

Student/intern information:

Name_____ Date_____ Class_____

Vehicle used for this activity:

Year_____ Make_____ Model_____

Odometer_____ VIN _____

Learning Objective / Task	CDX Tasksheet Number	2014 NATEF Priority Level	2014 NATEF Reference Number
• Perform system temperature, pressure, flow, and cycle time tests; determine needed action.	H539	P-1	8A3
• Verify placement of equipment/component safety labels and placards; determine needed action.	H540	P-1	8A4

Time off_____

Time on_____

Total time_____

Materials Required

- Vehicle with possible hydraulic concern
- Vehicle manufacturer's service information
- Manufacturer-specific tools depending on the concern
- Vehicle lifting equipment if applicable

Some Safety Issues to Consider

- Hydraulics systems operate under extremely high pressures! Injection of high-pressure hydraulic oil into human skin may require emergency surgery to stop the damage. Never use your hand to search for the source of a hydraulic leak. Wear appropriate safety equipment.
- Diagnosis of this fault may require test driving the vehicle on the school grounds or on a hoist, both of which carry severe risks. Attempt this task only with full permission from your supervisor/instructor and follow all the guidelines exactly.
- Caution: If you are working in an area where there could be "brake dust" present (may contain asbestos, which has been determined to cause cancer when inhaled or ingested), ensure you wear and use all OSHA-approved asbestos protective/removal equipment.
- Lifting equipment such as vehicle jacks and stands, vehicle hoists, and engine hoists are important tools that increase productivity and make the job easier. However, they can also cause severe injury or death if used improperly. Make sure you follow the manufacturer's operation procedures. Also make sure you have your supervisor/instructor's permission to use any particular type of lifting equipment.
- Comply with personal and environmental safety practices associated with clothing; eye protection; hand tools; power equipment; proper ventilation; and the handling, storage, and disposal of chemicals/materials in accordance with federal, state, and local regulations.
- Always wear the correct protective eyewear and clothing and use the appropriate safety equipment, as well as fender covers, seat protectors, and floor mat protectors.
- Make sure you understand and observe all legislative and personal safety procedures when carrying out practical assignments. If you are unsure of what these are, ask your supervisor/instructor.

Performance Standard

0–No exposure: No information or practice provided during the program; complete training required

1–Exposure only: General information provided with no practice time; close supervision needed; additional training required

2–Limited practice: Has practiced job during training program; additional training required to develop skill

3–Moderately skilled: Has performed job independently during training program; limited additional training may be required

4–Skilled: Can perform job independently with no additional training

Student/intern information:

Name_____ Date_____ Class_____

Vehicle used for this activity:

Year_____ Make_____ Model_____

Odometer_____ VIN _____

▶ TASK Verify placement of equipment/component safety labels and placards; determine needed action.

NATEF 8A4

Time off_____

Time on_____

Total time_____

CDX Tasksheet Number: H540

1. Research the procedure and specifications for the types of safety labels and placards and their correct positioning around the vehicle in the appropriate service information.
   a. List the appropriate safety labels and placards required by the manufacturer and relevant OSHA legislation:

   _____
   _____
   _____
   _____
   _____
   _____

2. Verify that each of these labels and placards (identified above) are correctly positioned and legible.
   a. Are they positioned correctly? Yes: _____ No: _____ Comments: _____

   _____
   _____

   b. Are they legible? Yes: _____ No: _____ Comments: _____

   _____
   _____

   c. Determine any necessary action(s):

   _____
   _____
   _____

3. Discuss the findings with your instructor.

Performance Rating

CDX Tasksheet Number: H540

☐ 0   ☐ 1   ☐ 2   ☐ 3   ☐ 4

Supervisor/instructor signature _____ Date_____

Welding & Hydraulics: Pumps 1

Student/intern information:

Name_____ Date_____ Class_____

Vehicle used for this activity:

Year_____ Make_____ Model_____

Odometer_____ VIN _____

Learning Objective / Task	CDX Tasksheet Number	2014 NATEF Priority Level	2014 NATEF Reference Number
• Identify system fluid type.	H541	P-1	8B1
• Identify causes of pump failure, unusual pump noises, temperature, flow, and leakage problems; determine needed action.	H542	P-1	8B2
• Determine pump type, rotation, and drive system.	H543	P-1	8B3

Time off_____

Time on_____

Total time_____

Materials Required

- Vehicle with possible hydraulic concern
- Vehicle manufacturer's service information
- Manufacturer-specific tools depending on the concern
- Vehicle lifting equipment if applicable

Some Safety Issues to Consider

- Hydraulics systems operate under extremely high pressures! Injection of high-pressure hydraulic oil into human skin may require emergency surgery to stop the damage. Never use your hand to search for the source of a hydraulic leak. Wear appropriate safety equipment.
- Diagnosis of this fault may require test driving the vehicle on the school grounds or on a hoist, both of which carry severe risks. Attempt this task only with full permission from your supervisor/instructor and follow all the guidelines exactly.
- Caution: If you are working in an area where there could be "brake dust" present (may contain asbestos, which has been determined to cause cancer when inhaled or ingested), ensure you wear and use all OSHA-approved asbestos protective/removal equipment.
- Lifting equipment such as vehicle jacks and stands, vehicle hoists, and engine hoists are important tools that increase productivity and make the job easier. However, they can also cause severe injury or death if used improperly. Make sure you follow the manufacturer's operation procedures. Also make sure you have your supervisor/instructor's permission to use any particular type of lifting equipment.
- Comply with personal and environmental safety practices associated with clothing; eye protection; hand tools; power equipment; proper ventilation; and the handling, storage, and disposal of chemicals/materials in accordance with federal, state, and local regulations.
- Always wear the correct protective eyewear and clothing and use the appropriate safety equipment, as well as fender covers, seat protectors, and floor mat protectors.
- Make sure you understand and observe all legislative and personal safety procedures when carrying out practical assignments. If you are unsure of what these are, ask your supervisor/instructor.

Performance Standard

0—No exposure: No information or practice provided during the program; complete training required

1—Exposure only: General information provided with no practice time; close supervision needed; additional training required

2—Limited practice: Has practiced job during training program; additional training required to develop skill

3—Moderately skilled: Has performed job independently during training program; limited additional training may be required

4—Skilled: Can perform job independently with no additional training

Student/intern information:

Name_____ Date_____ Class_____

Vehicle used for this activity:

Year_____ Make_____ Model_____

Odometer_____ VIN _____

▶ TASK Identify system fluid type.   NATEF 8B1

Time off_____

Time on_____

Total time_____

CDX Tasksheet Number: H541

1. Research the procedure and specifications for the correct fluid type in the appropriate service information.
    a. Type of specified oil: _____
    b. Main characteristics of this fluid:

    _____
    _____
    _____
    _____
    _____

2. Draw a sample of the hydraulic fluid into a sterile container for analysis. This is an important step when diagnosing a failure. Contaminated fluid can cause catastrophic failures.

3. If directed by your instructor, arrange for the oil sample to be analyzed for contamination and suitability.

4. Locate the hydraulic fluid supply within your workshop storage facilities and check the hydraulic fluid name, type, and suitability.
    a. Locate the hydraulic fluid in storage.
    b. Record the fluid's manufacturer's name: _____
    c. Record the fluid type: _____
        i. Does it meet manufacturer's specifications? Yes: _____ No: _____
            Comments: _____
            _____

        ii. Determine any necessary action(s):
            _____
            _____
            _____

5. Discuss the findings with your instructor.

Performance Rating

CDX Tasksheet Number: H541

☐	☐	☐	☐	☐
0	1	2	3	4

Supervisor/instructor signature _____ Date_____

Student/intern information:

Name_____ Date_____ Class_____

Vehicle used for this activity:

Year_____ Make_____ Model_____

Odometer_____ VIN _____

CDX Tasksheet Number: H542

1. Research the procedure and specifications for possible causes of hydraulic pump failure in the appropriate service information.
    a. Check for proper air flow across pump. Obstructions present? Yes: _____ No: _____
        Comments: _____
    b. Check for possible air in the system. Air bubble present? Yes: _____ No: _____
        Comments: _____
    c. Check for correct type of fluid. Proper type of fluid? Yes: _____ No: _____
        Comments: _____
    d. Check for properly routed lines. Are they kinking or twisted? Yes: _____ No: _____
        Comments: _____

2. Listen for possible abnormal noises coming from pump. Noises coming from pump?
    Yes: _____ No: _____ Comments: _____

    a. If yes, pump should be disassembled for inspection.

3. Check and record temperature of fluid in the reservoir: _____ degrees

    Note: Temperatures above 180°F (82°C) can cause failure of the hydraulic system. Proper viscosity and correct load specifications should be maintained. Overheating of fluid will cause a low pressure condition.

4. Check the flow of fluid using a pressure gauge to determine if there is a flow restriction.

5. Consult the appropriate service information for the proper desired pressure readings for the system being worked on.
    a. Desired pressure: _____ psi (kPa)
    b. Actual pressure: _____ psi (kPa)

6. Inspect all the components of the system for leakage.
    a. Leakage present? Yes: _____ No: _____ Comments: _____
        _____

    b. If yes, consult the appropriate service information for proper procedures to repair the system. Record the procedures.
        _____
        _____
        _____
        _____

7. Looking over your answers on the previous page, determine any necessary actions:

    _____
    _____
    _____

8. Discuss these findings with your instructor.

Performance Rating

☐   ☐   ☐   ☐   ☐
0   1   2   3   4

Supervisor/instructor signature _____ Date_____

Student/intern information:

Name_____ Date_____ Class_____

Vehicle used for this activity:

Year_____ Make_____ Model_____

Odometer_____ VIN _____

▶ **TASK** Determine pump type, rotation, and drive system. | NATEF 8B3 |

Time off_____

Time on_____

CDX Tasksheet Number: H543

1. Research the procedure and specifications for the correct identification of the attached product component in the appropriate service information.
   a. Identify the pump type: _____
   b. Identify the correct direction of rotation: Clockwise: _____ Counter-clockwise: _____
   c. Identify the pump drive system: _____

Total time_____

2. Discuss the findings with your instructor.

Performance Rating

CDX Tasksheet Number: H543

☐	☐	☐	☐	☐
0	1	2	3	4

Supervisor/instructor signature _____ Date_____

Welding & Hydraulics:
Pumps 2

Student/intern information:

Name_____ Date_____ Class_____

Vehicle used for this activity:

Year_____ Make_____ Model_____

Odometer_____ VIN _____

Learning Objective / Task	CDX Tasksheet Number	2014 NATEF Priority Level	2014 NATEF Reference Number
• Remove and install pump; prime and/or bleed system.	H544	P-2	8B4
• Inspect pump inlet for restrictions and leaks; determine needed action.	H545	P-2	8B5
• Inspect pump outlet for restrictions and leaks; determine needed action.	H546	P-2	8B6

Time off_____

Time on_____

Total time_____

Materials Required

- Vehicle with possible hydraulic concern
- Vehicle manufacturer's service information
- Manufacturer-specific tools depending on the concern
- Vehicle lifting equipment if applicable

Some Safety Issues to Consider

- Hydraulics systems operate under extremely high pressures! Injection of high-pressure hydraulic oil into human skin may require emergency surgery to stop the damage. Never use your hand to search for the source of a hydraulic leak. Wear appropriate safety equipment. Diagnosis of this fault may require test driving the vehicle on the school grounds or on a hoist, both of which carry severe risks. Attempt this task only with full permission from your supervisor/instructor and follow all the guidelines exactly.
- Caution: If you are working in an area where there could be "brake dust" present (may contain asbestos, which has been determined to cause cancer when inhaled or ingested), ensure you wear and use all OSHA-approved asbestos protective/removal equipment.
- Lifting equipment such as vehicle jacks and stands, vehicle hoists, and engine hoists are important tools that increase productivity and make the job easier. However, they can also cause severe injury or death if used improperly. Make sure you follow the manufacturer's operation procedures. Also make sure you have your supervisor/instructor's permission to use any particular type of lifting equipment.
- Comply with personal and environmental safety practices associated with clothing; eye protection; hand tools; power equipment; proper ventilation; and the handling, storage, and disposal of chemicals/materials in accordance with federal, state, and local regulations.
- Always wear the correct protective eyewear and clothing and use the appropriate safety equipment, as well as fender covers, seat protectors, and floor mat protectors.
- Make sure you understand and observe all legislative and personal safety procedures when carrying out practical assignments. If you are unsure of what these are, ask your supervisor/instructor.

Performance Standard

0—No exposure: No information or practice provided during the program; complete training required

1—Exposure only: General information provided with no practice time; close supervision needed; additional training required

2—Limited practice: Has practiced job during training program; additional training required to develop skill

3—Moderately skilled: Has performed job independently during training program; limited additional training may be required

4—Skilled: Can perform job independently with no additional training

Name_____ Date_____ Class_____

Vehicle used for this activity:

Year_____ Make_____ Model_____

Odometer_____ VIN _____

▶ **TASK** Remove and install pump; prime and/or bleed system. | **NATEF 8B4**

Time off_____

Time on_____

Total time_____

CDX Tasksheet Number: H544

1. Research the procedure and specifications for removing and installing the pump and priming and/or bleeding the system in the appropriate service information.
   a. List the procedure and all safety requirements for removing and installing the pump and priming and/or bleeding the system. Hydraulic systems create tremendous pressures and can cause serious bodily harm if system is ruptured. Always follow manufacturer recommended safety precautions.

   _____
   _____
   _____
   _____
   _____

2. Following the procedures outlined above, and taking into account all safety precautions, remove the hydraulic pump.
   a. While using a collection container adequate for the amount of oil to be drained, drain the power steering fluid.
   b. Collect an oil sample in a clean, sterile container to be sent for analysis with your instructor's approval.
   c. Remove the inlet and outlet hoses, collecting any fluid coming from the removed hoses.
   d. Remove the hydraulic pump and place on the work bench.

3. Inspect all components for wear and damage. List your observations:

   _____
   _____
   _____

4. Determine any necessary actions:

   _____
   _____

5. Have your instructor verify removal and your answers.
   Supervisor/instructor's initials: _____

6. Following the specified procedure, reinstall the pump.

7. Following the specified procedure, prime the pump.

© 2017 Jones & Bartlett Learning, LLC, an Ascend Learning Company

8. List any difficulties you experienced while performing this task:

   _____
   _____
   _____

9. Discuss the findings with your instructor.

Performance Rating

☐   ☐   ☐   ☐   ☐

0   1   2   3   4

Supervisor/instructor signature _____ Date_____

Student/intern information:

Name_____ Date_____ Class_____

Vehicle used for this activity:

Year_____ Make_____ Model_____

Odometer_____ VIN _____

© 2017 Jones & Bartlett Learning, LLC, an Ascend Learning Company

▶ **TASK** Inspect pump inlet for restrictions and leaks; determine needed action.   **NATEF 8B5**

CDX Tasksheet Number: H545

Time off_____

Time on_____

Total time_____

1. With the pump removed, inspect the inlets for any signs of restrictions and evidence of leakage.
    a. List your observations:

    _____
    _____
    _____
    _____
    _____

    b. Meets the manufacturer's specifications? Yes: _____ No: _____

    c. If no, list recommendations for repair or replacement of the component:

    _____
    _____
    _____
    _____
    _____

2. Select a replacement hydraulic pump and compare it with the removed original.

3. Inspect the inlets to ensure that there is no evidence of restrictions.

4. Discuss the findings with your instructor.

Performance Rating

CDX Tasksheet Number: H545

☐	☐	☐	☐	☐
0	1	2	3	4

Supervisor/instructor signature _____ Date_____

Student/intern information:

Name_____ Date_____ Class_____

Vehicle used for this activity:

Year_____ Make_____ Model_____

Odometer_____ VIN _____

▶ **TASK** Inspect pump outlet for restrictions and leaks; determine needed action.

NATEF 8B6

CDX Tasksheet Number: H546

1. With the pump removed, inspect the outlet for any signs of restrictions and any evidence of leakage.
    a. List your observations:

    _____
    _____
    _____
    _____
    _____

    b. Meets the manufacturer's specifications? Yes: _____ No: _____

    c. If no, list the areas and your recommendations:

    _____
    _____
    _____
    _____
    _____

2. Select a replacement hydraulic pump and compare it with the removed original.

3. Inspect the outlets to ensure that there is no evidence of restrictions.

4. Following the procedures outlined above, and taking into account all safety precautions, replace hydraulic pump.
    a. Change over the drive components if necessary.

    b. Prime the replacement pump and then plug the pump outlets.

    c. Refit the new hydraulic pump to the vehicle and torque all mounting bolts to the correct torque specification.
        i.   Manufacturer's recommended torque: _____
        ii. Actual torque: _____

    d. Remove the plugs and refit the hoses.

    e. Refill the pump with hydraulic fluid.
        i.   Correct type of fluid (name): _____
        ii. Recommended fluid quantity: _____
        iii. Actual amount of fluid added: _____

Time off_____

Time on_____

Total time_____

f. If applicable, bleed the hydraulic pump fluid system to remove air.

g. Start and run the engine; operate the hydraulic system and check for any leaks and security of the pump mounting.

h. Rectify any leaks.

5. Discuss the findings with your instructor.

Performance Rating

CDX Tasksheet Number: H546

☐	☐	☐	☐	☐
0	1	2	3	4

Supervisor/instructor signature _____ Date_____

Welding & Hydraulics:
Filtration and Reservoirs (Tanks)

Student/intern information:

Name_____ Date_____ Class_____

Vehicle used for this activity:

Year_____ Make_____ Model_____

Odometer_____ VIN _____

© 2017 Jones & Bartlett Learning, LLC, an Ascend Learning Company

Learning Objective / Task	CDX Tasksheet Number	2014 NATEF Priority Level	2014 NATEF Reference Number
• Identify type of filtration system; verify filter application and flow direction.	H547	P-1	8C1
• Service filters and breathers.	H548	P-1	8C2
• Identify causes of system contamination; determine needed action.	H549	P-2	8C3
• Take a hydraulic oil sample for analysis.	H550	P-1	8C4
• Check reservoir fluid level and condition; determine needed action.	H551	P-1	8C5
• Inspect and repair or replace reservoir, sight glass, vents, caps, mounts, valves, screens, supply and return lines.	H552	P-1	8C6

Time off_____

Time on_____

Total time_____

Materials Required

- Vehicle with possible hydraulic concern
- Vehicle manufacturer's service information
- Manufacturer-specific tools depending on the concern
- Vehicle lifting equipment if applicable

Some Safety Issues to Consider

- Hydraulics systems operate under extremely high pressures! Injection of high-pressure hydraulic oil into human skin may require emergency surgery to stop the damage. Never use your hand to search for the source of a hydraulic leak. Wear appropriate safety equipment.
- Diagnosis of this fault may require test driving the vehicle on the school grounds or on a hoist, both of which carry severe risks. Attempt this task only with full permission from your supervisor/instructor and follow all the guidelines exactly.
- Caution: If you are working in an area where there could be "brake dust" present (may contain asbestos, which has been determined to cause cancer when inhaled or ingested), ensure you wear and use all OSHA-approved asbestos protective/removal equipment.
- Lifting equipment such as vehicle jacks and stands, vehicle hoists, and engine hoists are important tools that increase productivity and make the job easier. However, they can also cause severe injury or death if used improperly. Make sure you follow the manufacturer's operation procedures. Also make sure you have your supervisor/instructor's permission to use any particular type of lifting equipment.
- Comply with personal and environmental safety practices associated with clothing; eye protection; hand tools; power equipment; proper ventilation; and the handling, storage, and disposal of chemicals/materials in accordance with federal, state, and local regulations.
- Always wear the correct protective eyewear and clothing and use the appropriate safety equipment, as well as fender covers, seat protectors, and floor mat protectors.

- Make sure you understand and observe all legislative and personal safety procedures when carrying out practical assignments. If you are unsure of what these are, ask your supervisor/instructor.

Performance Standard

0—No exposure: No information or practice provided during the program; complete training required

1—Exposure only: General information provided with no practice time; close supervision needed; additional training required

2—Limited practice: Has practiced job during training program; additional training required to develop skill

3—Moderately skilled: Has performed job independently during training program; limited additional training may be required

4—Skilled: Can perform job independently with no additional training

Student/intern information:

Name_____ Date_____ Class_____

Vehicle used for this activity:

Year_____ Make_____ Model_____

Odometer_____ VIN _____

▶ **TASK** Identify type of filtration system; verify filter application and flow direction.

NATEF 8C1

Time off_____

Time on_____

Total time_____

CDX Tasksheet Number: H547

1. Research the procedure and specifications to identify the type of filtration system in the appropriate service information.
   a. Manufacturer's recommended type of filtration system: _____

   b. Actual type of filtration system fitted to the vehicle: _____

2. Reference the appropriate service information for the procedure to verify filter application and flow direction.
   a. Manufacturer's recommended filter application: _____

   b. Actual filter application fitted to the vehicle: _____

   c. Manufacturer's applicable flow direction: _____

   d. Actual flow direction: _____

3. Gather your results of the inspection.
   a. Meets the manufacturer's specifications? Yes: _____ No: _____

   b. Determine any necessary action(s):
   _____
   _____
   _____
   _____
   _____

4. Discuss the findings with your instructor.

Performance Rating

CDX Tasksheet Number: H547

☐ 0   ☐ 1   ☐ 2   ☐ 3   ☐ 4

Supervisor/instructor signature _____ Date_____

Student/intern information:

Name_____ Date_____ Class_____

Vehicle used for this activity:

Year_____ Make_____ Model_____

Odometer_____ VIN _____

▶ **TASK** Service filters and breathers.   NATEF 8C2

Time off_____

Time on_____

Total time_____

CDX Tasksheet Number: H548

1. Research the procedure and specifications to service filters and breathers in the appropriate service information.
    a. List the procedure and all safety requirements to service filters and breathers:

    _____
    _____
    _____
    _____
    _____

2. Discuss the steps involved to service filters and breathers with your instructor.

3. Following all procedures and safety requirements, service the filters and breathers.
    a. Meets the manufacturer's specifications? Yes: _____ No: _____

    b. Determine any necessary action(s):

    _____
    _____
    _____
    _____
    _____

4. Discuss the findings with your instructor.

Performance Rating

CDX Tasksheet Number: H548

☐	☐	☐	☐	☐
0	1	2	3	4

Supervisor/instructor signature _____ Date_____

Student/intern information:

Name_____ Date_____ Class_____

Vehicle used for this activity:

Year_____ Make_____ Model_____

Odometer_____ VIN _____

© 2017 Jones & Bartlett Learning, LLC, an Ascend Learning Company

▶ **TASK** Identify causes of system contamination; determine needed action.   **NATEF 8C3**

CDX Tasksheet Number: H549

Time off_____

Time on_____

Total time_____

1. Research the procedure and specifications to identify the possible causes for system contamination in the appropriate service information.

    _____
    _____
    _____
    _____
    _____

    a. Other alternative causes:

        _____
        _____
        _____
        _____
        _____

2. From the list above, determine what actions should be taken to rectify these causes:

    _____
    _____
    _____
    _____
    _____

    a. Other alternative causes:

        _____
        _____
        _____
        _____
        _____

3. Discuss the findings with your instructor.

Performance Rating

CDX Tasksheet Number: H549

☐   ☐   ☐   ☐   ☐
0   1   2   3   4

Supervisor/instructor signature _____ Date_____

Student/intern information:

Name_____ Date_____ Class_____

Vehicle used for this activity:

Year_____ Make_____ Model_____

Odometer_____ VIN _____

▶ **TASK** Take a hydraulic oil sample for analysis.   NATEF 8C4

Time off_____

Time on_____

Total time_____

CDX Tasksheet Number: H550

1. Draw a sample of the hydraulic fluid into a sterile container for analysis.

    Note: Oil sampling is a good way to determine what caused a failure. Failure analysis is critical in diagnosing and preventing a failure from reoccurring again.

2. If directed by your instructor, arrange for the oil sample to be analyzed for contamination and suitability.

3. List the results of the oil analysis. If the oil is not being sent out, obtain a sample oil analysis report and list the results of that analysis.

    _____

    _____

    _____

    _____

    _____

    _____

    _____

    _____

    _____

4. Discuss the findings with your instructor.

Performance Rating

CDX Tasksheet Number: H550

☐   ☐   ☐   ☐   ☐

0   1   2   3   4

Supervisor/instructor signature _____ Date_____

Student/intern information:

Name_____ Date_____ Class_____

Vehicle used for this activity:

Year_____ Make_____ Model_____

Odometer_____ VIN _____

▶ **TASK** Check reservoir fluid level and condition; determine needed action. | NATEF 8C5

Time off_____

Time on_____

Total time_____

CDX Tasksheet Number: H551

1. Clean the cap area before you remove the cap of the reservoir.

2. Inspect the fluid level for the correct level.
    Note: It is good practice to check the level of the fluid when the fluid is hot to ensure that the fluid has penetrated the entire system.

    a. Is fluid level at the correct level: Yes: _____ No: _____ Comments: _____

    b. If no, consult the appropriate service information for the proper procedure to correct the fluid level.

3. Check the condition of the fluid. Look for burnt fluid or contamination.
    a. Condition of the fluid? Good: _____ Bad: _____ Comments: _____
    Note: It is good practice upon a system failure to draw out some of the fluid and send it out for analysis.

    b. If condition of the fluid is bad, consult the appropriate service information for the proper procedure to drain and flush the system and to refill the system with new fluid and record the steps below:

    _____
    _____
    _____
    _____
    _____

4. Discuss your findings with your instructor and record any recommendations below:

    _____
    _____
    _____
    _____
    _____

Performance Rating

CDX Tasksheet Number: H551

☐ 0   ☐ 1   ☐ 2   ☐ 3   ☐ 4

Supervisor/instructor signature _____ Date_____

Student/intern information:

Name_____ Date_____ Class_____

Vehicle used for this activity:

Year_____ Make_____ Model_____

Odometer_____ VIN _____

Inspect and repair or replace reservoir, sight glass, vents, caps, mounts, valves, screens, supply and return lines.   NATEF 8C6

Time off_____

Time on_____

Total time_____

CDX Tasksheet Number: H552

1.   Research the procedure and specifications to inspect and repair or replace the reservoir, sight glass, vents, caps, mounts, valves, screens, and supply and return lines in the appropriate service information. Carry out the inspection of the following components:

a.   Reservoir

i.   List your observations:

_____
_____
_____

ii. Meets the manufacturer's specifications? Yes: _____ No: _____
iii. If no, list your recommendations for rectification:

_____
_____
_____
_____

b.   Sight glass

Note: Sight glass is used to determine if there is air present in the system. If air is present, bubbles will be seen floating by in the flow of liquid.

i.   List your observations:

_____
_____
_____

ii. Meets the manufacturer's specifications? Yes: _____ No: _____
iii. If no, list your recommendations for rectification:

_____
_____
_____
_____

c.   Vents and caps

i.   List your observations:

_____
_____
_____

ii. Meets the manufacturer's specifications? Yes: _____ No: _____

iii. If no, list your recommendations for rectification:

_____
_____
_____
_____

    d. Mountings
       i. List your observations:

_____
_____
_____

      ii. Meets the manufacturer's specifications? Yes: _____ No: _____
     iii. If no, list your recommendations for rectification:

_____
_____
_____
_____

    e. Valves and screens
       i. List your observations:

_____
_____
_____

      ii. Meets the manufacturer's specifications? Yes: _____ No: _____
     iii. If no, list your recommendations for rectification:

_____
_____
_____
_____

    f. Supply and return lines
       i. List your observations:

_____
_____
_____

      ii. Meets the manufacturer's specifications? Yes: _____ No: _____
     iii. If no, list your recommendations for rectification:

_____
_____
_____
_____

2.   If directed by your instructor, carry out all necessary repairs/rectification.

3.   Discuss the findings with your instructor.

Performance Rating

CDX Tasksheet Number: H552

☐ 0   ☐ 1   ☐ 2   ☐ 3   ☐ 4

Supervisor/instructor signature _____ Date_____

© 2017 Jones & Bartlett Learning, LLC, an Ascend Learning Company

Welding & Hydraulics: Hoses, Fittings, and Connections

Student/intern information:

Name_____ Date_____ Class_____

Vehicle used for this activity:

Year_____ Make_____ Model_____

Odometer_____ VIN _____

Time off_____

Time on_____

Total time_____

Learning Objective / Task	CDX Tasksheet Number	2014 NATEF Priority Level	2014 NATEF Reference Number
• Diagnose causes of component leakage, damage, and restriction; determine needed action.	H553	P-2	8D1
• Inspect hoses and connections (length, size, routing, bend radii, and protection); repair or replace as needed.	H554	P-1	8D2
• Assemble hoses, tubes, connectors, and fittings in accordance with manufacturers' specifications; use proper procedures to avoid contamination.	H555	P-1	8D3
• Inspect and replace fitting seals and sealants.	H556	P-1	8D4

Materials Required

- Vehicle with possible hydraulic concern
- Vehicle manufacturer's service information
- Manufacturer-specific tools depending on the concern
- Vehicle lifting equipment if applicable

Some Safety Issues to Consider

- Hydraulics systems operate under extremely high pressures! Injection of high-pressure hydraulic oil into human skin may require emergency surgery to stop the damage. Never use your hand to search for the source of a hydraulic leak. Wear appropriate safety equipment.
- Diagnosis of this fault may require test driving the vehicle on the school grounds or on a hoist, both of which carry severe risks. Attempt this task only with full permission from your supervisor/instructor and follow all the guidelines exactly.
- Caution: If you are working in an area where there could be "brake dust" present (may contain asbestos, which has been determined to cause cancer when inhaled or ingested), ensure you wear and use all OSHA-approved asbestos protective/removal equipment.
- Lifting equipment such as vehicle jacks and stands, vehicle hoists, and engine hoists are important tools that increase productivity and make the job easier. However, they can also cause severe injury or death if used improperly. Make sure you follow the manufacturer's operation procedures. Also make sure you have your supervisor/instructor's permission to use any particular type of lifting equipment.
- Comply with personal and environmental safety practices associated with clothing; eye protection; hand tools; power equipment; proper ventilation; and the handling, storage, and disposal of chemicals/materials in accordance with federal, state, and local regulations.
- Always wear the correct protective eyewear and clothing and use the appropriate safety equipment, as well as fender covers, seat protectors, and floor mat protectors.

- Make sure you understand and observe all legislative and personal safety procedures when carrying out practical assignments. If you are unsure of what these are, ask your supervisor/instructor.

Performance Standard

0—No exposure: No information or practice provided during the program; complete training required

1—Exposure only: General information provided with no practice time; close supervision needed; additional training required

2—Limited practice: Has practiced job during training program; additional training required to develop skill

3—Moderately skilled: Has performed job independently during training program; limited additional training may be required

4—Skilled: Can perform job independently with no additional training

Name _____ Date _____ Class _____

Vehicle used for this activity:

Year _____ Make _____ Model _____

Odometer _____ VIN _____

▶ **TASK** Diagnose causes of component leakage, damage, and restriction; determine needed action.

NATEF 8D1

CDX Tasksheet Number: H553

1. Research the procedure and specifications to identify the possible causes of component leakage, damage, and restriction in the appropriate service information.

_____
_____
_____
_____
_____

   a. Other alternative causes:

_____
_____
_____
_____
_____

2. Determine any necessary action(s):

_____
_____
_____
_____
_____

3. Discuss the findings with your instructor.

Performance Rating

CDX Tasksheet Number: H553

☐ 0   ☐ 1   ☐ 2   ☐ 3   ☐ 4

Supervisor/instructor signature _____ Date _____

Student/intern information:

Name_____ Date_____ Class_____

Vehicle used for this activity:

Year_____ Make_____ Model_____

Odometer_____ VIN _____

▶ **TASK** Inspect hoses and connections (length, size, routing, bend radii, and protection); repair or replace as needed.

NATEF 8D2

Time off_____

Time on_____

Total time_____

CDX Tasksheet Number: H554

1. Research the procedure and specifications to inspect and repair hoses and connections (length, size, routing, bend radii, and protection) in the appropriate service information.

   a. Inspect hoses for cracks, signs of deterioration, and rubbing.

      i. List your observations:

      _____
      _____
      _____

      ii. Meets the manufacturer's specifications? Yes: _____ No: _____
      iii. If no, list your recommendations for rectification:

      _____
      _____
      _____
      _____

   b. Inspect hoses for correct length and sizing.

      i. List your observations:

      _____
      _____
      _____

      ii. Meets the manufacturer's specifications? Yes: _____ No: _____
      iii. If no, list your recommendations for rectification:

      _____
      _____
      _____
      _____

   c. Inspect hoses for correct routing, and bend radii.

      i. List your observations:

      _____
      _____
      _____

      ii. Meets the manufacturer's specifications? Yes: _____ No: _____
      iii. If no, list your recommendations for rectification:

      _____
      _____
      _____
      _____

d. Inspect hoses for correct/adequate protection and mounting.

i. List your observations:

_____

_____

_____

ii. Meets the manufacturer's specifications? Yes: _____ No: _____

iii. If no, list your recommendations for rectification:

_____

_____

_____

_____

2. If directed by your instructor, carry out all necessary repairs/rectification.

3. Discuss the findings with your instructor.

Performance Rating

CDX Tasksheet Number: H554

☐   ☐   ☐   ☐   ☐

0   1   2   3   4

Supervisor/instructor signature _____ Date_____

Student/intern information:

Name_____ Date_____ Class_____

Vehicle used for this activity:

Year_____ Make_____ Model_____

Odometer_____ VIN _____

▶ TASK Assemble hoses, tubes, connectors, and fittings in accordance with manufacturers' specifications; use proper procedures to avoid contamination.   NATEF 8D3

CDX Tasksheet Number: H555

Time off_____

Time on_____

Total time_____

1. All safety precautions must be executed at all times. Research the procedure and specifications to assemble the hoses, tubes, connectors, and fittings in the appropriate service information.
   a. Ensure you maintain your working area in a clean state to prevent contamination.

   b. Ensure the new hose pressure rating matches your system pressure requirements.
      i. List your observations:

      _____
      _____
      _____

      ii. Meets the manufacturer's specifications? Yes: _____ No: _____
      iii. If no, do not use. Source the correct hosing.

   c. Ensure the new hose meets the manufacturers' recommended temperature range.
      i. List your observations:

      _____
      _____
      _____

      ii. Meets the manufacturer's specifications? Yes: _____ No: _____
      iii. If no, do not use. Source the correct hosing.

   d. Ensure the new hose matches your system's fluid compatibility requirements.
      i. List your observations:

      _____
      _____
      _____

      ii. Meets the manufacturer's specifications? Yes: _____ No: _____
      iii. If no, do not use. Source the correct hosing.

   e. Ensure the new hose sizing matches the manufacturer's specification and your system requirements.
      i. List your observations:

      _____
      _____
      _____

      ii. Meets the manufacturer's specifications? Yes: _____ No: _____
      iii. If no, do not use. Source the correct hosing.

© 2017 Jones & Bartlett Learning, LLC, an Ascend Learning Company

Welding & Hydraulics 329

f. Determine the correct length of hose required to manufacturer the replacement hose.

g. Ensure the new hose and couplings compatibility matches the manufacturer's specification and your system requirements.
   i. List your observations:

   _____

   _____

   _____

   ii. Meets the manufacturer's specifications? Yes: _____ No: _____
   iii. If no, do not use. Source the correct hosing.

2. Discuss the findings with your instructor.

Performance Rating

CDX Tasksheet Number: H555

☐   ☐   ☐   ☐   ☐

0   1   2   3   4

Supervisor/instructor signature _____ Date_____

Name_____ Date_____ Class_____

Vehicle used for this activity:

Year_____ Make_____ Model_____

Odometer_____ VIN _____

▶ **TASK** Inspect and replace fitting seals and sealants.   NATEF 8D4

CDX Tasksheet Number: H556

Time off_____

Time on_____

Total time_____

1. Research the procedure and specifications to correctly inspect and replace the fitting seals and sealants in the appropriate service information.

2. Inspect the hydraulic fittings for leakage.
    a. List your observations:

    _____
    _____
    _____

    b. Meets the manufacturer's specifications? Yes: _____ No: _____

    c. Determine any necessary action(s):

    _____
    _____
    _____
    _____
    _____

3. If directed by your instructor, carry out all necessary repairs/rectification.

4. Discuss the findings with your instructor.

Performance Rating

CDX Tasksheet Number: H556

☐ 0   ☐ 1   ☐ 2   ☐ 3   ☐ 4

Supervisor/instructor signature _____ Date_____

Welding & Hydraulics: Control Valves

Student/intern information:

Name_____ Date_____ Class_____

Vehicle used for this activity:

Year_____ Make_____ Model_____

Odometer_____ VIN _____

Time off_____

Time on_____

Total time_____

Learning Objective / Task	CDX Tasksheet Number	2014 NATEF Priority Level	2014 NATEF Reference Number
• Pressure test system safety relief valve; determine needed action.	H557	P-1	8E1
• Perform control valve operating pressure and flow tests; determine needed action.	H558	P-1	8E2
• Inspect, test, and adjust valve controls (electrical/electronic, mechanical, and pneumatic).	H559	P-1	8E3
• Identify causes of control valve leakage problems (internal/external); determine needed action.	H560	P-1	8E4
• Inspect pilot control valve linkages, cables, and PTO controls; adjust, repair, or replace as needed.	H561	P-1	8E5

Materials Required

- Vehicle with possible hydraulic concern
- Vehicle manufacturer's service information
- Manufacturer-specific tools depending on the concern
- Vehicle lifting equipment if applicable

Some Safety Issues to Consider

- Hydraulics systems operate under extremely high pressures! Injection of high-pressure hydraulic oil into human skin may require emergency surgery to stop the damage. Never use your hand to search for the source of a hydraulic leak. Wear appropriate safety equipment.
- Diagnosis of this fault may require test driving the vehicle on the school grounds or on a hoist, both of which carry severe risks. Attempt this task only with full permission from your supervisor/instructor and follow all the guidelines exactly.
- Caution: If you are working in an area where there could be "brake dust" present (may contain asbestos, which has been determined to cause cancer when inhaled or ingested), ensure you wear and use all OSHA-approved asbestos protective/removal equipment.
- Lifting equipment such as vehicle jacks and stands, vehicle hoists, and engine hoists are important tools that increase productivity and make the job easier. However, they can also cause severe injury or death if used improperly. Make sure you follow the manufacturer's operation procedures. Also make sure you have your supervisor/instructor's permission to use any particular type of lifting equipment.
- Comply with personal and environmental safety practices associated with clothing; eye protection; hand tools; power equipment; proper ventilation; and the handling, storage, and disposal of chemicals/materials in accordance with federal, state, and local regulations.
- Always wear the correct protective eyewear and clothing and use the appropriate safety equipment, as well as fender covers, seat protectors, and floor mat protectors.

- Make sure you understand and observe all legislative and personal safety procedures when carrying out practical assignments. If you are unsure of what these are, ask your supervisor/instructor.

Performance Standard

0—No exposure: No information or practice provided during the program; complete training required

1—Exposure only: General information provided with no practice time; close supervision needed; additional training required

2—Limited practice: Has practiced job during training program; additional training required to develop skill

3—Moderately skilled: Has performed job independently during training program; limited additional training may be required

4—Skilled: Can perform job independently with no additional training

Student/intern information:

Name_____ Date_____ Class_____

Vehicle used for this activity:

Year_____ Make_____ Model_____

Odometer_____ VIN _____

▶ **TASK** Pressure test system safety relief valve; determine needed action. **NATEF 8E1**

CDX Tasksheet Number: H557

1. Research the procedure and specifications to pressure test the system safety relief valve in the appropriate service information.
    a. List the procedure and all safety requirements to pressure test the system safety relief valve:

    _____
    _____
    _____
    _____
    _____

2. While observing all safety and OSHA requirements, connect the hydraulic test equipment into the circuit.
    a. Ensure you collect any fluid that may leak when installing the test equipment.

3. Carry out the pressure test on the safety relief valve.
    a. List your observations:

    _____
    _____
    _____

    b. Meets the manufacturer's specifications? Yes: _____ No: _____

    c. Determine any necessary action(s):

    _____
    _____
    _____
    _____
    _____

4. Discuss the results with your instructor.

Performance Rating

CDX Tasksheet Number: H557

☐	☐	☐	☐	☐
0	1	2	3	4

Supervisor/instructor signature _____ Date_____

Student/intern information:

Name_____ Date_____ Class_____

Vehicle used for this activity:

Year_____ Make_____ Model_____

Odometer_____ VIN _____

▶ **TASK** Perform control valve operating pressure and flow tests; determine needed action.

NATEF 8E2

CDX Tasksheet Number: H558

1.   With the hydraulic test equipment still connected in the circuit, refer to the appropriate service information to perform the control valve operating pressure and flow tests.

2.   Carry out the pressure and flow tests on the control valve.
     a.   List your observations:

     _____
     _____
     _____

     b.   Meets the manufacturer's specifications? Yes: _____ No: _____

     c.   Determine any necessary action(s):

     _____
     _____
     _____
     _____
     _____

3.   Discuss the findings with your instructor.

Time off_____

Time on_____

Total time_____

Performance Rating

CDX Tasksheet Number: H558

☐   ☐   ☐   ☐   ☐
0   1   2   3   4

Supervisor/instructor signature _____ Date_____

Student/intern information:

Name_____ Date_____ Class_____

Vehicle used for this activity:

Year_____ Make_____ Model_____

Odometer_____ VIN _____

▶ **TASK** Inspect, test, and adjust valve controls (electrical/electronic, mechanical, and pneumatic).

NATEF 8E3

CDX Tasksheet Number: H559

1. Research the procedure and specifications to inspect, test, and adjust the valve controls (electrical/electronic, mechanical, and pneumatic) in the appropriate service information.
    a. List the procedure and all safety requirements to inspect, test, and adjust the valve controls (electrical/electronic, mechanical, and pneumatic):

    _____
    _____
    _____
    _____
    _____

2. Inspect, test, and adjust the valve controls (electrical/electronic, mechanical, and pneumatic).
    a. List your observations:

    _____
    _____
    _____

    b. Meets the manufacturer's specifications? Yes: _____ No: _____

    c. Determine any necessary action(s):

    _____
    _____
    _____
    _____
    _____

3. As directed by your instructor; remove the hydraulic test equipment and restore the hydraulic system.

4. Run the system and check for any leaks. Repair any leaks as directed.

5. Discuss the results with your instructor.

Performance Rating

CDX Tasksheet Number: H559

☐   ☐   ☐   ☐   ☐
0   1   2   3   4

Supervisor/instructor signature _____ Date_____

Time off_____

Time on_____

Total time_____

© 2017 Jones & Bartlett Learning, LLC, an Ascend Learning Company

Welding & Hydraulics   **339**

Name_____ Date_____ Class_____

Vehicle used for this activity:

Year_____ Make_____ Model_____

Odometer_____ VIN _____

▶ **TASK** Identify causes of control valve leakage problems (internal/external); determine needed action.

NATEF 8E4

Time off_____

Time on_____

Total time_____

CDX Tasksheet Number: H560

1. Research the procedure and specifications to identify the causes of control valve leakage problems (internal/external) in the appropriate service information.

   _____
   _____
   _____
   _____
   _____

   a. Other alternative causes:

   _____
   _____
   _____
   _____
   _____

2. Determine any necessary action(s):

   _____
   _____
   _____
   _____
   _____

3. Discuss the findings with your instructor.

Performance Rating

CDX Tasksheet Number: H560

☐ 0   ☐ 1   ☐ 2   ☐ 3   ☐ 4

Supervisor/instructor signature _____ Date_____

Name_____ Date_____ Class_____

Vehicle used for this activity:

Year_____ Make_____ Model_____

Odometer_____ VIN _____

▶ **TASK** Inspect pilot control valve linkages, cables, and PTO controls; adjust, repair, or
replace as needed.   **NATEF 8E5**

Time off_____

Time on_____

Total time_____

CDX Tasksheet Number: H561

1. Research the procedure and specifications to inspect or adjust the pilot control valve linkage
   and cables in the appropriate service information.
   a. Inspect and adjust the pilot control valve linkage and cables.
      i. List your observations:

      _____
      _____
      _____

      ii. Meets the manufacturer's specifications? Yes: _____ No: _____
      iii. Determine any necessary action(s):

      _____
      _____
      _____
      _____

   b. Inspect the power take-off (PTO) controls. PTOs are electrical or gear-driven and
      operate truck auxiliary components. Examples include dump body pumps or tow truck
      flatbed pumps.
      i. List your observations:

      _____
      _____
      _____

      ii. Meets the manufacturer's specifications? Yes: _____ No: _____
      iii. Determine any necessary action(s):

      _____
      _____
      _____
      _____

2. If directed by your instructor, carry out all necessary repairs/rectification.

3. Discuss the findings with your instructor.

Performance Rating

CDX Tasksheet Number: H561

☐   ☐   ☐   ☐   ☐
0   1   2   3   4

Supervisor/instructor signature _____ Date_____

Welding & Hydraulics: Actuators

Student/intern information:

Name_____ Date_____ Class_____

Vehicle used for this activity:

Year_____ Make_____ Model_____

Odometer_____ VIN _____

© 2017 Jones & Bartlett Learning, LLC, an Ascend Learning Company

Learning Objective / Task	CDX Tasksheet Number	2014 NATEF Priority Level	2014 NATEF Reference Number
• Identify actuator type (single/double acting, multi-stage/ telescopic, and motors).	H562	P-1	8F1
• Identify the cause of seal failure; determine needed repairs.	H563	P-1	8F2
• Identify the cause of incorrect actuator movement and leakage (internal and external); determine needed repairs.	H564	P-1	8F3
• Inspect actuator mounting, frame components, and hardware for looseness, cracks, and damage; determine needed action.	H565	P-1	8F4
• Remove, repair, and/or replace actuators in accordance with manufacturers' recommended procedures.	H566	P-1	8F5
• Inspect actuators for dents, cracks, damage, and leakage; determine needed action.	H567	P-1	8F6
• Purge and/or bleed system in accordance with manufacturers' recommended procedures.	H568	P-1	8F7

Time off_____

Time on_____

Total time_____

Materials Required

- Vehicle with possible hydraulic concern
- Vehicle manufacturer's service information
- Manufacturer-specific tools depending on the concern
- Vehicle lifting equipment if applicable

Some Safety Issues to Consider

- Hydraulics systems operate under extremely high pressures! Injection of high-pressure hydraulic oil into human skin may require emergency surgery to stop the damage. Never use your hand to search for the source of a hydraulic leak. Wear appropriate safety equipment.
- Comply with manufacturers' and industry accepted safety practices associated with equipment lock out/ tag out; pressure line release; implement/support (blocked or resting on ground); and articulated cylinder devices/machinery safety locks.
- Diagnosis of this fault may require test driving the vehicle on the school grounds or on a hoist, both of which carry severe risks. Attempt this task only with full permission from your supervisor/instructor and follow all the guidelines exactly.

- Caution: If you are working in an area where there could be "brake dust" present (may contain asbestos, which has been determined to cause cancer when inhaled or ingested), ensure you wear and use all OSHA-approved asbestos protective/removal equipment.
- Lifting equipment such as vehicle jacks and stands, vehicle hoists, and engine hoists are important tools that increase productivity and make the job easier. However, they can also cause severe injury or death if used improperly. Make sure you follow the manufacturer's operation procedures. Also make sure you have your supervisor/instructor's permission to use any particular type of lifting equipment.
- Comply with personal and environmental safety practices associated with clothing; eye protection; hand tools; power equipment; proper ventilation; and the handling, storage, and disposal of chemicals/materials in accordance with federal, state, and local regulations.
- Always wear the correct protective eyewear and clothing and use the appropriate safety equipment, as well as fender covers, seat protectors, and floor mat protectors.
- Make sure you understand and observe all legislative and personal safety procedures when carrying out practical assignments. If you are unsure of what these are, ask your supervisor/instructor.

Performance Standard

0—No exposure: No information or practice provided during the program; complete training required

1—Exposure only: General information provided with no practice time; close supervision needed; additional training required

2—Limited practice: Has practiced job during training program; additional training required to develop skill

3—Moderately skilled: Has performed job independently during training program; limited additional training may be required

4—Skilled: Can perform job independently with no additional training

Student/intern information:

Name_____ Date_____ Class_____

Vehicle used for this activity:

Year_____ Make_____ Model_____

Odometer_____ VIN _____

▶ TASK Identify actuator type (single/double acting, multi-stage/telescopic, and motors).

NATEF 8F1

Time off_____

Time on_____

Total time_____

CDX Tasksheet Number: H562

1. Research the procedure and specifications to identify the actuator type (single/double acting, multi-stage/telescopic, and motors) in the appropriate service information.

2. Carry out a visual inspection of your vehicle to determine the actuator types and motors.
   a. List the actuator types of the components fitted to your vehicle and their locations:

   _____

   _____

   _____

   _____

   _____

   _____

   _____

   _____

   _____

   b. Determine any necessary action(s):

   _____

   _____

   _____

3. Discuss the findings with your instructor.

Performance Rating

CDX Tasksheet Number: H562

☐ 0   ☐ 1   ☐ 2   ☐ 3   ☐ 4

Supervisor/instructor signature _____ Date_____

Name _____ Date _____ Class _____

Vehicle used for this activity:

Year _____ Make _____ Model _____

Odometer _____ VIN _____

▶ **TASK** Identify the cause of seal failure; determine needed repairs. _____ NATEF 8F2

CDX Tasksheet Number: H563

Time off _____

Time on _____

Total time _____

1. Research the procedure and specifications to identify the cause of seal failure in the appropriate service information.
   a. List all possible causes:

   _____
   _____
   _____
   _____
   _____

   b. Other alternative causes:

   _____
   _____
   _____
   _____
   _____

2. Determine any necessary action(s):

   _____
   _____
   _____

3. Carry out a visual inspection of the hydraulic components and seals fitted to your vehicle while referencing the service information.
   a. List your observations:

   _____
   _____
   _____

   b. Meets the manufacturer's specifications? Yes: _____ No: _____

   c. Determine any necessary action(s):

   _____
   _____

4. Discuss the findings with your instructor.

Performance Rating

CDX Tasksheet Number: H563

☐	☐	☐	☐	☐
0	1	2	3	4

Supervisor/instructor signature _____ Date _____

Student/intern information:

Name_____ Date_____ Class_____

Vehicle used for this activity:

Year_____ Make_____ Model_____

Odometer_____ VIN _____

▶ **TASK** Identify the cause of incorrect actuator movement and leakage (internal and external); determine needed repairs.   **NATEF 8F3**

Time off_____

Time on_____

Total time_____

CDX Tasksheet Number: H564

1. Research the procedure and specifications to identify the cause of incorrect actuator movement and leakage (internal and external) in the appropriate service information.
   a. List all possible causes:

   _____
   _____
   _____
   _____
   _____

   b. Other alternative causes:

   _____
   _____
   _____
   _____
   _____

2. Determine any necessary action(s):

   _____
   _____
   _____

3. Carry out a visual inspection of these hydraulic components fitted to your vehicle to determine incorrect actuator movement and leakage.
   a. List your observations:

   _____
   _____
   _____

   b. Meets the manufacturer's specifications? Yes: _____ No: _____

   c. Determine any necessary action(s):

   _____
   _____

4. Discuss the findings with your instructor.

Performance Rating

CDX Tasksheet Number: H564

☐ 0   ☐ 1   ☐ 2   ☐ 3   ☐ 4

Supervisor/instructor signature _____ Date_____

Student/intern information:

Name_____ Date_____ Class_____

Vehicle used for this activity:

Year_____ Make_____ Model_____

Odometer_____ VIN _____

▶ **TASK** Inspect actuator mounting, frame components, and hardware for looseness, cracks, and damage; determine needed action.   **NATEF 8F4**

CDX Tasksheet Number: H565

1. Inspect actuator mounting for any damage or looseness.
   a. Condition of actuator mounting? Good: _____ Bad: _____ Comments: _____
   _____

   b. If the actuator mounting is bad, determine any necessary actions:
   _____
   _____

2. Inspect all frame components and hardware for looseness and cracking.
   a. Looseness present? Yes: _____ No: _____ Comments: _____
   _____

   b. Cracking present? Yes: _____ No: _____ Comments: _____
   _____

   c. If looseness or cracking is present, determine any necessary actions:
   _____
   _____

3. If the frame is cracked, it must be repaired or replaced. Perform a frame alignment to bring it back to specification.

4. Discuss your findings with your instructor and record any recommendations:
   _____
   _____

Time off_____

Time on_____

Total time_____

Performance Rating   **CDX Tasksheet Number: H565**

☐   ☐   ☐   ☐   ☐
0   1   2   3   4

Supervisor/instructor signature _____ Date_____

Student/intern information:

Name _____ Date _____ Class _____

Vehicle used for this activity:

Year _____ Make _____ Model _____

Odometer _____ VIN _____

▶ TASK Remove, repair, and/or replace actuators in accordance with manufacturers'
recommended procedures.   **NATEF 8F5**

Time off _____

Time on _____

Total time _____

CDX Tasksheet Number: H566

1. Reference the manufacturer's service information for the correct procedure for removing,
    repairing, and/or replacing the actuators.
    a. List the procedure and all safety requirements for removing, repairing, and/or
        replacing the actuators:

        _____

        _____

        _____

        _____

        _____

2. Following the procedures outlined above, and taking into account all safety precautions,
    remove, repair, and/or replace the actuators.
    a. While using a collection container adequate for the amount of oil to be drained, drain
        the power steering fluid.
    b. With your instructor's approval, collect an oil sample in a clean, sterile container to be
        sent for analysis.
    c. Remove the inlet and outlet hoses, collecting any fluid coming from the removed
        hoses.
    d. Remove the hydraulic actuator and place on the work bench.

3. Inspect the actuator and any components. List your observations:

    _____

    _____

4. Determine any necessary action or correction:

    _____

    _____

5. Discuss the findings with your instructor.

Performance Rating

CDX Tasksheet Number: H566

☐   ☐   ☐   ☐   ☐
0   1   2   3   4

Supervisor/instructor signature _____ Date _____

Name_____ Date_____ Class_____

Vehicle used for this activity:

Year_____ Make_____ Model_____

Odometer_____ VIN _____

▶ **TASK** Inspect actuators for dents, cracks, damage, and leakage; determine needed action.

NATEF 8F6

Time off_____

Time on_____

Total time_____

CDX Tasksheet Number: H567

1. Research the procedure and specifications to inspect the actuator and determine the most appropriate course of action (repair or replace) in the appropriate service information.

2. With the actuator removed, inspect for dents, cracks, damage, and evidence of leakage.
   a. List your observations:

   _____
   _____
   _____

   b. Meets the manufacturer's specifications? Yes: _____ No: _____

   c. Determine any necessary action(s):

   _____
   _____
   _____
   _____
   _____

3. If directed by your instructor to replace the actuator:
   a. Select a replacement hydraulic actuator and compare it with the removed original.

   b. Inspect the inlets and outlets to ensure that there is no evidence of restrictions.

4. List your observations:

   _____
   _____
   _____

5. Discuss the findings with your instructor.

Performance Rating

CDX Tasksheet Number: H567

☐	☐	☐	☐	☐
0	1	2	3	4

Supervisor/instructor signature _____ Date_____

Performance Rating

CDX Tasksheet Number: H568

☐	☐	☐	☐	☐
0	1	2	3	4

Supervisor/instructor signature _____ Date_____

Preventive Maintenance Inspection, DT110

CONTENTS

Preventive Maintenance Inspection:
Engine System—Engine

Student/intern information:

Name_____ Date_____ Class_____

Vehicle used for this activity:

Year_____ Make_____ Model_____

Odometer_____ VIN _____

© 2017 Jones & Bartlett Learning, LLC, an Ascend Learning Company

Learning Objective / Task	CDX Tasksheet Number	2014 NATEF Priority Level	2014 NATEF Reference Number
• Check engine starting/operation (including unusual noises, vibrations, exhaust smoke, etc.); record idle and governed rpm.	H394	P-1	7A1.1
• Inspect vibration damper.	H395	P-1	7A1.2
• Inspect belts, tensioners, and pulleys; check and adjust belt tension; check belt alignment.	H396	P-1	7A1.3
• Check engine oil level and condition; check dipstick seal.	H397	P-1	7A1.4
• Inspect engine mounts for looseness and deterioration.	H398	P-1	7A1.5
• Check engine for oil, coolant, air, fuel and exhaust leaks (engine off and running).	H399	P-1	7A1.6
• Check engine compartment wiring harnesses, connectors, and seals for damage and proper routing.	H400	P-1	7A1.7

Time off_____

Time on_____

Total time_____

Materials Required

- Vehicle with possible engine concern
- Vehicle manufacturer's service information
- Manufacturer-specific tools, depending on the concern
- Vehicle lifting equipment, if applicable

Some Safety Issues to Consider

- Diagnosis of this fault may require test driving the vehicle on the school grounds or on a hoist, both of which carry severe risks. Attempt this task only with full permission from your supervisor/instructor and follow all the guidelines exactly.
- **Caution:** If you are working in an area where there could be brake dust present (may contain asbestos, which has been determined to cause cancer when inhaled or ingested), wear and use all OSHA-approved asbestos protective/removal equipment.
- Lifting equipment such as vehicle jacks and stands, vehicle hoists, and engine hoists are important tools that increase productivity and make the job easier. However, they can also cause severe injury or death if used improperly. Make sure you follow the manufacturer's operation procedures. Also make sure you have your supervisor/instructor's permission to use any particular type of lifting equipment.

- Comply with personal and environmental safety practices associated with clothing; eye protection; hand tools; power equipment; proper ventilation; and the handling, storage, and disposal of chemicals/materials in accordance with federal, state, and local regulations.
- Always wear the correct protective eyewear and clothing and use the appropriate safety equipment, as well as fender covers, seat protectors, and floor mat protectors.
- Make sure you understand and observe all legislative and personal safety procedures when carrying out practical assignments. If you are unsure of what these are, ask your supervisor/instructor.

Performance Standard

0—No exposure: No information or practice provided during the program; complete training required

1—Exposure only: General information provided with no practice time; close supervision needed; additional training required

2—Limited practice: Has practiced job during training program; additional training required to develop skill

3—Moderately skilled: Has performed job independently during training program; limited additional training may be required

4—Skilled: Can perform job independently with no additional training

Student/intern information:

Name_____ Date_____ Class_____

Vehicle used for this activity:

Year_____ Make_____ Model_____

Odometer_____ VIN _____

▶ **TASK** Check engine starting/operation (including unusual noises, vibrations, exhaust smoke, etc.); record idle and governed rpm.　　　　　　　　　　　　　**NATEF 7A1.1**

Time off_____

Time on_____

Total time_____

CDX Tasksheet Number: H394

　　1.　List engine noises that you will be looking for when starting and running the engine:

　　　　_____

　　　　_____

　　　　_____

　　　　_____

　　2.　Check engine starting/operation (including unusual noises, vibrations, exhaust smoke, etc.); record idle and governed rpm.
　　　　a.　Battery voltage before starting the engine: _____ V
　　　　b.　Cranking ampere: _____ amps
　　　　c.　With the engine running:
　　　　　　i.　Idle RPM: _____
　　　　　　ii.　Governed RPM: _____
　　　　　　iii.　Color of the exhaust smoke from the stack: _____
　　　　　　iv.　List any unusual noises from the engine (if any).

　　　　　　　　_____

　　　　　　　　_____

　　　　　　　　_____

　　　　　　v.　Are there any vibrations coming from the engine? Yes: _____ No: _____
　　　　　　　　a.　If yes, where are the vibrations coming from?

　　　　　　　　　_____

　　　　　　　　　_____

　　　　　　　　　_____

　　3.　Discuss the finding(s) with your instructor.

Performance Rating

CDX Tasksheet Number: H394

☐	☐	☐	☐	☐
0	1	2	3	4

Supervisor/instructor signature _____ Date_____

Name_____ Date_____ Class_____

Vehicle used for this activity:

Year_____ Make_____ Model_____

Odometer_____ VIN _____

▶ **TASK** Inspect vibration damper.   **NATEF 7A1.2**

CDX Tasksheet Number: H395

1. Research the procedure and specifications for inspecting the vibration damper in the appropriate service information.
    a. Specified maximum vibration damper run out: _____ in/mm

2. Inspect the viscous dampers for dents which could render it unusable.
    a. Check for run out using a dial indicator.
        i.   Record the reading: _____
        ii. Compare the reading to manufacturer's specifications.

3. Determine any necessary action(s):

    _____
    _____
    _____
    _____
    _____

4. Discuss the finding(s) with your instructor.

Performance Rating

CDX Tasksheet Number: H395

☐   ☐   ☐   ☐   ☐
0   1   2   3   4

Supervisor/instructor signature _____ Date_____

Student/intern information:

Name_____ Date_____ Class_____

Vehicle used for this activity:

Year_____ Make_____ Model_____

Odometer_____ VIN _____

▶ **TASK** Inspect belts, tensioners, and pulleys; check and adjust belt tension; check belt alignment. NATEF 7A1.3

CDX Tasksheet Number: H396

1. Inspect belts, tensioners, and pulleys. Look for dry rot and cracking.
   a. Record condition of drive belts: Good: _____ Need replacing: _____
      Comments: _____

   b. Record condition of belt tensioners: Good: _____ Need replacing: _____
      Comments: _____

   c. Record condition of drive pulleys: Good: _____ Need replacing: _____
      Comments: _____

2. Check and adjust belt tension utilizing the proper belt tension gauge.
   a. Record belt tension before adjustment: _____ ft-lb (Nm)
   b. Record belt tension after adjustment: _____ ft-lb (Nm)

3. Check belt alignment.
   a. List your observations:
      _____
      _____

   Note: If belt alignment is off, this will require replacement of drive parts.

4. Determine any necessary actions or corrections:
   _____
   _____
   _____

5. Discuss the finding(s) with your instructor.

Time off_____
Time on_____
Total time_____

Performance Rating

CDX Tasksheet Number: H396

☐ 0   ☐ 1   ☐ 2   ☐ 3   ☐ 4

Supervisor/instructor signature _____ Date_____

© 2017 Jones & Bartlett Learning, LLC, an Ascend Learning Company

Preventive Maintenance Inspection **369**

Student/intern information:

Name_____ Date_____ Class_____

Vehicle used for this activity:

Year_____ Make_____ Model_____

Odometer_____ VIN _____

▶ **TASK** Check engine oil level and condition; check dipstick seal. | NATEF 7A1.4 |

CDX Tasksheet Number: H397

1. Engine oil level: Good: _____ Needs adjustment: _____
    a. If oil is needed, how much? _____ pints (liters)

2. Engine oil condition:
    _____
    _____
    _____
    _____
    _____

3. Recheck for any engine oil leaks. Are there any oil leaks? Yes: _____ No: _____
    a. If yes, where is oil leaking and what actions are required?
    _____
    _____
    _____
    _____

4. Check the dipstick seal. Condition: Good: _____ Bad: _____
    Comments: _____

5. Determine any necessary actions or corrections:
    _____
    _____

6. Discuss the finding(s) with your instructor.

Performance Rating

CDX Tasksheet Number: H397

☐	☐	☐	☐	☐
0	1	2	3	4

Supervisor/instructor signature _____ Date_____

Student/intern information:

Name_____ Date_____ Class_____

Vehicle used for this activity:

Year_____ Make_____ Model_____

Odometer_____ VIN _____

▶ **TASK** Inspect engine mounts for looseness or deterioration.   NATEF 7A1.5

Time off_____

Time on_____

Total time_____

CDX Tasksheet Number: H398

1. Is there evidence of looseness? Yes: _____ No: _____
   Comments: _____

   a. If looseness is evident, try to re-torque the attaching bolts.
   b. Recommended torque setting for engine mounting bolts: _____ ft-lb (Nm)

2. Is there evidence of deterioration? Yes: _____ No: _____
   Comments: _____

   a. If there is evidence of deterioration, this will require replacement of the mount.

   b. Research the procedure and specifications for replacing the motor mounts in the appropriate service information. Record the procedures:

   _____
   _____
   _____
   _____

3. Determine any necessary action(s):

   _____
   _____
   _____

4. Discuss the finding(s) with the instructor.

Performance Rating

CDX Tasksheet Number: H398

☐	☐	☐	☐	☐
0	1	2	3	4

Supervisor/instructor signature _____ Date_____

© 2017 Jones & Bartlett Learning, LLC, an Ascend Learning Company

Preventive Maintenance Inspection **373**

Name_____ Date_____ Class_____

Vehicle used for this activity:

Year_____ Make_____ Model_____

Odometer_____ VIN _____

▶ TASK Check engine for oil, coolant, air, fuel, and exhaust leaks (engine off and running).

NATEF 7A1.6

Time off_____

Time on_____

Total time_____

CDX Tasksheet Number: H399

1. Check for any engine oil leaks. Are there any oil leaks? Yes: _____ No: _____
   a. If yes, where is oil leaking and what actions are required?

   _____
   _____
   _____

2. Check for any coolant leaks. Are there any coolant leaks? Yes: _____ No: _____
   a. If yes, where is coolant leaking and what actions are required?

   _____
   _____
   _____

3. Check for any air leaks. Are there any air leaks? Yes: _____ No: _____
   a. If yes, where is the air leak and what actions are required?

   _____
   _____
   _____

4. Check for any fuel leaks. Are there any fuel leaks? Yes: _____ No: _____
   a. If yes, where is fuel leaking and what actions are required?

   _____
   _____
   _____

5. Check for any exhaust leaks. Are there any exhaust leaks? Yes: _____ No: _____
   a. If yes, where is the exhaust leak and what actions are required?

   _____
   _____
   _____

6. Shut the engine down and discuss the finding(s) with the instructor.

Performance Rating

CDX Tasksheet Number: H399

☐	☐	☐	☐	☐
0	1	2	3	4

Supervisor/instructor signature _____ Date_____

Student/intern information:

Name_____ Date_____ Class_____

Vehicle used for this activity:

Year_____ Make_____ Model_____

Odometer_____ VIN _____

© 2017 Jones & Bartlett Learning, LLC, an Ascend Learning Company

▶ **TASK** Check engine compartment wiring harnesses, connectors, and seals for damage and proper routing.   NATEF 7A1.7

Time off_____

Time on_____

Total time_____

CDX Tasksheet Number: H400

1. Research the procedure and specifications for checking and inspecting engine compartment wiring, connectors, seals, and harnesses for damage and proper routing in the appropriate service information.

2. Consult the appropriate service information's schematics for all wiring associated with the model vehicle you are working on.
   a. Inspect wiring for any rubbing, missing insulation and/or bareness.
   b. Condition of wiring? Good: _____ Bad: _____
      Comments: _____
   c. If the condition of the wiring is bad, consult the appropriate service information to repair it.

3. Check the connectors and seals for any signs of weather related damage.
   a. Condition of connectors and seals? Good: _____ Bad: _____
      Comments: _____
   b. If the condition of the connectors and/or seals is bad, consult the appropriate service information to make a repair.

4. Inspect all harnesses for damage and proper routing.
   Note: Harnesses may be suspended using factory fasteners and may come loose over time. If this is the case, make sure to tighten the fasteners properly.
   a. Condition of harnesses? Good: _____ Bad: _____
      Comments: _____
   b. Are the harnesses properly routed? Yes: _____ No: _____
      Comments: _____
   c. If the condition of the harnesses is bad, consult the appropriate service information to repair any damage or looseness that exists.

5. Determine any necessary action(s):
   _____
   _____

6. Discuss your findings with your instructor.

Performance Rating

CDX Tasksheet Number: H400

☐   ☐   ☐   ☐   ☐
0   1   2   3   4

Supervisor/instructor signature _____ Date_____

Preventive Maintenance Inspection:
Engine System–Fuel System

Student/intern information:

Name_____ Date_____ Class_____

Vehicle used for this activity:

Year_____ Make_____ Model_____

Odometer_____ VIN _____

Learning Objective / Task	CDX Tasksheet Number	2014 NATEF Priority Level	2014 NATEF Reference Number
• Check fuel tanks, mountings, lines, caps, and vents.	H401	P-1	7A2.1
• Drain water from fuel system.	H402	P-1	7A2.2
• Service water separator/fuel heater; replace fuel filter(s); prime and bleed fuel system.	H403	P-1	7A2.3

Time off_____

Time on_____

Total time_____

Materials Required

- Vehicle with possible engine fuel concern
- Vehicle manufacturer's service information
- Manufacturer-specific tools, depending on the concern
- Vehicle lifting equipment, if applicable

Some Safety Issues to Consider

- Diagnosis of this fault may require test driving the vehicle on the school grounds or on a hoist, both of which carry severe risks. Attempt this task only with full permission from your supervisor/instructor and follow all the guidelines exactly.
- **Caution:** If you are working in an area where there could be brake dust present (may contain asbestos, which has been determined to cause cancer when inhaled or ingested), wear and use all OSHA-approved asbestos protective/removal equipment.
- Lifting equipment such as vehicle jacks and stands, vehicle hoists, and engine hoists are important tools that increase productivity and make the job easier. However, they can also cause severe injury or death if used improperly. Make sure you follow the manufacturer's operation procedures. Also make sure you have your supervisor/instructor's permission to use any particular type of lifting equipment.
- Comply with personal and environmental safety practices associated with clothing; eye protection; hand tools; power equipment; proper ventilation; and the handling, storage, and disposal of chemicals/materials in accordance with federal, state, and local regulations.
- Always wear the correct protective eyewear and clothing and use the appropriate safety equipment, as well as fender covers, seat protectors, and floor mat protectors.
- Make sure you understand and observe all legislative and personal safety procedures when carrying out practical assignments. If you are unsure of what these are, ask your supervisor/instructor.

Performance Standard

0–No exposure: No information or practice provided during the program; complete training required

1–Exposure only: General information provided with no practice time; close supervision needed; additional training required

2–Limited practice: Has practiced job during training program; additional training required to develop skill

3–Moderately skilled: Has performed job independently during training program; limited additional training may be required

4–Skilled: Can perform job independently with no additional training

Student/intern information:

Name_____ Date_____ Class_____

Vehicle used for this activity:

Year_____ Make_____ Model_____

Odometer_____ VIN _____

▶ **TASK** Check fuel tanks, mountings, lines, caps, and vents. | **NATEF 7A2.1**

Time off_____

Time on_____

Total time_____

CDX Tasksheet Number: H401

1. Check fuel tanks.
    a. Any signs of structural damage? Yes: _____ No: _____
        i. If yes, list the damaged area:

        _____
        _____
        _____

    b. Is there fuel leaking from any of the structural damaged areas? Yes: _____ No: _____
        i. If yes, detail what repairs need to be carried out:

        _____
        _____
        _____

2. Check fuel tanks mounts.
    a. Any signs of structural damage? Yes: _____ No: _____
        i. If yes, list the damaged area:

        _____
        _____
        _____

    b. Are fuel tank mounting bolts correctly torqued to the manufacturer's specifications?
        i. Manufacturer's recommended torque setting: _____ ft-lb (Nm)
        ii. Have the mounting bolts been torqued to specifications?
            Yes: _____ and to _____ ft-lb (Nm) No: _____
            a. If no, detail why these mounts have not been torqued to specifications.

            _____
            _____
            _____

3. Check fuel lines.
    a. Any signs of damage/deterioration? Yes: _____ No: _____
        i. If yes, list the damaged/deteriorated fuel line location:

        _____
        _____
        _____

4. Check fuel tank cap and vents.
    a. Any signs of damage/blockage? Yes: _____ No: _____
        i. If yes, list steps to rectify:

        _____
        _____
        _____

5. Determine any necessary actions or corrections:

    _____
    _____

6. Discuss the finding(s) with the instructor.

Performance Rating

CDX Tasksheet Number: H401

☐	☐	☐	☐	☐
0	1	2	3	4

Supervisor/instructor signature _____ Date_____

Student/intern information:

Name_____ Date_____ Class_____

Vehicle used for this activity:

Year_____ Make_____ Model_____

Odometer_____ VIN _____

CDX Tasksheet Number: H402

Time off_____

Time on_____

Total time_____

1. Drain water from the fuel system and inspect the tank for any signs of water contamination:
    a. Any signs of water contamination? Yes: _____ No: _____
        Comments: _____
        _____

    i. If yes, place a suitable drain capturing device under the fuel tank drain plug
        and drain off any water sediment contained within the fuel tank.

        Note: If water is found in the fuel tank, it is recommended to install a water
        separator to prevent injector and cylinder block damage.

2. Determine any necessary action(s):
    _____
    _____
    _____

3. Discuss the finding(s) with the instructor.

Performance Rating

CDX Tasksheet Number: H402

☐   ☐   ☐   ☐   ☐
0   1   2   3   4

Supervisor/instructor signature _____ Date_____

Student/intern information:

Name_____ Date_____ Class_____

Vehicle used for this activity:

Year_____ Make_____ Model_____

Odometer_____ VIN _____

Service water separator/fuel heater; replace fuel filter(s); prime and bleed fuel system.

NATEF 7A2.3

Time off_____

Time on_____

Total time_____

CDX Tasksheet Number: H403

1. Locate the fuel filter water trap, if fitted:
   a. Is there water visible in the water trap fuel bowl? Yes: _____ No: _____
      i. If yes, place a drain container under the sediment bowl of the filter and remove. Clean and dry the sediment bowl.

2. If a fuel heater is installed, inspect the wiring harness for any signs of damage or loose connections:
   a. Any signs of damage or loose connections? Yes: _____ No: _____
      i. If yes, list the damaged area:
      _____
      _____

3. Referencing the manufacturer's specifications, locate the specification for the fuel heater:
   a. Manufacturer's recommended voltage: _____ Volts
   b. Manufacturer's recommended wattage: _____ Watts

4. Measure and record fuel heater voltage with ignition off and ignition on:
   a. Ignition OFF voltage: _____ Volts
   b. Ignition ON voltage: _____ Volts
   c. If not within specifications, what is (are) your recommendation(s)?
      _____
      _____
      _____

5. As directed by your instructor, replace fuel filter(s).

6. Replace water separation bowl on appropriate fuel filter.

7. Ensure the sealing gasket is in good condition.

8. Ensure the bowl is tightened to the manufacturer's recommendation.

9. Prime the replacement filters and check for any signs of leaking.
   Note: Screw on filters should be hand tightened. Over tightening will cause leaks.

10. Bleed the fuel system to expel any air from the system.
11. If directed by your instructor, start the engine and check for any signs of fuel leakage.

12. Shut the engine down and undertake a final inspection of the fuel system.

13. Determine any necessary action(s):

_____

_____

_____

14. Discuss the finding(s) with the instructor.

Performance Rating

☐   ☐   ☐   ☐   ☐
0   1   2   3   4

Supervisor/instructor signature _____ Date_____

Preventive Maintenance Inspection:
Engine System—Air Induction and Exhaust Systems

Student/intern information:

Name_____ Date_____ Class_____

Vehicle used for this activity:

Year_____ Make_____ Model_____

Odometer_____ VIN _____

© 2017 Jones & Bartlett Learning, LLC, an Ascend Learning Company

Learning Objective / Task	CDX Tasksheet Number	2014 NATEF Priority Level	2014 NATEF Reference Number
• Check exhaust system mountings for looseness and damage.	H404	P-1	7A3.1
• Check engine exhaust system for leaks, proper routing, and damaged or missing components to include exhaust gas recirculation (EGR) system and after treatment devices, if equipped.	H405	P-1	7A3.2
• Check air induction system: piping, charge air cooler, hoses, clamps, and mountings; check for air restrictions and leaks.	H406	P-1	7A3.3
• Inspect turbocharger for leaks; check mountings and connections.	H407	P-1	7A3.4
• Check operation of engine compression/exhaust brake.	H408	P-2	7A3.5
• Service or replace air filter as needed; check and reset air filter restriction indicator.	H409	P-1	7A3.6
• Inspect and service crankcase ventilation system.	H410	P-1	7A3.7
• Inspect diesel exhaust fluid (DEF) system, to include tanks, lines, gauge pump, and filter.	H411	P-1	7A3.8
• Inspect selective catalyst reduction (SCR) system; including diesel exhaust fluid (DEF) for proper levels, leaks, mounting and connections.	H412	P-2	7A3.9

Time off_____

Time on_____

Total time_____

Materials Required
- Vehicle with possible engine fuel concern
- Vehicle manufacturer's service information
- Manufacturer-specific tools, depending on the concern
- Vehicle lifting equipment, if applicable

Some Safety Issues to Consider
- Diagnosis of this fault may require test driving the vehicle on the school grounds or on a hoist, both of which carry severe risks. Attempt this task only with full permission from your supervisor/instructor and follow all the guidelines exactly.
- **Caution:** If you are working in an area where there could be brake dust present (may contain asbestos, which has been determined to cause cancer when inhaled or ingested), wear and use all OSHA-approved asbestos protective/removal equipment.

- Lifting equipment such as vehicle jacks and stands, vehicle hoists, and engine hoists are important tools that increase productivity and make the job easier. However, they can also cause severe injury or death if used improperly. Make sure you follow the manufacturer's operation procedures. Also make sure you have your supervisor/instructor's permission to use any particular type of lifting equipment.
- Comply with personal and environmental safety practices associated with clothing; eye protection; hand tools; power equipment; proper ventilation; and the handling, storage, and disposal of chemicals/materials in accordance with federal, state, and local regulations.
- Always wear the correct protective eyewear and clothing and use the appropriate safety equipment, as well as fender covers, seat protectors, and floor mat protectors.
- Make sure you understand and observe all legislative and personal safety procedures when carrying out practical assignments. If you are unsure of what these are, ask your supervisor/instructor.

Performance Standard

0—No exposure: No information or practice provided during the program; complete training required

1—Exposure only: General information provided with no practice time; close supervision needed; additional training required

2—Limited practice: Has practiced job during training program; additional training required to develop skill

3—Moderately skilled: Has performed job independently during training program; limited additional training may be required

4—Skilled: Can perform job independently with no additional training

Student/intern information:

Name_____ Date_____ Class_____

Vehicle used for this activity:

Year_____ Make_____ Model_____

Odometer_____ VIN _____

▶ **TASK** Check exhaust system mountings for looseness and damage. | NATEF 7A3.1

Time off_____

Time on_____

Total time_____

CDX Tasksheet Number: H404

1. Research the procedure and specifications to inspect and service the exhaust system in the appropriate service information.

2. Today's exhaust systems are equipped with exhaust treatment systems.

3. Check the exhaust for loose and/or damaged mountings.
   a. Condition of exhaust mountings? Good: _____ Bad: _____
      Comments: _____
      _____

   b. If the condition of the exhaust mountings is bad, consult the appropriate service information for the proper procedures to replace or repair damaged parts.

4. Check the exhaust treatment systems for proper mounting and/or looseness.
   a. Condition of exhaust treatment systems? Good: _____ Bad: _____
      Comments: _____
      _____

   b. If the condition of the exhaust treatment systems is bad, consult the appropriate service information for the proper procedures to replace or repair damaged parts.

      Note: Exhaust systems endure harsh conditions and components may become corroded and oxidized. Many states have inspection rules regarding exhaust leakage. Consult local, state and government regulations regarding this subject.

5. Determine any necessary action(s):
   _____
   _____
   _____
   _____

6. Discuss your findings with your instructor.

Performance Rating

CDX Tasksheet Number: H404

☐   ☐   ☐   ☐   ☐

0   1   2   3   4

Supervisor/instructor signature _____ Date_____

Student/intern information:

Name_____ Date_____ Class_____

Vehicle used for this activity:

Year_____ Make_____ Model_____

Odometer_____ VIN _____

▶ **TASK** Check engine exhaust system for leaks, proper routing, and damaged or missing components to include exhaust gas recirculation (EGR) system and after treatment devices, if equipped.   NATEF 7A3.2

Time off_____

Time on_____

Total time_____

CDX Tasksheet Number: H405

1. Any sign of leaks? Yes: _____ No: _____ Comments: _____
    _____

    a. If yes, detail what repairs need to be carried out:
        _____
        _____
        _____

2. Check engine exhaust system. Look for faulty routing, damage, or missing components:
    a. List your observations:
        _____
        _____
        _____

    b. Does the system meet the manufacturer's specifications? Yes: _____ No: _____
        i. If no, what repairs are necessary to rectify the system?
            _____
            _____
            _____

3. Research the procedure and specifications to inspect and service the EGR system and aftertreatment device systems in the appropriate service information. Record the procedures:
    _____
    _____
    _____

4. Discuss the finding(s) with the instructor.

Performance Rating

CDX Tasksheet Number: H405

☐ 0   ☐ 1   ☐ 2   ☐ 3   ☐ 4

Supervisor/instructor signature _____ Date_____

© 2017 Jones & Bartlett Learning, LLC, an Ascend Learning Company

Student/intern information:

Name_____ Date_____ Class_____

Vehicle used for this activity:

Year_____ Make_____ Model_____

Odometer_____ VIN _____

▶ TASK Check air induction system: piping, charge air cooler, hoses, clamps, and mountings; check for air restrictions and leaks. NATEF 7A3.3

CDX Tasksheet Number: H406

1. Any signs of structural damage? Yes: _____ No: _____
   a. If yes, list the damaged area(s):
   _____
   _____

2. Piping: Good: _____ Needs replacing: _____ Comments: _____
   _____

3. Charged air cooler: Good: _____ Needs replacing: _____ Comments: _____
   _____

4. Air induction hoses: Good: _____ Needs replacing: _____ Comments: _____
   _____

5. Hose clamps and mountings: Good: _____ Needs replacing: _____
   Comments: _____

   a. Manufacturer's torque setting–hose clamps: _____ in-lb (Nm)
   b. Hose clamps tightened to: _____ in-lb (Nm)
   c. Any clamps extremely loose? Yes: _____ No: _____
      Comments: _____

      i. If yes, remove that pipe and check for any signs of dust entry.
   d. Any evidence of dust leakage at joint? Yes: _____ No: _____
      Comments: _____

      i. If yes, determine any necessary actions or corrections:
      _____
      _____

6. Are the mounting bolts correctly torqued to manufacturer's specifications?
   a. Manufacturer's recommended torque setting: _____ ft-lb (Nm)
   b. Have the mounting bolts been torqued to specifications?
      Yes: _____ and to _____ ft-lb (Nm) No: _____
      i. If no, why have these mounts not been torqued to specifications?
      _____

7. Remove air cleaner and check serviceability for element: Clean and reuse: _____
   Requires replacing: _____ Comments: _____
   _____

8. Does air cleaner element housing show signs of dust entry? Yes: _____ No: _____

9. Determine any necessary actions:
   _____
   _____
   _____

10. Discuss the finding(s) with the instructor.

Performance Rating

CDX Tasksheet Number: H406

☐　　　　☐　　　　☐　　　　☐　　　　☐
0　　　　1　　　　2　　　　3　　　　4

Supervisor/instructor signature _____ Date_____

Student/intern information:

Name_____ Date_____ Class_____

Vehicle used for this activity:

Year_____ Make_____ Model_____

Odometer_____ VIN _____

▶ **TASK** Inspect turbocharger for leaks; check mountings and connections. _____ NATEF 7A3.4

CDX Tasksheet Number: H407

1. Any signs of damage/leakage? Yes: _____ No: _____
   a. If yes, list the damaged area(s):
   _____
   _____

2. Are mounting bolts correctly torqued to manufacturer's specifications?
   a. Manufacturer's recommended torque setting: _____ ft-lb (Nm)
   b. Have the mounting bolts been torqued to specifications?
      Yes: _____ and to _____ ft-lb (Nm) No: _____
      i. If no, why have these mounts not been torqued to specifications?
      _____
      _____

3. Turbocharger connections: Good: _____ Needs replacing: _____
   Comments: _____
   a. Manufacturer's torque setting–hose clamps: _____ ft-lb (Nm)
   b. Hose clamps tightened to: _____ ft-lb (Nm)

4. Checking back pressure by utilizing an exhaust back pressure tool or manometer for leaks may be required.

5. Discuss the finding(s) with the instructor.

Performance Rating

CDX Tasksheet Number: H407

☐ ☐ ☐ ☐ ☐
0   1   2   3   4

Supervisor/instructor signature _____ Date_____

Time off_____

Time on_____

Total time_____

© 2017 Jones & Bartlett Learning, LLC, an Ascend Learning Company

Student/intern information:

Name_____ Date_____ Class_____

Vehicle used for this activity:

Year_____ Make_____ Model_____

Odometer_____ VIN _____

Time off_____

CDX Tasksheet Number: H408

Time on_____

1. 12-volt system: Power supply should be between 12-14V: Actual voltage: _____ Volts

2. 24-volt system: Power supply should be between 24-28V: Actual voltage: _____ Volts

Total time_____

3. Research the procedure and specifications to check voltage drop across closed switches regarding engine braking (e.g., a Jacob's engine brake) in the appropriate service information.
   a. Dash switch: _____ Voltage drop
   b. Clutch switch: _____ Voltage drop
   c. Throttle switch: _____ Voltage drop

4. Are these results within the manufacturer's specification? Yes: _____ No: _____
   a. If no, determine any necessary actions or corrections:
   _____
   _____

5. Check all wiring harnesses for soundness, correct routing, and condition:
   a. To perform a final check of the operation of the engine compression brake, you may be required to test drive the vehicle on the school grounds or on a hoist, both of which carry severe risks. Before attempting this task, you must seek and have full permission from your supervisor/instructor and follow all the college/instructor guidelines exactly. Results of test drive (if approved and undertaken): Pass: _____ Fail: _____
      i. If failed, determine any necessary actions:
      _____
      _____

6. Discuss the finding(s) with the instructor.

Performance Rating

CDX Tasksheet Number: H408

☐	☐	☐	☐	☐
0	1	2	3	4

Supervisor/instructor signature _____ Date_____

Name_____ Date_____ Class_____

Vehicle used for this activity:

Year_____ Make_____ Model_____

Odometer_____ VIN _____

▶ **TASK** Service or replace air filter as needed; check and reset air filter restriction indicator.

NATEF 7A3.6

Time off_____

Time on_____

Total time_____

CDX Tasksheet Number: H409

1. Research the procedure and specifications to service or replace the air cleaner in the appropriate service information.
   a. Specified filter part number: _____
   b. Record actions:
      i. Serviced: Yes: _____ No: _____ Comments: _____
      _____
      ii. Replaced: Yes: _____ No: _____ Comments: _____
      _____
   c. With reference to appropriate service information, reset air filter restriction indicator.

2. Determine any necessary action(s):
   _____
   _____
   _____

3. Discuss the finding(s) with the instructor.

Performance Rating

CDX Tasksheet Number: H409

☐ 0   ☐ 1   ☐ 2   ☐ 3   ☐ 4

Supervisor/instructor signature _____ Date_____

Name_____ Date_____ Class_____

Vehicle used for this activity:

Year_____ Make_____ Model_____

Odometer_____ VIN _____

▶ **TASK** Inspect and service crankcase ventilation system.   **NATEF 7A3.7**

CDX Tasksheet Number: H410

Time off_____

Time on_____

Total time_____

1. Research the procedure and specifications to inspect and service the crankcase ventilation system in the appropriate service information.

    Note: Crankcase ventilation is crucial to ensure that crankcase pressure does not rise and cause catastrophic engine damage. This can be tested with a crankcase pressure tool or manometer.

2. Inspect the crankcase ventilation system. List your observations:

    _____

    _____

3. Determine any necessary actions:

    _____

    _____

4. Record actions:
    a. Serviced: Yes: _____ No: _____
    b. Replaced: Yes: _____ No: _____

5. Discuss the finding(s) with the instructor.

Performance Rating

CDX Tasksheet Number: H410

☐   ☐   ☐   ☐   ☐

0   1   2   3   4

Supervisor/instructor signature _____ Date_____

Student/intern information:

Name_____ Date_____ Class_____

Vehicle used for this activity:

Year_____ Make_____ Model_____

Odometer_____ VIN _____

▶ **TASK** Inspect diesel exhaust fluid (DEF) system, to include tanks, lines, gauge pump, and filter. **NATEF 7A3.8**

© 2017 Jones & Bartlett Learning, LLC, an Ascend Learning Company

Time off_____

Time on_____

Total time_____

CDX Tasksheet Number: H411

1. Research the procedure and specifications for inspection of all diesel exhaust fluid (DEF) system components in the appropriate service information.

2. Inspect fluid tank for any damage or leakage that would result in depletion of exhaust fluid.
   a. Is there damage present? Yes: _____ No: _____ Comments: _____
   _____

   b. Is there leakage present? Yes: _____ No: _____ Comments: _____
   _____

   Note: When the fluid level is low, engine performance will suffer resulting in a possible limp mode or a no start condition.

3. Inspect all lines for proper routing and any kinking that may result in improper operation of the exhaust fluid system.
   a. Condition of lines? Good: _____ Bad: _____ Comments: _____
   _____

4. Check fluid gauge for proper operation.
   a. Operation of fluid gauge? Good: _____ Bad: _____ Comments: _____
   _____

5. Inspect pump and filter for proper operation.
   a. Operation of pump and filter? Good: _____ Bad: _____ Comments: _____
   _____

6. Determine any necessary actions or corrections:
   _____
   _____
   _____

7. Discuss your findings with your instructor.

Performance Rating

CDX Tasksheet Number: H411

☐ 0   ☐ 1   ☐ 2   ☐ 3   ☐ 4

Supervisor/instructor signature _____ Date_____

Student/intern information:

Name_____ Date_____ Class_____

Vehicle used for this activity:

Year_____ Make_____ Model_____

Odometer_____ VIN _____

© 2017 Jones & Bartlett Learning, LLC, an Ascend Learning Company

▶ TASK Inspect selective catalyst reduction (SCR) system; including diesel exhaust fluid (DEF) for proper levels, leaks, mounting and connections. **NATEF 7A3.9**

Time off_____

Time on_____

Total time_____

CDX Tasksheet Number: H412

1. Research the procedure and specifications to properly inspect the selective catalyst reduction system in the appropriate service information.

2. Proper measurement of the exhaust fluid can include a visual inspection of the tank level or by using a dash mounted gauge for ongoing monitoring of the level.
   a. Level of fluid? Low: _____ High: _____

   b. If the level of the fluid is low, consult the appropriate service information for the proper procedure to refill the fluid and the type of fluid needed for operation.

3. Inspect tanks for any physical damage or leakage present.
   a. Damage present? Yes: _____ No: _____ Comments: _____
   _____

   b. Leakage present? Yes: _____ No: _____ Comments: _____
   _____

4. Check all mountings and check the tank for loose or missing hardware.
   a. Condition of mountings? Good: _____ Bad: _____ Comments: _____
   _____

   b. Condition of tank hardware? Good: _____ Bad: _____ Comments: _____
   _____

5. Check all connections for tightness and leakage.
   a. Leakage present? Yes: _____ No: _____ Comments: _____
   _____

6. Discuss your findings with your instructor.

Performance Rating

CDX Tasksheet Number: H412

0	1	2	3	4
☐	☐	☐	☐	☐

Supervisor/instructor signature _____ Date_____

Preventive Maintenance Inspection: Engine System–Cooling Systems

© 2017 Jones & Bartlett Learning, LLC, an Ascend Learning Company

Student/intern information:

Name_____ Date_____ Class_____

Vehicle used for this activity:

Year_____ Make_____ Model_____

Odometer_____ VIN _____

Learning Objective / Task	CDX Tasksheet Number	2014 NATEF Priority Level	2014 NATEF Reference Number
• Check operation of fan clutch.	H413	P-1	7A4.1
• Inspect radiator (including air flow restriction, leaks, and damage) and mountings.	H414	P-1	7A4.2
• Inspect fan assembly and shroud.	H415	P-1	7A4.3
• Pressure test cooling system and radiator cap.	H416	P-1	7A4.4
• Inspect coolant hoses and clamps.	H417	P-1	7A4.5
• Inspect coolant recovery system.	H418	P-1	7A4.6
• Check coolant for contamination, additive package concentration, aeration, and protection level (freeze point).	H419	P-1	7A4.7
• Service coolant filter.	H420	P-1	7A4.8
• Inspect water pump.	H421	P-1	7A4.9

Time off_____

Time on_____

Total time_____

Materials Required

- Vehicle with possible engine fuel concern
- Vehicle manufacturer's service information
- Manufacturer-specific tools, depending on the concern
- Vehicle lifting equipment, if applicable
- Cooling system testing equipment
- Workshop tools
- Hand tools

Some Safety Issues to Consider

- Diagnosis of this fault may require test driving the vehicle on the school grounds or on a hoist, both of which carry severe risks. Attempt this task only with full permission from your supervisor/instructor and follow all the guidelines exactly.
- **Caution:** If you are working in an area where there could be brake dust present (may contain asbestos, which has been determined to cause cancer when inhaled or ingested), wear and use all OSHA-approved asbestos protective/removal equipment.
- Lifting equipment such as vehicle jacks and stands, vehicle hoists, and engine hoists are important tools that increase productivity and make the job easier. However, they can also cause severe injury or death if used improperly. Make sure you follow the manufacturer's operation procedures. Also make sure you have your supervisor/instructor's permission to use any particular type of lifting equipment.
- Comply with personal and environmental safety practices associated with clothing; eye protection; hand tools; power equipment; proper ventilation; and the handling, storage, and disposal of chemicals/materials in accordance with federal, state, and local regulations.

- Always wear the correct protective eyewear and clothing and use the appropriate safety equipment, as well as fender covers, seat protectors, and floor mat protectors.
- Make sure you understand and observe all legislative and personal safety procedures when carrying out practical assignments. If you are unsure of what these are, ask your supervisor/instructor.

Performance Standard

0—No exposure: No information or practice provided during the program; complete training required

1—Exposure only: General information provided with no practice time; close supervision needed; additional training required

2—Limited practice: Has practiced job during training program; additional training required to develop skill

3—Moderately skilled: Has performed job independently during training program; limited additional training may be required

4—Skilled: Can perform job independently with no additional training

Name_____ Date_____ Class_____

Vehicle used for this activity:

Year_____ Make_____ Model_____

Odometer_____ VIN _____

▶ TASK Check operation of fan clutch.   NATEF 7A4.1

Time off_____

Time on_____

Total time_____

CDX Tasksheet Number: H413

1. Research the operation and testing procedure for the fan clutch. List the steps to follow to verify that it is operating properly:

    _____

    _____

    _____

    _____

2. Check the operation of the fan clutch. Is the fan clutch operating in accordance with the manufacturer's specifications? Yes: _____ No: _____ Comments: _____

    _____

    a. If no, determine any necessary actions or corrections:

        _____

        _____

        _____

3. Discuss the finding(s) with the instructor.

Performance Rating

CDX Tasksheet Number: H413

☐   ☐   ☐   ☐   ☐

0   1   2   3   4

Supervisor/instructor signature _____ Date_____

Student/intern information:

Name_____ Date_____ Class_____

Vehicle used for this activity:

Year_____ Make_____ Model_____

Odometer_____ VIN _____

▶ **TASK** Inspect radiator (including air flow restriction, leaks, and damage) and mountings.

NATEF 7A4.2

Time off_____

Time on_____

Total time_____

CDX Tasksheet Number: H414

1. Carry out a visual inspection of the radiator and its componentry:
   a. List any damage observed during visual inspection:
   _____
   _____

2. Check the air flow through the radiator core:
   a. Are the radiator core and fins unrestricted? Yes: _____ No: _____
      Comments: _____
      i. If no, clean and repair radiator core cooling fins.

3. Check radiator cooling system for any leaks:
   a. Are there any leaks? Yes: _____ No: _____ Comments: _____
      _____

      i. If yes, detail what repairs need to be carried out:
      _____
      _____

4. Check radiator cooling system mountings:
   a. Do the radiator mounts meet the manufacturer's specifications?
      Yes: _____ No: _____ Comments: _____
      _____

      i. If no, determine any necessary action(s):
      _____
      _____

5. Discuss the finding(s) with the instructor.

Performance Rating

CDX Tasksheet Number: H414

☐ 0   ☐ 1   ☐ 2   ☐ 3   ☐ 4

Supervisor/instructor signature _____ Date_____

© 2017 Jones & Bartlett Learning, LLC, an Ascend Learning Company

Name_____ Date_____ Class_____

Vehicle used for this activity:

Year_____ Make_____ Model_____

Odometer_____ VIN _____

▶ **TASK** Inspect fan assembly and shroud.　　　　　　　　　　　　　**NATEF 7A4.3**

Time off_____

Time on_____

Total time_____

CDX Tasksheet Number: H415

1. Do the fan assembly and shroud meet the manufacturer's specifications? Yes: _____ No: _____
   Comments: _____
   a. If no, determine any necessary action(s):
   _____
   _____
   _____

2. Inspect fan blades for straightness and/or missing blades.
   a. Condition of fan? Good: _____ Bad: _____ Comments: _____
   _____

   b. If the condition of the fan is bad, consult the appropriate service information for the proper procedures to replace the fan blade. Record the procedure:
   _____
   _____
   _____

3. Inspect the shroud for any obstructions or broken pieces that would cause air not to flow properly over the engine.
   a. Condition of shroud? Good: _____ Bad: _____ Comments: _____
   _____

   b. If the condition of the shroud is bad, consult the appropriate service information for the procedures to repair or replace damaged parts. Record the procedures:
   _____
   _____
   _____

4. Discuss the finding(s) with the instructor.

Performance Rating

CDX Tasksheet Number: H415

☐ 　　　　☐ 　　　　☐ 　　　　☐ 　　　　☐
0 　　　　1 　　　　2 　　　　3 　　　　4

Supervisor/instructor signature _____ Date_____

Student/intern information:

Name_____ Date_____ Class_____

Vehicle used for this activity:

Year_____ Make_____ Model_____

Odometer_____ VIN _____

▶ **TASK** Pressure test cooling system and radiator cap.   NATEF 7A4.4

CDX Tasksheet Number: H416

Time off_____

Time on_____

Total time_____

1. Pressure test radiator cap for serviceability:
   a. Manufacturer's specification: _____ psi (kPa)
   b. Radiator cap tested at: _____ psi (kPa)
   c. Radiator cap: Good: _____ Needs replacing: _____
      Comments: _____

2. Pressure test radiator system: Good: _____ System leaking down: _____
   a. If leak down is evident, where is the system leaking and what are your recommendations?
      _____
      _____
      _____

3. Are the mounting bolts correctly torqued to manufacturer's specifications?
   a. Manufacturer's recommended torque setting: _____ ft-lb (Nm)
   b. Have the mounting bolts been torqued to specifications?
      Yes: _____ and to _____ ft-lb (Nm) No: _____
      i. If no, why have these mounts not been torqued to specifications?
         _____
         _____
         _____

4. Discuss the finding(s) with the instructor.

Performance Rating

CDX Tasksheet Number: H416

☐ 0   ☐ 1   ☐ 2   ☐ 3   ☐ 4

Supervisor/instructor signature _____ Date_____

Student/intern information:

Name_____ Date_____ Class_____

Vehicle used for this activity:

Year_____ Make_____ Model_____

Odometer_____ VIN _____

▶ **TASK**   Inspect coolant hoses and clamps.   NATEF 7A4.5

CDX Tasksheet Number: H417

Time off_____

Time on_____

Total time_____

1. Inspect the coolant hoses and clamps. Serviceability of the hoses should be done if hoses are dry rotted or kinked. If engine overhaul was done, these should be replaced.
   a. Are the radiator hoses serviceable? Yes: _____ No: _____
      i. If no, list the damaged hoses:

      _____

      _____

   b. What is the condition of the hose clamps? Check hose clamps for tightness and rust. If evidence of coolant is seen, clamps should be replaced. Good: _____ Need replacing: _____ Comments: _____
      i. Manufacturer's torque setting for hose clamps: _____ in-lb (Nm)
      ii. Hose clamps tightened to: _____ in-lb (Nm)
      iii. Are any clamps extremely loose? Yes: _____ No: _____
         Comments: _____

2. Discuss the findings with the instructor.

Performance Rating

CDX Tasksheet Number: H417

☐ 0   ☐ 1   ☐ 2   ☐ 3   ☐ 4

Supervisor/instructor signature _____ Date_____

Student/intern information:

Name_____ Date_____ Class_____

Vehicle used for this activity:

Year_____ Make_____ Model_____

Odometer_____ VIN _____

© 2017 Jones & Bartlett Learning, LLC, an Ascend Learning Company

▶ **TASK** Inspect coolant recovery system.   **NATEF 7A4.6**

Time off_____

Time on_____

CDX Tasksheet Number: H418

1. Inspect the coolant recovery system and all attaching hoses.
   a. Inspect the coolant bottle for cracks and leaks. Condition of coolant bottle:
      Good: _____ Bad: _____ Comments: _____
      _____

Total time_____

   b. Inspect all hoses that are connected to the coolant bottle for dry rotting and kinking.
      Condition of hoses: Good: _____ Bad: _____ Comments: _____
      _____

   c. If any of these components are bad, record the procedure to replace or repair the
      coolant recovery system below:
      _____
      _____
      _____

2. Discuss the finding(s) with the instructor.

Performance Rating

CDX Tasksheet Number: H418

☐   ☐   ☐   ☐   ☐

0   1   2   3   4

Supervisor/instructor signature _____ Date_____

Student/intern information:

Name_____ Date_____ Class_____

Vehicle used for this activity:

Year_____ Make_____ Model_____

Odometer_____ VIN _____

▶ **TASK** Check coolant for contamination, additive package concentration, aeration, and protection level (freeze point).   NATEF 7A4.7

CDX Tasksheet Number: H419

Time off_____

Time on_____

Total time_____

1.   Check the cooling system functionality and serviceability.
      a. Is the coolant color bright, in accordance with manufacturer's specifications?
          Yes: _____ No: _____ Comments: _____
          _____

          i.   If no, determine any necessary actions or corrections:
               _____
               _____
               _____

      b. Check the coolant for additive package concentration, aeration, and protection level (freeze point). The manufacturer recommends 3-Way Coolant Test Strips:
          i.   If the engine has been running or the coolant is hot, observe all OSHA requirements and carefully remove the radiator cap and dip the strip into the coolant, covering all the test spots for about 70 seconds.

          ii. Compare the test strip coloring against the color chart supplied.
               a. Is the result within the manufacturer's specifications?
                   Yes: _____ No: _____ Comments: _____
                   _____

                   i.   If no, determine any necessary action(s):
                        _____
                        _____

      c. Check antifreeze levels. A number of methods are available for this test. Check with your instructor to ascertain what method is available in your workshop.
          i.   Option #1: Use an antifreeze tester (cheapest method; level desired is as close to 50% as possible or listed in the manufacturer's specifications):
               a. Remove the radiator cap, observing all OSHA requirements.
               b. Insert the nozzle of the tester into the coolant and draw up coolant into the visual chamber. Record the freeze protection level reached on the floating scale: _____
               c. Is the result within the manufacturer's specifications?
                   Yes: _____ No: _____
                   i.   If no, determine any necessary action(s):
                        _____
                        _____

ii. Option #2: Use a refractometer (more accurate method, but equipment is more expensive):

    a. Remove the radiator cap, observing all OSHA requirements.

    b. Draw up coolant into a tube. Place a drop of coolant on the refractometer window and close the lid. Look through the focused eye piece and record the freeze point protection level: _____

    c. Is the result within the manufacturer's specifications?
       Yes: _____ No: _____

       i. If no, determine any necessary action(s):

         _____

         _____

2. Discuss the findings with the instructor.

Performance Rating

CDX Tasksheet Number: H419

☐   ☐   ☐   ☐   ☐

0   1   2   3   4

Supervisor/instructor signature _____ Date_____

Name_____ Date_____ Class_____

Vehicle used for this activity:

Year_____ Make_____ Model_____

Odometer_____ VIN _____

▶ **TASK** Service coolant filter.   **NATEF 7A4.8**

CDX Tasksheet Number: H420

Time off_____

Time on_____

Total time_____

1. Research the procedure to service the coolant filter in the appropriate service information. List the steps:

   _____
   _____
   _____
   _____

2. Remove coolant filter. Inspect the filter and list your observations:

   _____
   _____
   _____

3. Have your instructor verify removal and your answers.
   Supervisor/instructor's initials: _____

4. Prime replacement coolant filter and fit.

5. Top coolant system with the appropriate coolant.

6. Does the cooling system require bleeding after filter change? Yes: _____ No: _____
   a. If yes, list the procedure for bleeding the coolant system in accordance with manufacturer's specifications:

   _____
   _____
   _____
   _____

7. Discuss the findings with the instructor.

Performance Rating

CDX Tasksheet Number: H420

☐	☐	☐	☐	☐
0	1	2	3	4

Supervisor/instructor signature _____ Date_____

Student/intern information:

Name_____ Date_____ Class_____

Vehicle used for this activity:

Year_____ Make_____ Model_____

Odometer_____ VIN _____

▶ **TASK** Inspect water pump.   NATEF 7A4.9

CDX Tasksheet Number: H421

1. Research the procedure and specifications to inspect the water pump in the appropriate service information.

2. Visually inspect the water pump for leakage at the weep hole and around the pump shaft.
   a. Condition of weep hole and shaft? Good: _____ Bad: _____
      Comments: _____

   b. If the condition of the weep hole and/or shaft is bad, record the recommended procedure to replace the pump.

      _____
      _____
      _____

3. Inspect the water pump mountings and gaskets for any leakage that may be present.
   a. Condition of mountings and gaskets? Good: _____ Bad: _____
      Comments: _____

   b. If the condition of the mountings and/or gaskets is bad, record the recommended procedure to repair or replace the mountings and/or gaskets:

      _____
      _____
      _____

4. Discuss the finding(s) with the instructor.

Performance Rating

CDX Tasksheet Number: H421

☐	☐	☐	☐	☐
0	1	2	3	4

Supervisor/instructor signature _____ Date_____

Preventive Maintenance Inspection: Engine System—Lubrication System

Student/intern information:

Name_____ Date_____ Class_____

Vehicle used for this activity:

Year_____ Make_____ Model_____

Odometer_____ VIN _____

Learning Objective / Task	CDX Tasksheet Number	2014 NATEF Priority Level	2014 NATEF Reference Number
• Change engine oil and filters; visually check oil for coolant or fuel contamination; inspect and clean magnetic drain plugs.	H422	P-1	7A5.1
• Take an engine oil sample for analysis.	H423	P-1	7A5.2

Time off_____

Time on_____

Total time_____

Materials Required

- Vehicle with possible engine fuel concern
- Vehicle manufacturer's service information
- Manufacturer-specific tools, depending on the concern
- Vehicle lifting equipment, if applicable
- Workshop tools
- Hand tools
- Engine lubricants
- Engine oil filters
- Approved drainage containers

Some Safety Issues to Consider

- Diagnosis of this fault may require test driving the vehicle on the school grounds or on a hoist, both of which carry severe risks. Attempt this task only with full permission from your supervisor/instructor and follow all the guidelines exactly.
- **Caution:** If you are working in an area where there could be brake dust present (may contain asbestos, which has been determined to cause cancer when inhaled or ingested), wear and use all OSHA-approved asbestos protective/removal equipment.
- Lifting equipment such as vehicle jacks and stands, vehicle hoists, and engine hoists are important tools that increase productivity and make the job easier. However, they can also cause severe injury or death if used improperly. Make sure you follow the manufacturer's operation procedures. Also make sure you have your supervisor/instructor's permission to use any particular type of lifting equipment.
- Comply with personal and environmental safety practices associated with clothing; eye protection; hand tools; power equipment; proper ventilation; and the handling, storage, and disposal of chemicals/materials in accordance with federal, state, and local regulations.
- Always wear the correct protective eyewear and clothing and use the appropriate safety equipment, as well as fender covers, seat protectors, and floor mat protectors.
- Make sure you understand and observe all legislative and personal safety procedures when carrying out practical assignments. If you are unsure of what these are, ask your supervisor/instructor.

© 2017 Jones & Bartlett Learning, LLC, an Ascend Learning Company

Performance Standard

0—No exposure: No information or practice provided during the program; complete training required

1—Exposure only: General information provided with no practice time; close supervision needed; additional training required

2—Limited practice: Has practiced job during training program; additional training required to develop skill

3—Moderately skilled: Has performed job independently during training program; limited additional training may be required

4—Skilled: Can perform job independently with no additional training

Student/intern information:

Name_____ Date_____ Class_____

Vehicle used for this activity:

Year_____ Make_____ Model_____

Odometer_____ VIN _____

▶ **TASK** Change engine oil and filters; visually check oil for coolant or fuel contamination; inspect and clean magnetic drain plugs. 　　　　　　　　　　NATEF 7A5.1

Time off_____

Time on_____

Total time_____

CDX Tasksheet Number: H422

1. Change engine oil and filters.
    a. Ensure that you have new oil filters before commencing (reference the appropriate service information and specification).
    b. Using an adequate sized collection drain container, clean around sump plug.
    c. Using the appropriate sump plug tool, remove sump plug and collect used engine oil in accordance with manufacturer's specifications and governmental environmental protection legislation.
    d. With your instructor's approval, as the oil is draining from engine sump, collect an oil sample in a clean, sterile container to be sent for analysis.
    e. Visually check the sump oil for signs of coolant or fuel contamination.
    f. Are there any visual signs of oil contamination? Yes: _____ No: _____
       Comments: _____
        i. If yes, list the suspected causes of contamination:
           _____
           _____
           _____

    g. Clean sump plug and replace sealing gasket.
    h. Wipe around sump plug location and reinstall the sump plug and torque to manufacturer's specification:
        i. Manufacturer's specified torque: _____ ft-lb (Nm)
        ii. Sump plug torqued to: _____ ft-lb (Nm)

2. Remove and renew oil filters.
    a. Clean the area around the oil filter(s).
    b. Ensure that you have an oil collection container under the oil filter location.
    c. Remove oil filter and housing.
    d. Inspect the oil filter and housing for any signs of contamination, iron filings, etc.
        i. List your observations:
           _____
           _____

    e. Clean and dry oil filter housing.
    f. Remove old sealing O-rings and replace with new sealing rings.
    g. Have your instructor verify removal and your answers.
       Supervisor/instructor's initials: _____
    h. Fit new oil filter into its housing.
    i. Torque retaining bolts to manufacturer's specifications:
        i. Manufacturer's specified torque: _____ ft-lb (Nm)
        ii. Oil filter housing torqued to: _____ ft-lb (Nm)

3. Refill engine sump with fresh lubricating oil.
   a. Reference the appropriate service information or oil company reference charts for the correct oil type and quantity:
      i. Specified engine oil type: _____
      ii. Specified engine oil capacity: _____ gallons/quarts (liters)

   b. Clean around engine oil filler cap.
   c. Add the recommended quantity of correct engine oil.
   d. Allow oil to drain down; check oil level with dipstick.
   e. Start and run engine, but do not rev engine. If oil pressure does not go out within a few seconds, shut the engine down.
   f. With the engine running, check that oil filter housings are not leaking.
   g. Shut engine down and wait a few minutes for oil to drain back into sump.
   h. Recheck oil level and adjust as necessary. Do not overfill the engine oil sump.
   i. On the repair order, record the final quantity of engine oil used: Quantity: _____

4. Dispose of the waste oil in a manner approved by the environmental protection agencies.

5. Discuss the finding(s) with the instructor and have the instructor evaluate the engine for any undue leaks.

Performance Rating

CDX Tasksheet Number: H422

☐   ☐   ☐   ☐   ☐

0   1   2   3   4

Supervisor/instructor signature _____ Date_____

Name_____ Date_____ Class_____

Vehicle used for this activity:

Year_____ Make_____ Model_____

Odometer_____ VIN _____

▶ **TASK** Take an engine oil sample for analysis.   **NATEF 7A5.2**

CDX Tasksheet Number: H423

Time off_____

Time on_____

Total time_____

1. Research the procedure and specifications for oil sampling and analysis in the appropriate service information.

2. Draw a small amount of oil for analysis by removing the oil filter and draining it into a clean container to be sent to the lab.
   a. Oil amount: _____ ounces (ml)

3. A visual inspection of the oil sample will reveal if particles are present.
   a. Particles present? Yes: _____ No: _____ Comments: _____
   _____

   Note: Oil analysis can identify contaminants and engine particles that may be present do to progressive wear. Oil change intervals can be determined from the test so as to prevent premature engine failure.

4. Send the oil out to a lab for analysis and discuss findings and recommendations with the customer.

5. List the results of the oil analysis. If the oil is not being sent out, obtain a sample oil analysis report and list the results of that analysis.
   _____
   _____
   _____
   _____
   _____
   _____

6. Discuss your findings with your instructor.

Performance Rating

CDX Tasksheet Number: H423

☐   ☐   ☐   ☐   ☐

0   1   2   3   4

Supervisor/instructor signature _____ Date_____

Preventive Maintenance Inspection:
Cab and Hood—Instruments and Controls

Student/intern information:

Name_____ Date_____ Class_____

Vehicle used for this activity:

Year_____ Make_____ Model_____

Odometer_____ VIN _____

Learning Objective / Task	CDX Tasksheet Number	2014 NATEF Priority Level	2014 NATEF Reference Number
• Inspect key condition and operation of ignition switch.	H424	P-1	7B1.1
• Check warning indicators.	H425	P-1	7B1.2
• Check instruments; record oil pressure and system voltage.	H426	P-1	7B1.3
• Check operation of electronic power take off (PTO) and engine idle speed controls, if applicable.	H427	P-2	7B1.4
• Check heater, ventilation, and air conditioning (HVAC) controls.	H428	P-1	7B1.5
• Check operation of all accessories.	H429	P-1	7B1.6
• Using electronic service tool or on-board diagnostic system, retrieve engine monitoring information; check and record diagnostic codes and trip/operational data (including engine, transmission, ABS, and other systems).	H430	P-1	7B1.7

Materials Required

- Vehicle with possible cab and hood concern
- Vehicle manufacturer's service information
- Manufacturer-specific tools, depending on the concern
- Vehicle lifting equipment, if applicable
- Electrical and electronic test equipment
- Diagnostic tools
- Workshop tools
- Hand tools

Some Safety Issues to Consider

- Diagnosis of this fault may require test driving the vehicle on the school grounds or on a hoist, both of which carry severe risks. Attempt this task only with full permission from your supervisor/instructor and follow all the guidelines exactly.
- **Caution:** If you are working in an area where there could be brake dust present (may contain asbestos, which has been determined to cause cancer when inhaled or ingested), wear and use all OSHA-approved asbestos protective/removal equipment.
- Lifting equipment such as vehicle jacks and stands, vehicle hoists, and engine hoists are important tools that increase productivity and make the job easier. However, they can also cause severe injury or death if used improperly. Make sure you follow the manufacturer's operation procedures. Also make sure you have your supervisor/instructor's permission to use any particular type of lifting equipment.

- Comply with personal and environmental safety practices associated with clothing; eye protection; hand tools; power equipment; proper ventilation; and the handling, storage, and disposal of chemicals/materials in accordance with federal, state, and local regulations.
- Always wear the correct protective eyewear and clothing and use the appropriate safety equipment, as well as fender covers, seat protectors, and floor mat protectors.
- Make sure you understand and observe all legislative and personal safety procedures when carrying out practical assignments. If you are unsure of what these are, ask your supervisor/instructor.

Performance Standard

0—No exposure: No information or practice provided during the program; complete training required

1—Exposure only: General information provided with no practice time; close supervision needed; additional training required

2—Limited practice: Has practiced job during training program; additional training required to develop skill

3—Moderately skilled: Has performed job independently during training program; limited additional training may be required

4—Skilled: Can perform job independently with no additional training

Name_____ Date_____ Class_____

Vehicle used for this activity:

Year_____ Make_____ Model_____

Odometer_____ VIN _____

▶ **TASK** Inspect key condition and operation of ignition switch.   **NATEF 7B1.1**

Time off_____

Time on_____

Total time_____

CDX Tasksheet Number: H424

ENGINE "OFF"

1. Inspect the key blade to ensure that it is not bent, severely worn, or cracked:
   a. Is the key blade in good condition? Yes: _____ No: _____
      i. If no, list the problems and your recommendation(s):

      _____
      _____
      _____

2. Fit the key into the ignition barrel and turn the key to each of the ignition positions:
   a. Does the ignition key bind in any position? Yes: _____ No: _____
      i. If no, list the problems and your recommendation(s):

      _____
      _____
      _____

3. Lock and unlock the vehicle doors:
   a. Do the door locks operate in accordance with manufacturer's specifications?
      Yes: _____ No: _____
      i. If no, list the problems and your recommendation(s):

      _____
      _____
      _____

4. Discuss the findings with the instructor.

Performance Rating

CDX Tasksheet Number: H424

□	□	□	□	□
0	1	2	3	4

Supervisor/instructor signature _____ Date_____

Student/intern information:

Name_____ Date_____ Class_____

Vehicle used for this activity:

Year_____ Make_____ Model_____

Odometer_____ VIN _____

▶ **TASK** Check warning indicators.   NATEF 7B1.2

CDX Tasksheet Number: H425

Time off_____

Time on_____

Total time_____

1. Carry out a visual inspection of the warning indicator components and check manual operation of these warning devices.
    a. List any damage observed during visual inspection.

    _____

    _____

    b. Are the warning devices working in accordance with the manufacturer's specifications? Yes: _____ No: _____
        i. If no, list the problems and your recommendation(s):

        _____

        _____

        _____

    c. Check for proper timing of the warning indicators to ensure both sides are working at the same rate of speed.
        i. Indicator speed? Good: _____ Bad: _____
        ii. If the indicator speed is bad, consult the appropriate service information for the procedures to repair the warning indicators. Record the procedures:

        _____

        _____

        _____

2. Discuss the finding(s) with the instructor.

Performance Rating

CDX Tasksheet Number: H425

☐	☐	☐	☐	☐
0	1	2	3	4

Supervisor/instructor signature _____ Date_____

Student/intern information:

Name_____ Date_____ Class_____

Vehicle used for this activity:

Year_____ Make_____ Model_____

Odometer_____ VIN _____

▶ **TASK** Check instruments; record oil pressure and system voltage.   NATEF 7B1.3

Time off_____

Time on_____

Total time_____

CDX Tasksheet Number: H426

ENGINE "ON"

1. Turn the dash lights and ignition switch "on," but do not start the engine.
    a. Are all the dash gauges illuminated, activating and working in accordance with the manufacturer's specifications? Yes: _____ No: _____
        i. If no, list the problems and your recommendation(s):

        _____

        _____

        _____

    b. Start the engine and record the engine oil pressure and battery voltage, then shut the engine down:
        i.   Engine oil pressure at idle: _____ psi (kPa)
        ii.   Engine oil pressure at 1,500 rpm: _____ psi (kPa)
        iii. Battery voltage at idle: _____ Volts
        iv.   Battery voltage at 1,500 rpm: _____ Volts

2. Discuss the findings with the instructor.

Performance Rating

CDX Tasksheet Number: H426

☐ 0   ☐ 1   ☐ 2   ☐ 3   ☐ 4

Supervisor/instructor signature _____ Date_____

Name_____ Date_____ Class_____

Vehicle used for this activity:

Year_____ Make_____ Model_____

Odometer_____ VIN _____

▶ **TASK** Check operation of electronic power take off (PTO) and engine idle speed controls
(if applicable). **NATEF 7B1.4**

CDX Tasksheet Number: H427

Time off_____

Time on_____

Total time_____

1. Research the procedure and specifications for the power take-off and engine idle speed
controls in the appropriate service information.

   Note: Power take-offs are small gear boxes attached to the transmission to operate hydraulic
   equipment such as dump bodies and trash truck compactors.

2. Operation of the power take-off can be controlled by either an electronic control or a manual
cable-type control.

3. Most PTO's require that the vehicle is in neutral when engaging the unit.
   a. Put the vehicle in neutral.
   b. Engage the PTO cable or switch.
   c. Does the PTO engage properly? Yes: _____ No: _____
      Comments: _____
      _____

   d. If the PTO does not engage properly, consult the appropriate service information for
      the procedure to repair or replace the PTO unit. Record the procedure:
      _____
      _____
      _____
      _____

   e. If there is a problem with control engagement, consult the appropriate service
      information for the procedure to adjust or troubleshoot the control units or cables.
      Record the procedure:
      _____
      _____
      _____
      _____

4. Discuss your findings with your instructor.

Performance Rating

CDX Tasksheet Number: H427

☐ 0   ☐ 1   ☐ 2   ☐ 3   ☐ 4

Supervisor/instructor signature _____ Date_____

Name_____ Date_____ Class_____

Vehicle used for this activity:

Year_____ Make_____ Model_____

Odometer_____ VIN _____

▶ **TASK** Check HVAC controls.   NATEF 7B1.5

CDX Tasksheet Number: H428

Time off_____

Time on_____

Total time_____

1. With the engine at operating temperature, turn cabin heater "on."
    a. Heater controls movement without any binding or hesitations? Yes: _____ No: _____
        Comments: _____
        _____

        i. If no, rectify heater control movement to ensure smooth operation.

    b. With the control lever in the maximum heat position, is the heater delivering hot air through the vents? Yes: _____ No: _____

        Comments: _____
        _____

        i. If no, inspect heater circuit to determine where the problem lies. Results of inspection:
            _____
            _____
            _____

2. Turn heater "off."

3. Are all vent outlet louvres free to move/rotate? Yes: _____ No: _____
    Comments: _____
    _____

    a. If no, rectify to ensure smooth operation.

4. Move ventilation controls to "on" position.

5. With the fan speed control on each speed level, check the air flow through the vent outlets.
    a. Low speed: Good: _____ Inadequate: _____
        Comments: _____
    b. Intermediate speed: Good: _____ Inadequate: _____
        Comments: _____
    c. Full/high speed: Good: _____ Inadequate: _____
        Comments: _____

6. Turn ventilation fans "off."

7. Turn A/C "on;" set temperature to lowest setting and at lowest fan speed.
   a. Check air temperature at air vents with a digital thermometer:
      i. Temperature at lowest fan speed: _____ °F (_____ °C)
      ii. Temperature at highest fan speed: _____ °F (_____ °C)

   b. Are these readings within the manufacturer's specifications: Yes: _____ No: _____
      i. If no, inspect A/C circuit to ascertain where the problem lies. Results of inspection:

      _____
      _____
      _____

8. Turn ventilation fans "off."

9. Discuss the finding(s) with the instructor.

Performance Rating

CDX Tasksheet Number: H428

☐   ☐   ☐   ☐   ☐

0   1   2   3   4

Supervisor/instructor signature _____ Date_____

Student/intern information:

Name_____ Date_____ Class_____

Vehicle used for this activity:

Year_____ Make_____ Model_____

Odometer_____ VIN _____

CDX Tasksheet Number: H429

ENGINE "ON" OR "OFF"

1. Check all accessory devices fitted and ensure that they are activating and working in accordance with the manufacturer's specifications:
   a. For example, is the CD player and radio operating as described in the service information? Yes: _____ No: _____
      i. If no, list the problems and your recommendation(s):

      _____
      _____
      _____

   b. Test additional accessories and record your findings:

      _____
      _____
      _____
      _____
      _____
      _____
      _____
      _____
      _____
      _____

2. Discuss the findings with the instructor.

Performance Rating

CDX Tasksheet Number: H429

☐	☐	☐	☐	☐
0	1	2	3	4

Supervisor/instructor signature _____ Date_____

Time off_____

Time on_____

Total time_____

Student/intern information:

Name_____ Date_____ Class_____

Vehicle used for this activity:

Year_____ Make_____ Model_____

Odometer_____ VIN _____

▶ TASK Using electronic service tool(s) or on-board diagnostic system; retrieve engine monitoring information; check and record diagnostic codes and trip/operational data (including engine, transmission, ABS, and other systems). **NATEF 7B1.7**

Time off_____

Time on_____

Total time_____

CDX Tasksheet Number: H430

1. Using electronic service tool(s) or on-board diagnostic system, retrieve engine monitoring information:
   a. Are there any fault codes listed in diagnostic tester? Yes: _____ No: _____
      i. If yes, list the code(s) and their descriptions:

   _____
   _____
   _____
   _____
   _____
   _____
   _____
   _____
   _____
   _____

2. Discuss findings with your instructor. If directed by your instructor, clear any stored codes.

Performance Rating

CDX Tasksheet Number: H430

☐   ☐   ☐   ☐   ☐
0   1   2   3   4

Supervisor/instructor signature _____ Date_____

Preventive Maintenance Inspection: Cab and Hood–Safety Equipment

Student/intern information:

Name_____ Date_____ Class_____

Vehicle used for this activity:

Year_____ Make_____ Model_____

Odometer_____ VIN _____

Time off_____

Time on_____

Total time_____

Learning Objective / Task	CDX Tasksheet Number	2014 NATEF Priority Level	2014 NATEF Reference Number
• Check operation of electric/air horns and reverse warning devices.	H431	P-1	7B2.1
• Check condition of spare fuses, safety triangles, fire extinguisher, and all required decals.	H432	P-1	7B2.2
• Inspect seat belts and sleeper restraints.	H433	P-1	7B2.3
• Inspect wiper blades and arms.	H434	P-1	7B2.4

Materials Required

- Vehicle with possible cab and hood concern
- Vehicle manufacturer's service information
- Manufacturer-specific tools, depending on the concern
- Vehicle lifting equipment, if applicable
- Diagnostic tools
- Workshop tools
- Hand tools

Some Safety Issues to Consider

- Diagnosis of this fault may require test driving the vehicle on the school grounds or on a hoist, both of which carry severe risks. Attempt this task only with full permission from your supervisor/instructor and follow all the guidelines exactly.
- **Caution:** If you are working in an area where there could be brake dust present (may contain asbestos, which has been determined to cause cancer when inhaled or ingested), wear and use all OSHA-approved asbestos protective/removal equipment.
- Lifting equipment such as vehicle jacks and stands, vehicle hoists, and engine hoists are important tools that increase productivity and make the job easier. However, they can also cause severe injury or death if used improperly. Make sure you follow the manufacturer's operation procedures. Also make sure you have your supervisor/instructor's permission to use any particular type of lifting equipment.
- Comply with personal and environmental safety practices associated with clothing; eye protection; hand tools; power equipment; proper ventilation; and the handling, storage, and disposal of chemicals/materials in accordance with federal, state, and local regulations.
- Always wear the correct protective eyewear and clothing and use the appropriate safety equipment, as well as fender covers, seat protectors, and floor mat protectors.
- Make sure you understand and observe all legislative and personal safety procedures when carrying out practical assignments. If you are unsure of what these are, ask your supervisor/instructor.

Performance Standard

0–No exposure: No information or practice provided during the program; complete training required

1–Exposure only: General information provided with no practice time; close supervision needed; additional training required

2–Limited practice: Has practiced job during training program; additional training required to develop skill

3–Moderately skilled: Has performed job independently during training program; limited additional training may be required

4–Skilled: Can perform job independently with no additional training

Student/intern information:

Name_____ Date_____ Class_____

Vehicle used for this activity:

Year_____ Make_____ Model_____

Odometer_____ VIN _____

▶ **TASK** Check operation of electric/air horns and reverse warning devices.   **NATEF 7B2.1**

CDX Tasksheet Number: H431

1. Check and test the operation of the audible warning device(s):
   a. Electric horn: Good: _____ Faulty: _____
      i. If faulty, list the problems and your recommendation(s):
      _____
      _____
      _____

   b. Air horn: Good: _____ Faulty: _____
      i. If faulty, list the problems and your recommendation(s):
      _____
      _____
      _____

   c. Back-up (or reversing) warning device: Good: _____ Faulty: _____
      i. If faulty, list the problems and your recommendation(s):
      _____
      _____
      _____

2. Discuss the findings with the instructor.

Time off_____

Time on_____

Total time_____

Performance Rating

CDX Tasksheet Number: H431

☐	☐	☐	☐	☐
0	1	2	3	4

Supervisor/instructor signature _____ Date_____

© 2017 Jones & Bartlett Learning, LLC, an Ascend Learning Company

Student/intern information:

Name_____ Date_____ Class_____

Vehicle used for this activity:

Year_____ Make_____ Model_____

Odometer_____ VIN _____

▶ **TASK** Check condition of spare fuses, safety triangles, fire extinguisher, and all required
decals.   **NATEF 7B2.2**

CDX Tasksheet Number: H432

© 2017 Jones & Bartlett Learning, LLC, an Ascend Learning Company

1.   Check condition of all safety equipment as required by current national/federal legislative acts/
     regulations.
     a. Safety flares (if required by law):
         i.   Are they stored correctly and do they meet current legislative requirements?
              Yes: _____ No: _____
              a.   If no, list the problems and your recommendation(s):

              _____
              _____
              _____

     b. Fire extinguishers (if required by law):
         i.   Are they secured correctly and do they meet current legislative requirements?
              Yes: _____ No: _____
              a.   If no, list the problems and your recommendation(s):

              _____
              _____
              _____

     c. Emergency triangles (if required by law):
         i.   Are they secured correctly and do they meet current legislative requirements?
              Yes: _____ No: _____
              a.   If no, list the problems and your recommendation(s):

              _____
              _____
              _____

     d. Spare fuses (if required by law):
         i.   Are they in a secured location and do they meet current legislative requirements?
              Yes: _____ No: _____
              a.   If no, list the problems and your recommendation(s):

              _____
              _____
              _____

Time off_____

Time on_____

Total time_____

e. Vehicle decals (if required by law):
    i. Are they in a sound condition and do they meet current legislative requirements? Yes: _____ No: _____
        a. If no, list the problems and your recommendation(s):

        _____

        _____

        _____

2. Discuss the findings with the instructor.

Performance Rating

CDX Tasksheet Number: H432

☐   ☐   ☐   ☐   ☐
0   1   2   3   4

Supervisor/instructor signature _____ Date_____

Student/intern information:

Name_____ Date_____ Class_____

Vehicle used for this activity:

Year_____ Make_____ Model_____

Odometer_____ VIN _____

▶ **TASK** Inspect seat belts and sleeper restraints.   **NATEF 7B2.3**

Time off_____

Time on_____

Total time_____

CDX Tasksheet Number: H433

1. Check and test the operation and condition of:
    a. Seat belt operation: Good: _____ Faulty: _____
        i. If faulty, list the problems and your recommendation(s):

        _____
        _____
        _____

    b. Seat belts compliant with national/federal safety legislation? Yes: _____ No: _____
        i. If no, list the problems and your recommendation(s):

        _____
        _____
        _____

    c. Sleeper compartment restraints operation: Good: _____ Faulty: _____
        i. If faulty, list the problems and your recommendation(s):

        _____
        _____
        _____

    d. Sleeper compartment restraints compliant with national/federal safety legislation?
        Yes: _____ No: _____
        i. If no, list the problems and your recommendation(s):

        _____
        _____
        _____

2. Discuss the findings with the instructor.

Performance Rating

CDX Tasksheet Number: H433

☐   ☐   ☐   ☐   ☐
0   1   2   3   4

Supervisor/instructor signature _____ Date_____

Student/intern information:

Name_____ Date_____ Class_____

Vehicle used for this activity:

Year_____ Make_____ Model_____

Odometer_____ VIN _____

▶ **TASK** Inspect wiper blades and arms.   NATEF 7B2.4

Time off_____

Time on_____

Total time_____

CDX Tasksheet Number: H434

1. Inspect the condition of the windshield wiper blades. Inspect for split rubber or missing rubber.
   Check for hardening of the blade. Good: _____ Faulty: _____
   a. If faulty, list the problems and your recommendation(s):

   _____

   _____

   _____

2. Inspect the condition of wiper arms: Good: _____ Faulty: _____
   a. If faulty, list the problems and your recommendation:

   _____

   _____

   _____

3. Discuss the finding(s) with the instructor.

Performance Rating

CDX Tasksheet Number: H434

☐	☐	☐	☐	☐
0	1	2	3	4

Supervisor/instructor signature _____ Date_____

© 2017 Jones & Bartlett Learning, LLC, an Ascend Learning Company

Preventive Maintenance Inspection: Cab and Hood—Hardware

Student/intern information:

Name_____ Date_____ Class_____

Vehicle used for this activity:

Year_____ Make_____ Model_____

Odometer_____ VIN _____

Learning Objective / Task	CDX Tasksheet Number	2014 NATEF Priority Level	2014 NATEF Reference Number
• Check operation of wiper and washer.	H435	P-1	7B3.1
• Inspect windshield glass for cracks or discoloration; check sun visor.	H436	P-1	7B3.2
• Check seat condition, operation, and mounting.	H437	P-1	7B3.3
• Check door glass and window operation.	H438	P-1	7B3.4
• Inspect steps and grab handles.	H439	P-1	7B3.5
• Inspect mirrors, mountings, brackets, and glass.	H440	P-1	7B3.6
• Record all observed physical damage.	H441	P-2	7B3.7
• Lubricate all cab and hood grease fittings.	H442	P-2	7B3.8
• Inspect and lubricate door and hood hinges, latches, strikers, lock cylinders, safety latches, linkages, and cables.	H443	P-1	7B3.9
• Inspect cab mountings, hinges, latches, linkages, and ride height; service as needed.	H444	P-1	7B3.10

Time off_____

Time on_____

Total time_____

Materials Required

- Vehicle with possible cab and hood concern
- Vehicle manufacturer's service information
- Manufacturer-specific tools, depending on the concern
- Vehicle lifting equipment, if applicable
- Diagnostic tools
- Workshop tools
- Hand tools

Some Safety Issues to Consider

- Diagnosis of this fault may require test driving the vehicle on the school grounds or on a hoist, both of which carry severe risks. Attempt this task only with full permission from your supervisor/instructor and follow all the guidelines exactly.
- **Caution:** If you are working in an area where there could be brake dust present (may contain asbestos, which has been determined to cause cancer when inhaled or ingested), wear and use all OSHA-approved asbestos protective/removal equipment.
- Lifting equipment such as vehicle jacks and stands, vehicle hoists, and engine hoists are important tools that increase productivity and make the job easier. However, they can also cause severe injury or death if used improperly. Make sure you follow the manufacturer's operation procedures. Also make sure you have your supervisor/instructor's permission to use any particular type of lifting equipment.

- Comply with personal and environmental safety practices associated with clothing; eye protection; hand tools; power equipment; proper ventilation; and the handling, storage, and disposal of chemicals/materials in accordance with federal, state, and local regulations.
- Always wear the correct protective eyewear and clothing and use the appropriate safety equipment, as well as fender covers, seat protectors, and floor mat protectors.
- Make sure you understand and observe all legislative and personal safety procedures when carrying out practical assignments. If you are unsure of what these are, ask your supervisor/instructor.

Performance Standard

0—No exposure: No information or practice provided during the program; complete training required

1—Exposure only: General information provided with no practice time; close supervision needed; additional training required

2—Limited practice: Has practiced job during training program; additional training required to develop skill

3—Moderately skilled: Has performed job independently during training program; limited additional training may be required

4—Skilled: Can perform job independently with no additional training

Student/intern information:

Name_____ Date_____ Class_____

Vehicle used for this activity:

Year_____ Make_____ Model_____

Odometer_____ VIN _____

▶ **TASK** Check operation of wiper and washer.   NATEF 7B3.1

Time off_____

Time on_____

Total time_____

CDX Tasksheet Number: H435

1. Inspect and check the operation of windshield wiper blades (ensure that the windshield is wet before operating wipers) and note condition: Good: _____ Needs repair/replacement: _____
    a. If faulty, list the problems and your recommendation(s):

    _____
    _____
    _____

2. Check operation of the windshield washer system for correct spray pattern and volume.
    a. Condition of washer spray? Good: _____ Bad: _____

    Comments: _____
    _____

    b. If the condition of the washer spray is bad, consult the appropriate service information for the proper procedures to repair or replace the washer system. Record the procedures:

    _____
    _____
    _____

3. Discuss the findings with the instructor.

Performance Rating

CDX Tasksheet Number: H435

☐   ☐   ☐   ☐   ☐
0   1   2   3   4

Supervisor/instructor signature _____ Date_____

Student/intern information:

Name_____ Date_____ Class_____

Vehicle used for this activity:

Year_____ Make_____ Model_____

Odometer_____ VIN _____

▶ **TASK** Inspect windshield glass for cracks or discoloration; check sun visor.   **NATEF 7B3.2**

CDX Tasksheet Number: H436

1. Inspect the windshield for any damage—cracks, chips, scratches, or visual deterioration:
    Good: _____ Needs repair/replacement: _____
    a. If needs repair/replacement, list the problems and your recommendation(s):

    _____

    _____

    _____

    Note: Upon replacement of a windshield, ensure that it is AS1 compliant.

2. Check sun visor. Good: _____ Needs repair/replacement: _____
    a. If needs repair/replacement, list the problems and your recommendation(s):

    _____

    _____

    _____

3. Discuss the findings with the instructor.

Time off_____

Time on_____

Total time_____

Performance Rating

CDX Tasksheet Number: H436

☐	☐	☐	☐	☐
0	1	2	3	4

Supervisor/instructor signature _____ Date_____

Student/intern information:

Name_____ Date_____ Class_____

Vehicle used for this activity:

Year_____ Make_____ Model_____

Odometer_____ VIN _____

▶ **TASK** Check seat condition, operation, and mounting.　　　　　　NATEF 7B3.3

CDX Tasksheet Number: H437

1. Check seat condition, operation, and mounting:
   a. Seat condition: Are they in good condition and meet current legislative requirements? Yes: _____ No: _____
      i. If no, list the problems and your recommendation(s):

      _____
      _____
      _____

   b. Seat operation: Are they operating in accordance with manufacturer's specification and current legislative requirements? Yes: _____ No: _____
      i. If no, list the problems and your recommendation(s):

      _____
      _____
      _____

   c. Seat mounting(s): Are they secured in accordance with manufacturer's specification and current legislative requirements? Yes: _____ No: _____
      i. If no, list the problems and your recommendation(s):

      _____
      _____
      _____

2. Discuss the findings with the instructor.

Performance Rating

CDX Tasksheet Number: H437

☐	☐	☐	☐	☐
0	1	2	3	4

Supervisor/instructor signature _____ Date_____

Student/intern information:

Name_____ Date_____ Class_____

Vehicle used for this activity:

Year_____ Make_____ Model_____

Odometer_____ VIN _____

▶ **TASK** Check door glass and window operation.   NATEF 7B3.4

Time off_____

Time on_____

Total time_____

CDX Tasksheet Number: H438

    1.   Check door glass and window operation:
        a. Door window(s) operation: Good: _____ Faulty: _____
            i. If faulty, list the problems and your recommendation(s):

              _____
              _____
              _____

        b. Condition of door window(s): Good: _____ Needs repair/replacement: _____
            i. If needs repair/replacement, list the problems and your recommendation(s):

              _____
              _____
              _____

    2.   Discuss the findings with the instructor.

Performance Rating

CDX Tasksheet Number: H438

☐	☐	☐	☐	☐
0	1	2	3	4

Supervisor/instructor signature _____ Date_____

Student/intern information:

Name_____ Date_____ Class_____

Vehicle used for this activity:

Year_____ Make_____ Model_____

Odometer_____ VIN _____

▶ **TASK** Inspect steps and grab handles.   NATEF 7B3.5

Time off_____

Time on_____

CDX Tasksheet Number: H439

1. Inspect vehicle entry safety items fitted to this vehicle.
    a. Check the security of cabin entry steps and grab handles:
        Good: _____ Needs repair/replacement: _____
        i. If faulty, list the problems and your recommendation(s):

        _____
        _____
        _____

Total time_____

    b. Check the suitability and condition of cabin entry steps and grab handles (e.g., any rust, jagged edges, etc.): Good: _____ Needs repair/replacement: _____
        i. If faulty, list the problems and your recommendation(s):

        _____
        _____
        _____

2. Discuss the findings with the instructor.

Performance Rating

CDX Tasksheet Number: H439

☐	☐	☐	☐	☐
0	1	2	3	4

Supervisor/instructor signature _____ Date_____

Student/intern information:

Name_____ Date_____ Class_____

Vehicle used for this activity:

Year_____ Make_____ Model_____

Odometer_____ VIN _____

▶ **TASK** Inspect mirrors, mountings, brackets, and glass. **NATEF 7B3.6**

Time off_____

Time on_____

Total time_____

CDX Tasksheet Number: H440

1. Inspect vehicle glass external mirrors fitted to this vehicle (if required by national/federal law).
   a. External mirror glass condition: Good: _____ Faulty: _____
      i. If faulty, list the problems and your recommendation(s):

      _____

      _____

      _____

   b. Condition of external mirror mounting and bracket(s):
      Good: _____ Needs repair/replacement: _____
      i. If needs repair/replacement, list the problems and your recommendation(s):

      _____

      _____

      _____

2. Discuss the findings with the instructor.

Performance Rating

CDX Tasksheet Number: H440

☐	☐	☐	☐	☐
0	1	2	3	4

Supervisor/instructor signature _____ Date_____

Student/intern information:

Name_____ Date_____ Class_____

Vehicle used for this activity:

Year_____ Make_____ Model_____

Odometer_____ VIN _____

▶ **TASK** Record all observed physical damage. NATEF 7B3.7

Time off_____

Time on_____

Total time_____

CDX Tasksheet Number: H441

1. Pre-trip inspections are required before a vehicle can be operated on the highway.

2. Part of the pre-trip inspection is to observe any physical damage that might be present and/or cause harm to the vehicle or another vehicle.

3. Check the outside of the cab for any physical damage. Record your findings:

_____
_____
_____
_____
_____

4. Check the frame and axles for any visible physical damage. Record your findings:

_____
_____
_____
_____
_____

   Note: Guidelines for pre-trip inspections can be found online or through the state Department of Transportation offices.

5. Discuss your findings with your instructor and record any recommendations necessary:

_____
_____
_____

Performance Rating

CDX Tasksheet Number: H441

☐	☐	☐	☐	☐
0	1	2	3	4

Supervisor/instructor signature _____ Date_____

© 2017 Jones & Bartlett Learning, LLC, an Ascend Learning Company

▶ **TASK** Lubricate all cab and hood grease fittings.   **NATEF 7B3.8**

Time off_____

CDX Tasksheet Number: H442

Time on_____

1. Research the procedure and specifications for the correct lubricant/grease in the appropriate service information. Grease all appropriate locations.
   a. Specified lubricant: _____

   Total time_____

   b. List the areas lubricated.

   _____
   _____
   _____
   _____
   _____
   _____
   _____

2. Discuss the findings with the instructor.

Performance Rating

CDX Tasksheet Number: H442

☐	☐	☐	☐	☐
0	1	2	3	4

Supervisor/instructor signature _____ Date_____

Student/intern information:

Name_____ Date_____ Class_____

Vehicle used for this activity:

Year_____ Make_____ Model_____

Odometer_____ VIN _____

© 2017 Jones & Bartlett Learning, LLC, an Ascend Learning Company

▶ **TASK** Inspect and lubricate door and hood hinges, latches, strikers, lock cylinders, safety latches, linkages, and cables.   **NATEF 7B3.9**

Time off_____

Time on_____

Total time_____

CDX Tasksheet Number: H443

1. Inspect and lubricate all interior components requiring periodic lubrication.
   a. Specified lubricant: _____
   b. Door(s) and hood hinges condition: Good: _____ Needs repair/replacement: _____
      i. If needs repair/replacement, list the problems and your recommendation(s):
         _____
         _____
         _____

      ii. Lubricated? Yes: _____ No: _____
         a. If no, why:
            _____

   c. Latches, strikers, and safety latches condition:
      Good: _____ Needs repair/replacement: _____
      i. If needs repair/replacement, list the problems and your recommendation(s):
         _____
         _____
         _____

      ii. Lubricated? Yes: _____ No: _____
         a. If no, why:
            _____

   d. Lock cylinders, linkages, and cables condition:
      Good: _____ Needs repair/replacement: _____
      i. If needs repair/replacement, list the problems and your recommendation(s):
         _____
         _____
         _____

      ii. Lubricated? Yes: _____ No: _____
         a. If no, why:
            _____

2. Discuss the findings with the instructor.

Performance Rating

CDX Tasksheet Number: H443

☐	☐	☐	☐	☐
0	1	2	3	4

Supervisor/instructor signature _____ Date_____

Student/intern information:

Name_____ Date_____ Class_____

Vehicle used for this activity:

Year_____ Make_____ Model_____

Odometer_____ VIN _____

▶ **TASK** Inspect cab mountings, hinges, latches, linkages, and ride height; service as needed.

NATEF 7B3.10

CDX Tasksheet Number: H444

. Inspect cab mounting components.
   a. Condition and suitability of cab mounting(s):
      Good: _____ Needs repair/replacement: _____
      i. If needs repair/replacement, list the problems and your recommendation(s):
      _____
      _____
      _____

   b. Condition and suitability of cab hinges:
      Good: _____ Needs repair/replacement: _____
      i. If needs repair/replacement, list the problems and your recommendation(s):
      _____
      _____
      _____

   c. Condition and suitability of cab mounting latches:
      Good: _____ Needs repair/replacement: _____
      i. If needs repair/replacement, list the problems and your recommendation(s):
      _____
      _____
      _____

   d. Condition and suitability of cab mounting linkage and ride height:
      i. Record manufacturer specified ride height: _____
      ii. Record actual ride height: _____
      iii. If needs servicing/adjustment, reference the appropriate service information for procedure to adjust ride height. With your instructor's permission, adjust ride height.

2. Discuss the finding(s) with the instructor.

Time off_____

Time on_____

Total time_____

Performance Rating

CDX Tasksheet Number: H444

☐ 0   ☐ 1   ☐ 2   ☐ 3   ☐ 4

Supervisor/instructor signature _____ Date_____

017 Jones & Bartlett Learning, LLC, an Ascend Learning Company

Preventive Maintenance Inspection   479

Preventive Maintenance Inspection:
Cab and Hood—Heating, Ventilation & Air Conditioning (HVAC)

Student/intern information:

Name_____ Date_____ Class_____

Vehicle used for this activity:

Year_____ Make_____ Model_____

Odometer_____ VIN _____

Learning Objective / Task	CDX Tasksheet Number	2014 NATEF Priority Level	2014 NATEF Reference Number
• Inspect A/C condenser and lines for condition and visible leaks; check mountings.	H445	P-2	7B4.1
• Inspect A/C compressor and lines for condition and visible leaks; check mountings.	H446	P-2	7B4.2
• Check A/C system condition and operation; check A/C monitoring system, if applicable.	H447	P-1	7B4.3
• Check HVAC air inlet filters and ducts; service as needed.	H448	P-1	7B4.4

Time off_____

Time on_____

Total time_____

Materials Required

- Vehicle with possible cab and hood concern
- Vehicle manufacturer's service information
- Manufacturer-specific tools, depending on the concern
- Vehicle lifting equipment, if applicable
- Diagnostic tools
- Workshop tools
- Hand tools

Some Safety Issues to Consider

- Diagnosis of this fault may require test driving the vehicle on the school grounds or on a hoist, both of which carry severe risks. Attempt this task only with full permission from your supervisor/instructor and follow all the guidelines exactly.
- **Caution:** If you are working in an area where there could be brake dust present (may contain asbestos, which has been determined to cause cancer when inhaled or ingested), wear and use all OSHA-approved asbestos protective/removal equipment.
- Lifting equipment such as vehicle jacks and stands, vehicle hoists, and engine hoists are important tools that increase productivity and make the job easier. However, they can also cause severe injury or death if used improperly. Make sure you follow the manufacturer's operation procedures. Also make sure you have your supervisor/instructor's permission to use any particular type of lifting equipment.
- Comply with personal and environmental safety practices associated with clothing; eye protection; hand tools; power equipment; proper ventilation; and the handling, storage, and disposal of chemicals/materials in accordance with federal, state, and local regulations.
- Always wear the correct protective eyewear and clothing and use the appropriate safety equipment, as well as fender covers, seat protectors, and floor mat protectors.
- Make sure you understand and observe all legislative and personal safety procedures when carrying out practical assignments. If you are unsure of what these are, ask your supervisor/instructor.

© 2017 Jones & Bartlett Learning, LLC, an Ascend Learning Company

Performance Standard

0—No exposure: No information or practice provided during the program; complete training required

1—Exposure only: General information provided with no practice time; close supervision needed; additional training required

2—Limited practice: Has practiced job during training program; additional training required to develop skill

3—Moderately skilled: Has performed job independently during training program; limited additional training may be required

4—Skilled: Can perform job independently with no additional training

Student/intern information:

Name_____ Date_____ Class_____

Vehicle used for this activity:

Year_____ Make_____ Model_____

Odometer_____ VIN _____

▶ TASK Inspect A/C condenser and lines for condition and visible leaks; check mountings.

NATEF 7B4.1

CDX Tasksheet Number: H445

1. Inspect condenser lines and condition.
   a. Inspect A/C condenser and lines for condition:
      Good: _____ Needs repair/replacement: _____
      i. If needs repair/replacement, list the problems and your recommendation(s):
      _____
      _____
      _____

   b. Inspect A/C condenser and lines for visible leaks:
      Good: _____ Needs repair/replacement: _____
      i. If needs repair/replacement, list the problems and your recommendation(s):
      _____
      _____
      _____

   c. Inspect A/C condenser mountings: Good: _____ Needs repair/replacement: _____
      i. If needs repair/replacement, list the problems and your recommendation(s):
      _____
      _____
      _____

2. Discuss the findings with the instructor.

Time off_____

Time on_____

Total time_____

Performance Rating

CDX Tasksheet Number: H445

☐ 0   ☐ 1   ☐ 2   ☐ 3   ☐ 4

Supervisor/instructor signature _____ Date_____

© 2017 Jones & Bartlett Learning, LLC, an Ascend Learning Company

Student/intern information:

Name_____ Date_____ Class_____

Vehicle used for this activity:

Year_____ Make_____ Model_____

Odometer_____ VIN _____

▶ **TASK** Inspect A/C compressor and lines for condition and visible leaks; check mountings.

NATEF 7B4.2

CDX Tasksheet Number: H446

1. Inspect compressor lines and condition.
   a. Inspect A/C compressor and lines for condition:
      Good: _____ Needs repair/replacement: _____
      i. If needs repair/replacement, list the problems and your recommendation(s):
      _____
      _____
      _____

   b. Inspect A/C compressor and lines for visible leaks:
      Good: _____ Needs repair/replacement: _____
      i. If needs repair/replacement, list the problems and your recommendation(s):
      _____
      _____
      _____

   c. Inspect A/C compressor mountings: Good: _____ Needs repair/replacement: _____
      i. If needs repair/replacement, list the problems and your recommendation(s):
      _____
      _____
      _____

2. Discuss the findings with the instructor.

Performance Rating

CDX Tasksheet Number: H446

☐	☐	☐	☐	☐
0	1	2	3	4

Supervisor/instructor signature _____ Date_____

Student/intern information:

Name_____ Date_____ Class_____

Vehicle used for this activity:

Year_____ Make_____ Model_____

Odometer_____ VIN _____

▶ **TASK** Check A/C system condition and operation; check A/C monitoring system, if applicable.

NATEF 7B4.3

CDX Tasksheet Number: H447

1. Check HVAC controls and filters.
   a. Check that all vent outlet louvres are free to move/rotate: Yes: _____ No: _____
      Comments: _____
      _____

      i. If no, rectify to ensure smooth operation. List your actions:
         _____
         _____

   b. Move ventilation controls to the "on" position. With the fan speed control on each speed level, check the air flow through the vent outlets:
      i. Low speed: Good: _____ Inadequate: _____
         Comments: _____

      ii. Intermediate speed: Good: _____ Inadequate: _____
          Comments: _____

      iii. Full/high speed: Good: _____ Inadequate: _____
           Comments: _____

   c. Turn ventilation fans "off."

   d. Turn A/C "on;" set temperature to lowest setting and lowest fan speed:
      i. Check air temperature at air vents with a digital thermometer:
         a. Temperature at lowest fan speed: _____ °F (_____ °C)
         b. Temperature at highest fan speed: _____ °F (_____ °C)
      ii. Are these readings within the manufacturer's specifications:
          Yes: _____ No: _____

   e. Turn A/C and engine "off."
      i. Determine any necessary actions or corrections:
         _____
         _____

2. Discuss the findings with the instructor.

Performance Rating

CDX Tasksheet Number: H447

☐   ☐   ☐   ☐   ☐

0   1   2   3   4

Supervisor/instructor signature _____ Date_____

Student/intern information:

Name_____ Date_____ Class_____

Vehicle used for this activity:

Year_____ Make_____ Model_____

Odometer_____ VIN _____

CDX Tasksheet Number: H448

Time off_____

Time on_____

Total time_____

1. Inspect A/C air inlet filters. Research the procedure and specifications for locations of filters in the appropriate service information. Good: _____ Needs cleaning/replacement: _____
   a. If needs cleaning, list the procedure and your recommendation(s):
   _____
   _____
   _____

   b. If needs repair/replacement, list the problems and your recommendation(s):
   _____
   _____
   _____

2. Check air inlet ducts. Good: _____ Needs cleaning/replacement: _____
   a. If needs cleaning, list the procedure and your recommendation(s):
   _____
   _____
   _____

   b. If needs repair/replacement, list the problems and your recommendation(s):
   _____
   _____
   _____

3. Discuss the finding(s) with the instructor.

Performance Rating

CDX Tasksheet Number: H448

☐	☐	☐	☐	☐
0	1	2	3	4

Supervisor/instructor signature _____ Date_____

Preventive Maintenance Inspection:
Electrical/Electronics–Battery and Starting Systems

Student/intern information:

Name_____ Date_____ Class_____

Vehicle used for this activity:

Year_____ Make_____ Model_____

Odometer_____ VIN _____

Learning Objective / Task	CDX Tasksheet Number	2014 NATEF Priority Level	2014 NATEF Reference Number
• Inspect battery box(es), cover(s), and mountings.	H449	P-1	7C1.1
• Inspect battery hold-downs, connections, cables, and cable routing; service as needed.	H450	P-1	7C1.2
• Check/record battery state-of-charge (open-circuit voltage) and condition.	H451	P-1	7C1.3
• Perform battery test (load and/or capacitance).	H452	P-1	7C1.4
• Inspect starter, mounting, and connections.	H453	P-1	7C1.5
• Engage starter; check for unusual noises, starter drag, and starting difficulty.	H454	P-1	7C1.6

Time off_____

Time on_____

Total time_____

Materials Required

- Vehicle
- Vehicle manufacturer's service information
- Manufacturer-specific tools, depending on the concern
- Vehicle lifting equipment, if applicable
- Diagnostic tools
- Battery testing equipment
- Electrical/electronic testing equipment
- Workshop tools
- Hand tools

Some Safety Issues to Consider

- Diagnosis of this fault may require test driving the vehicle on the school grounds or on a hoist, both of which carry severe risks. Attempt this task only with full permission from your supervisor/instructor and follow all the guidelines exactly.
- **Caution:** If you are working in an area where there could be brake dust present (may contain asbestos, which has been determined to cause cancer when inhaled or ingested), wear and use all OSHA-approved asbestos protective/removal equipment.
- Lifting equipment such as vehicle jacks and stands, vehicle hoists, and engine hoists are important tools that increase productivity and make the job easier. However, they can also cause severe injury or death if used improperly. Make sure you follow the manufacturer's operation procedures. Also make sure you have your supervisor/instructor's permission to use any particular type of lifting equipment.
- Comply with personal and environmental safety practices associated with clothing; eye protection; hand tools; power equipment; proper ventilation; and the handling, storage, and disposal of chemicals/materials in accordance with federal, state, and local regulations.
- Always wear the correct protective eyewear and clothing and use the appropriate safety equipment, as well as fender covers, seat protectors, and floor mat protectors.

- Make sure you understand and observe all legislative and personal safety procedures when carrying out practical assignments. If you are unsure of what these are, ask your supervisor/instructor.

Performance Standard

0—No exposure: No information or practice provided during the program; complete training required

1—Exposure only: General information provided with no practice time; close supervision needed; additional training required

2—Limited practice: Has practiced job during training program; additional training required to develop skill

3—Moderately skilled: Has performed job independently during training program; limited additional training may be required

4—Skilled: Can perform job independently with no additional training

Name_____ Date_____ Class_____

Vehicle used for this activity:

Year_____ Make_____ Model_____

Odometer_____ VIN _____

▶ **TASK** Inspect battery box(es), cover(s), and mountings.   NATEF 7C1.1

CDX Tasksheet Number: H449

Time off_____	
Time on_____	
Total time_____	

1. Is the battery box(es), including battery box cover(s), in good condition? Yes: _____ No: _____
   a. If no, list the problems and your recommendation(s):

   _____

   _____

   _____

2. Is the battery box(es) mounting(s) secured to the chassis/vehicle? Yes: _____ No: _____
   a. If no, list the problems and your recommendation(s):

   _____

   _____

   _____

3. Is the battery cabling secured to the battery/chassis/vehicle? Yes: _____ No: _____
   a. If no, list the problems and your recommendation(s):

   _____

   _____

   _____

4. Discuss the findings with the instructor.

Performance Rating

CDX Tasksheet Number: H449

☐ 0   ☐ 1   ☐ 2   ☐ 3   ☐ 4

Supervisor/instructor signature _____ Date_____

Student/intern information:

Name_____ Date_____ Class_____

Vehicle used for this activity:

Year_____ Make_____ Model_____

Odometer_____ VIN _____

▶ **TASK** Inspect battery hold-downs, connections, cables, and cable routing; service as needed.

NATEF 7C1.2

CDX Tasksheet Number: H450

Time off_____

Time on_____

Total time_____

Note: Batteries give off hydrogen gas while they are being charged. Hydrogen is a highly explosive gas that is easily ignited by a spark. Batteries are filled with sulfuric acid, which is an additional hazard. Use caution and do not make a spark around batteries.

1. Remove battery cover(s). Are the hold-downs and connection(s) secure and in good condition?
    Yes: _____ No: _____
    a. If no, list the problems and your recommendation(s):
        _____
        _____
        _____

2. Are the battery cables in good condition and not chafing on chassis? Yes: _____ No: _____
    a. If no, list the problems and your recommendation(s):
        _____
        _____
        _____

3. Determine any necessary actions or corrections:
    _____
    _____
    _____

4. Discuss the findings with the instructor.

Performance Rating

CDX Tasksheet Number: H450

☐ 0   ☐ 1   ☐ 2   ☐ 3   ☐ 4

Supervisor/instructor signature _____ Date_____

Student/intern information:

Name_____ Date_____ Class_____

Vehicle used for this activity:

Year_____ Make_____ Model_____

Odometer_____ VIN _____

▶ **TASK** Check/record battery state-of-charge (open-circuit voltage) and condition.

Time off_____

Time on_____

Total time_____

CDX Tasksheet Number: H451

Note: Batteries give off hydrogen gas while they are being charged. Hydrogen is a highly explosive gas that is easily ignited by a spark. Batteries are filled with sulfuric acid, which is an additional hazard. Use caution and do not make a spark around batteries.

1. With battery cover(s) removed, check battery condition.
   a. Using an appropriate battery tester, check battery voltage at rest:
      i. First battery voltage at rest: _____ Volts
      ii. Second battery voltage at rest: _____ Volts
      iii. If third battery fitted, third battery voltage at rest: _____ Volts
      iv. Specific gravity (SG) for each cell (first battery; if more than one is used, record their details as well):

First Battery		Second Battery		Third Battery		Fourth Battery	
Cell	SG	Cell	SG	Cell	SG	Cell	SG
1		1		1		1	
2		2		2		2	
3		3		3		3	
4		4		4		4	
5		5		5		5	
6		6		6		6	

   b. Condition of battery (or batteries): Serviceable: _____ Unserviceable: _____
      Comments: _____

      _____

      i. If unserviceable, list your recommendation(s):

         _____

         _____

         _____

c. Are the battery cables in good condition and not chafing on chassis?
Yes: _____ No: _____

　　i. If no, list the problems and your recommendation(s):

_____

_____

_____

d. Rectify any problems discovered during inspection.

2. Discuss the findings with the instructor.

Performance Rating

CDX Tasksheet Number: H451

☐	☐	☐	☐	☐
0	1	2	3	4

Supervisor/instructor signature _____ Date _____

Student/intern information:

Name_____ Date_____ Class_____

Vehicle used for this activity:

Year_____ Make_____ Model_____

Odometer_____ VIN _____

▶ **TASK** Perform battery test (load and/or capacitance).   **NATEF 7C1.4**

CDX Tasksheet Number: H452

Time off_____

Time on_____

Total time_____

1. List the CCA rating of each battery:
   a. First battery: _____ CCA
   b. Second battery: _____ CCA
   c. Third battery: _____ CCA

2. If using an appropriate battery load tester, record the battery test results:
   a. First battery: Voltage at end of load test: _____ Volts Pass: _____ Fail: _____
   b. Second battery: Voltage at end of load test: _____ Volts Pass: _____ Fail: _____
   c. Third battery: Voltage at end of load test: _____ Volts Pass: _____ Fail: _____
   d. Based on the above results, determine any necessary actions for each battery:

   _____
   _____
   _____
   _____

3. If using an appropriate capacitance tester, record the battery test results:
   a. First battery: Actual battery capacity: _____ CCAs Pass: _____ Fail: _____
   b. Second battery: Actual battery capacity: _____ CCAs Pass: _____ Fail: _____
   c. Third battery: Actual battery capacity: _____ CCAs Pass: _____ Fail: _____
   d. Based on the above results, determine any necessary actions for each battery:

   _____
   _____
   _____
   _____

4. Discuss these findings with your instructor.

Performance Rating

CDX Tasksheet Number: H452

☐ 0   ☐ 1   ☐ 2   ☐ 3   ☐ 4

Supervisor/instructor signature _____ Date_____

© 2017 Jones & Bartlett Learning, LLC, an Ascend Learning Company

Preventive Maintenance Inspection   **499**

▶ **TASK** Inspect starter, mounting, and connections.   **NATEF 7C1.5**

Time off_____

Time on_____

CDX Tasksheet Number: H453

1. Is the starter motor fully secured to engine block and are the mounting bolts tight?
   Yes: _____ No: _____
   a. If no, list the problems and your recommendation(s):

   _____
   _____
   _____

Total time_____

2. Are the starter motor electrical connections tight and is the connector in good condition?
   Yes: _____ No: _____
   a. If no, list the problems and your recommendation(s):

   _____
   _____
   _____

   Note: When servicing the connections on the starter, be careful to disconnect the battery or electrical shorting can result.

3. Discuss the findings with the instructor.

Performance Rating

CDX Tasksheet Number: H453

☐	☐	☐	☐	☐
0	1	2	3	4

Supervisor/instructor signature _____ Date_____

Student/intern information:

Name_____ Date_____ Class_____

Vehicle used for this activity:

Year_____ Make_____ Model_____

Odometer_____ VIN _____

▶ **TASK** Engage starter; check for unusual noises, starter drag, and starting difficulty.

NATEF 7C1.6

Time off_____

Time on_____

Total time_____

CDX Tasksheet Number: H454

1. Insert key into the ignition, ensure that the vehicle is out of gear, and start the engine:
    a. Did the starter engage smoothly, no unusual noises? Yes: _____ No: _____
        i. If no, list the problems and your recommendation(s):

        _____
        _____
        _____

    b. Did the starter drag while the engine was cranking? Yes: _____ No: _____
        i. If the starter dragged while the engine was cranking, list the problems and your recommendation(s):

        _____
        _____
        _____

    c. Were there any other difficulties while starting the engine? Yes: _____ No: _____

    d. If there were other difficulties, describe the symptoms and your recommendation(s):

        _____
        _____
        _____

2. Discuss the finding(s) with the instructor.

Performance Rating

CDX Tasksheet Number: H454

☐ 0   ☐ 1   ☐ 2   ☐ 3   ☐ 4

Supervisor/instructor signature _____ Date_____

Preventive Maintenance Inspection:
Electrical/Electronics–Charging System

Student/intern information:

Name_____ Date_____ Class_____

Vehicle used for this activity:

Year_____ Make_____ Model_____

Odometer_____ VIN _____

Time off_____

Time on_____

Total time_____

Learning Objective / Task	CDX Tasksheet Number	2014 NATEF Priority Level	2014 NATEF Reference Number
• Inspect alternator, mountings, cable, wiring, and wiring routing; determine needed action.	H455	P-1	7C2.1
• Perform alternator output tests.	H456	P-1	7C2.2

Materials Required

- Vehicle
- Vehicle manufacturer's service information
- Manufacturer-specific tools, depending on the concern
- Vehicle lifting equipment, if applicable
- Diagnostic tools
- Battery testing equipment
- Electrical/electronic testing equipment
- Workshop tools
- Hand tools

Some Safety Issues to Consider

- Diagnosis of this fault may require test driving the vehicle on the school grounds or on a hoist, both of which carry severe risks. Attempt this task only with full permission from your supervisor/instructor and follow all the guidelines exactly.
- **Caution:** If you are working in an area where there could be brake dust present (may contain asbestos, which has been determined to cause cancer when inhaled or ingested), wear and use all OSHA-approved asbestos protective/removal equipment.
- Lifting equipment such as vehicle jacks and stands, vehicle hoists, and engine hoists are important tools that increase productivity and make the job easier. However, they can also cause severe injury or death if used improperly. Make sure you follow the manufacturer's operation procedures. Also make sure you have your supervisor/instructor's permission to use any particular type of lifting equipment.
- Comply with personal and environmental safety practices associated with clothing; eye protection; hand tools; power equipment; proper ventilation; and the handling, storage, and disposal of chemicals/materials in accordance with federal, state, and local regulations.
- Always wear the correct protective eyewear and clothing and use the appropriate safety equipment, as well as fender covers, seat protectors, and floor mat protectors.
- Make sure you understand and observe all legislative and personal safety procedures when carrying out practical assignments. If you are unsure of what these are, ask your supervisor/instructor.

Performance Standard

0—No exposure: No information or practice provided during the program; complete training required

1—Exposure only: General information provided with no practice time; close supervision needed; additional training required

2—Limited practice: Has practiced job during training program; additional training required to develop skill

3—Moderately skilled: Has performed job independently during training program; limited additional training may be required

4—Skilled: Can perform job independently with no additional training

Name_____ Date_____ Class_____

Vehicle used for this activity:

Year_____ Make_____ Model_____

Odometer_____ VIN _____

▶TASK Inspect alternator, mountings, cable, wiring, and wiring routing; determine needed action.

NATEF 7C2.1

Time off_____

Time on_____

Total time_____

CDX Tasksheet Number: H455

1. Check alternator mounting security; check that mounting bolts are tight:
    Good: _____ Requires servicing: _____
    a. If requires servicing, list the problems and your recommendation(s):
    _____
    _____
    _____

2. Check alternator wiring connectors and terminal for security and no chafing:
    Good: _____ Requires servicing: _____
    a. If requires servicing, list the problems and your recommendation(s):
    _____
    _____
    _____

3. Check alternator wiring routing for security and no chafing:
    Good: _____ Requires servicing: _____
    a. If requires servicing, list the problems and your recommendation(s):
    _____
    _____
    _____

4. Discuss the findings with the instructor.

Performance Rating

CDX Tasksheet Number: H455

☐   ☐   ☐   ☐   ☐

0   1   2   3   4

Supervisor/instructor signature _____ Date_____

Name_____ Date_____ Class_____

Vehicle used for this activity:

Year_____ Make_____ Model_____

Odometer_____ VIN _____

▶ **TASK** Perform alternator output tests.   NATEF 7C2.2

Time off_____

Time on_____

Total time_____

CDX Tasksheet Number: H456

1. Research the procedure and specifications for performing alternator output tests in the appropriate service information.
   a. Specified regulated charging system voltage: _____ Volts
   b. Specified alternator output: _____ Amps

2. Using an appropriate voltmeter tester, connect the "+" lead of the voltmeter to the "+" output connector of the alternator and the "–" lead of the voltmeter to a grounded location on the chassis (as outlined in the appropriate service information).

3. Start and run engine.

4. Check and record alternator output voltage. _____ Volts

5. Shut engine "off."

6. Disconnect the voltmeter cables.

7. Using an appropriate ammeter tester, connect the amperage tester inductive probe to the alternator output wire. Set the tester for amperage output (depending on equipment manufacturer).

8. Start and run engine.

9. Check and record alternator output amperage. _____ A

10. Shut engine "off."

11. Disconnect the ammeter cables.

12. Reconnect alternator output cable.

13. Discuss the finding(s) with the instructor.

Performance Rating

CDX Tasksheet Number: H456

☐ 0   ☐ 1   ☐ 2   ☐ 3   ☐ 4

Supervisor/instructor signature _____ Date_____

Preventive Maintenance Inspection: Electrical/Electronics–Lighting System

Student/intern information:

Name_____ Date_____ Class_____

Vehicle used for this activity:

Year_____ Make_____ Model_____

Odometer_____ VIN _____

<table>
<tr><td rowspan="2">Learning Objective / Task</td><td>CDX Tasksheet Number</td><td>2014 NATEF Priority Level</td><td>2014 NATEF Reference Number</td></tr>
<tr><td></td><td></td><td></td></tr>
<tr><td>• Check operation of interior lights; determine needed action.</td><td>H457</td><td>P-1</td><td>7C3.1</td></tr>
<tr><td>• Check all exterior lights, lenses, reflectors, and conspicuity tape; check headlight alignment; determine needed action.</td><td>H458</td><td>P-1</td><td>7C3.2</td></tr>
<tr><td>• Inspect and test tractor-to-trailer multi-wire connector(s), cable(s), and holder(s); determine needed action.</td><td>H459</td><td>P-1</td><td>7C3.3</td></tr>
</table>

Time off_____

Time on_____

Total time_____

Materials Required

- Vehicle
- Vehicle manufacturer's service information
- Manufacturer-specific tools, depending on the concern
- Vehicle lifting equipment, if applicable
- Diagnostic tools
- Battery testing equipment
- Electrical/electronic testing equipment
- Workshop tools
- Hand tools

Some Safety Issues to Consider

- Diagnosis of this fault may require test driving the vehicle on the school grounds or on a hoist, both of which carry severe risks. Attempt this task only with full permission from your supervisor/instructor and follow all the guidelines exactly.
- **Caution:** If you are working in an area where there could be brake dust present (may contain asbestos, which has been determined to cause cancer when inhaled or ingested), wear and use all OSHA-approved asbestos protective/removal equipment.
- Lifting equipment such as vehicle jacks and stands, vehicle hoists, and engine hoists are important tools that increase productivity and make the job easier. However, they can also cause severe injury or death if used improperly. Make sure you follow the manufacturer's operation procedures. Also make sure you have your supervisor/instructor's permission to use any particular type of lifting equipment.
- Comply with personal and environmental safety practices associated with clothing; eye protection; hand tools; power equipment; proper ventilation; and the handling, storage, and disposal of chemicals/materials in accordance with federal, state, and local regulations.
- Always wear the correct protective eyewear and clothing and use the appropriate safety equipment, as well as fender covers, seat protectors, and floor mat protectors.
- Make sure you understand and observe all legislative and personal safety procedures when carrying out practical assignments. If you are unsure of what these are, ask your supervisor/instructor.

Performance Standard

0—No exposure: No information or practice provided during the program; complete training required

1—Exposure only: General information provided with no practice time; close supervision needed; additional training required

2—Limited practice: Has practiced job during training program; additional training required to develop skill

3—Moderately skilled: Has performed job independently during training program; limited additional training may be required

4—Skilled: Can perform job independently with no additional training

Name_____ Date_____ Class_____

Vehicle used for this activity:

Year_____ Make_____ Model_____

Odometer_____ VIN _____

▶ **TASK** Check operation of interior lights; determine needed action.   NATEF 7C3.1

CDX Tasksheet Number: H457

1. Check the operation of all interior lights, including sleeper compartment, if applicable:
   All operational: _____ Require servicing: _____
   a. If requires servicing, list the problem light(s) and your recommendation(s):

   _____
   _____
   _____

2. Check light covers of all interior lights, including sleeper compartment, if applicable:
   Good condition: _____ Require servicing: _____
   a. If requires servicing, list the problem light(s) and cover(s) and your recommendation(s):

   _____
   _____
   _____

3. Discuss the findings with the instructor.

Time off_____

Time on_____

Total time_____

Performance Rating

CDX Tasksheet Number: H457

☐ 0   ☐ 1   ☐ 2   ☐ 3   ☐ 4

Supervisor/instructor signature _____ Date_____

Student/intern information:

Name_____ Date_____ Class_____

Vehicle used for this activity:

Year_____ Make_____ Model_____

Odometer_____ VIN _____

▶ **TASK** Check all exterior lights, lenses, reflectors, and conspicuity tape; check headlight alignment; determine needed action.   NATEF 7C3.2

Time off_____

Time on_____

Total time_____

CDX Tasksheet Number: H458

1. Check the operation of all exterior lights, including any auxiliary clearance lights, if applicable:
   All operational: _____ Require servicing: _____
   a. If requires servicing, list the problem light(s) and your recommendation(s):
   _____
   _____
   _____

2. Check light covers of all exterior lights, including any auxiliary clearance lights, if applicable:
   Good: _____ Require servicing: _____
   a. If requires servicing, list the problem light(s) and your recommendation(s):
   _____
   _____
   _____

3. Check all exterior lenses, reflectors, and conspicuity tape:
   Good: _____ Require servicing: _____
   a. If requires servicing, list the problem light(s) and your recommendation(s):
   _____
   _____
   _____

4. Check headlight alignment: Good: _____ Require adjusting: _____
   a. If requires servicing, list the problem light(s) and your recommendation(s):
   _____
   _____

5. After discussing procedure with your instructor, if directed, carry out headlight adjustment. List the steps you performed:
   _____
   _____
   _____

6. Discuss the findings with the instructor.

Performance Rating

CDX Tasksheet Number: H458

☐   ☐   ☐   ☐   ☐
0   1   2   3   4

Supervisor/instructor signature _____ Date_____

Name_____ Date_____ Class_____

Vehicle used for this activity:

Year_____ Make_____ Model_____

Odometer_____ VIN _____

▶ **TASK** Inspect and test tractor-to-trailer multi-wire connector(s), cable(s), and holder(s); determine needed action.

NATEF 7C3.3

Time off_____

Time on_____

Total time_____

CDX Tasksheet Number: H459

1. Check the serviceability of tractor-to-trailer multi-wired connector(s):
   Serviceable: _____ Unserviceable: _____
   a. If unserviceable, list the problems and your recommendation(s):

   _____

   _____

   _____

2. Check the serviceability of tractor-to-trailer multi-wired cable(s) and holder(s):
   Serviceable: _____ Unserviceable: _____
   a. If unserviceable, list the problems and your recommendation(s):

   _____

   _____

   _____

3. Discuss the finding(s) with the instructor.

Performance Rating

CDX Tasksheet Number: H459

☐	☐	☐	☐	☐
0	1	2	3	4

Supervisor/instructor signature _____ Date_____

Preventive Maintenance Inspection:
Frame and Chassis–Air Brakes Part 1

Student/intern information:

Name_____ Date_____ Class_____

Vehicle used for this activity:

Year_____ Make_____ Model_____

Odometer_____ VIN _____

Time off_____

Time on_____

Total time_____

Learning Objective / Task	CDX Tasksheet Number	2014 NATEF Priority Level	2014 NATEF Reference Number
• Check operation of parking brake.	H460	P-1	7D1.1
• Record air governor cut-in and cut-out setting (psi).	H461	P-1	7D1.2
• Check operation of air reservoir/tank drain valves.	H462	P-1	7D1.3
• Check air system for leaks (brakes released).	H463	P-1	7D1.4
• Check air system for leaks (brakes applied).	H464	P-1	7D1.5
• Test one-way and double-check valves.	H465	P-1	7D1.6
• Check low air pressure warning devices.	H466	P-1	7D1.7

Materials Required

- Vehicle
- Vehicle manufacturer's service information
- Manufacturer-specific tools, depending on the concern
- Vehicle lifting equipment, if applicable
- Diagnostic tools
- Electrical/electronic testing equipment
- Measuring equipment
- Workshop tools
- Hand tools

Some Safety Issues to Consider

- Diagnosis of this fault may require test driving the vehicle on the school grounds or on a hoist, both of which carry severe risks. Attempt this task only with full permission from your supervisor/instructor and follow all the guidelines exactly.
- **Caution:** If you are working in an area where there could be brake dust present (may contain asbestos, which has been determined to cause cancer when inhaled or ingested), wear and use all OSHA-approved asbestos protective/removal equipment.
- Lifting equipment such as vehicle jacks and stands, vehicle hoists, and engine hoists are important tools that increase productivity and make the job easier. However, they can also cause severe injury or death if used improperly. Make sure you follow the manufacturer's operation procedures. Also make sure you have your supervisor/instructor's permission to use any particular type of lifting equipment.
- Comply with personal and environmental safety practices associated with clothing; eye protection; hand tools; power equipment; proper ventilation; and the handling, storage, and disposal of chemicals/materials in accordance with federal, state, and local regulations.
- Always wear the correct protective eyewear and clothing and use the appropriate safety equipment, as well as fender covers, seat protectors, and floor mat protectors.

- Make sure you understand and observe all legislative and personal safety procedures when carrying out practical assignments. If you are unsure of what these are, ask your supervisor/instructor.

Performance Standard

0—No exposure: No information or practice provided during the program; complete training required

1—Exposure only: General information provided with no practice time; close supervision needed; additional training required

2—Limited practice: Has practiced job during training program; additional training required to develop skill

3—Moderately skilled: Has performed job independently during training program; limited additional training may be required

4—Skilled: Can perform job independently with no additional training

Name_____ Date_____ Class_____

Vehicle used for this activity:

Year_____ Make_____ Model_____

Odometer_____ VIN _____

▶ **TASK** Check operation of parking brake.   NATEF 7D1.1

CDX Tasksheet Number: H460

Time off_____

Time on_____

Total time_____

1.   Ensure that the air pressure has been completely built up; apply the parking brake:
     Operational: _____ Requires servicing: _____
     a. If requires servicing, list the problem(s) and your recommendation(s):

     _____
     _____
     _____

2.   Ensure that all parking brake chambers have been applied: Yes: _____ No: _____
     a. If no, list the problem and your recommendation(s):

     _____
     _____
     _____

3.   Release the parking brake and inspect to see if all chambers have released.
     a. Chambers released? Yes: _____ No: _____
     b. If no, list the problem and your recommendation(s):

     _____
     _____
     _____

4.   Discuss the findings with the instructor.

Performance Rating

CDX Tasksheet Number: H460

☐   ☐   ☐   ☐   ☐
0   1   2   3   4

Supervisor/instructor signature _____ Date_____

Name_____ Date_____ Class_____

Vehicle used for this activity:

Year_____ Make_____ Model_____

Odometer_____ VIN _____

▶ **TASK** Record air governor cut-in and cut-out setting (psi).　　　　　**NATEF 7D1.2**

CDX Tasksheet Number: H461

Time off_____

Time on_____

Total time_____

1. Reference manufacturer's service information. Record the specified "governor cut-out pressure": _____ psi (kPa)

2. Check air governor cut-in pressure.
   a. Check air compressor governor "cut-out" pressure operation.

   b. By pumping the air brake pedal, remove the air from the system until governor cut-in allows air to be replenished to the system.

      Note: Air governor cut-in pressure should be approximately 90–95 psi (621–655 kPa) and cut-out pressure should be approximately 118–122 psi (814–841 kPa).

   c. Did the governor cut-in occur as specified? Yes: _____ No: _____
      Comments: _____
      _____

   d. If the governor cut-in did not occur as specified, consult the appropriate service information for the proper procedures to repair or replace the air governor. Record the procedures:
      _____
      _____
      _____

3. Discuss the findings with the instructor.

Performance Rating

CDX Tasksheet Number: H461

☐	☐	☐	☐	☐
0	1	2	3	4

Supervisor/instructor signature _____ Date_____

Student/intern information:

Name_____ Date_____ Class_____

Vehicle used for this activity:

Year_____ Make_____ Model_____

Odometer_____ VIN _____

▶ **TASK** Check operation of air reservoir/tank drain valves.   **NATEF 7D1.3**

Time off_____

Time on_____

Total time_____

CDX Tasksheet Number: H462

1. Research the procedure and specifications for checking the air reservoir/tank drain valve operation in the appropriate service information.

2. Following the procedure from the service information, test the air reservoir/tank drain valve(s) operation: Operational: _____ Requires servicing: _____

    a. If requires servicing, list the problem and your recommendation(s):

    _____
    _____
    _____

    Note: Testing can be performed by manually pulling on the release cables attached to the bottom of the valve or by tipping the center valve on the automatic drain valves with a small screw driver.

3. Discuss the findings with the instructor.

Performance Rating

CDX Tasksheet Number: H462

☐   ☐   ☐   ☐   ☐
0   1   2   3   4

Supervisor/instructor signature _____ Date_____

Name_____ Date_____ Class_____

Vehicle used for this activity:

Year_____ Make_____ Model_____

Odometer_____ VIN _____

▶ **TASK** Check air system for leaks (brakes released).   NATEF 7D1.4

CDX Tasksheet Number: H463

Time off_____

Time on_____

Total time_____

1. Research the procedure and specifications for checking the air brake system components for air leaks (brakes released) in the appropriate service information.

2. Following the specified procedure, inspect the air system for leaks. No leaks: _____ Leaks: _____

   a. If leaks are detected, list the areas and your recommendation(s):

   _____

   _____

   _____

   Note: Leaks can be tested by utilizing a soap and water solution in a thermistor bottle. Spray all connections and lines and look for soap bubbles. This process will reveal the source of the leak.

3. Discuss the findings with the instructor.

Performance Rating

CDX Tasksheet Number: H463

☐	☐	☐	☐	☐
0	1	2	3	4

Supervisor/instructor signature _____ Date_____

Student/intern information:

Name_____ Date_____ Class_____

Vehicle used for this activity:

Year_____ Make_____ Model_____

Odometer_____ VIN _____

▶ **TASK** Check air system for leaks (brakes applied).   NATEF 7D1.5

CDX Tasksheet Number: H464

<table>
<tr><td>Time off_____</td></tr>
<tr><td>Time on_____</td></tr>
<tr><td>Total time_____</td></tr>
</table>

1. Research the procedure and specifications for rechecking the air brake system components for air leaks (brakes applied) in the appropriate service information.

2. Following the specified procedure, inspect the air brake system for leaks (brakes applied).
   No leaks: _____ Leaks: _____
   a. If leaks are detected, list the areas and your recommendation(s):

   _____
   _____
   _____

   Note: Leaks can be tested by utilizing a soap and water solution in a thermistor bottle. Spray all connections and lines and look for soap bubbles. This process will reveal the source of the leak.

3. Discuss the findings with the instructor.

Performance Rating

CDX Tasksheet Number: H464

☐	☐	☐	☐	☐
0	1	2	3	4

Supervisor/instructor signature _____ Date_____

Name_____ Date_____ Class_____

Vehicle used for this activity:

Year_____ Make_____ Model_____

Odometer_____ VIN _____

▶ **TASK** Test one-way and double-check valves.   NATEF 7D1.6

CDX Tasksheet Number: H465

Time off_____

Time on_____

Total time_____

1. Following the procedure from the appropriate service information, ensure that the air brake reservoirs are full; with engine "off," remove the inlet pipe to the first air reservoir. Check the fitting on the reservoir for air leaks: No leaks: _____ Leaks: _____
   a. If leaks are detected, list the areas and your recommendation(s):

   _____

   _____

   _____

2. Discuss the findings with the instructor.

Performance Rating

CDX Tasksheet Number: H465

☐	☐	☐	☐	☐
0	1	2	3	4

Supervisor/instructor signature _____ Date_____

Student/intern information:

Name_____ Date_____ Class_____

Vehicle used for this activity:

Year_____ Make_____ Model_____

Odometer_____ VIN _____

▶ **TASK** Check low air pressure warning devices.   **NATEF 7D1.7**

CDX Tasksheet Number: H466

1. Following the procedure from the appropriate service information, ensure that the air brake reservoirs are full; with key "on" and engine "off," apply and release brake pedal until air pressure drops and "low air pressure warning device" is activated:

    a. Air pressure when activated: _____ psi (kPa)

    b. Specifications for air pressure when activated: _____ psi (kPa)

    c. Determine any necessary actions:

    _____

    _____

    _____

2. Discuss the finding(s) with the instructor.

Performance Rating

CDX Tasksheet Number: H466

☐	☐	☐	☐	☐
0	1	2	3	4

Supervisor/instructor signature _____ Date_____

Preventive Maintenance Inspection:
Frame and Chassis—Air Brakes Part 2

Student/intern information:

Name_____ Date_____ Class_____

Vehicle used for this activity:

Year_____ Make_____ Model_____

Odometer_____ VIN _____

Time off_____

Time on_____

Total time_____

Learning Objective / Task	CDX Tasksheet Number	2014 NATEF Priority Level	2014 NATEF Reference Number
• Check emergency (spring) brake control/modulator valve, if applicable.	H467	P-1	7D1.8
• Check tractor protection valve.	H468	P-1	7D1.9
• Test air pressure build-up time.	H469	P-1	7D1.10
• Inspect coupling air lines, holders, and gladhands.	H470	P-1	7D1.11
• Check brake chambers and air lines for secure mounting and damage.	H471	P-1	7D1.12
• Check operation of air drier.	H472	P-1	7D1.13
• Inspect and record brake shoe/pad condition, thickness, and contamination.	H473	P-1	7D1.14
• Inspect and record condition of brake drums/rotors.	H474	P-1	7D1.15

Materials Required

- Vehicle
- Vehicle manufacturer's service information
- Manufacturer-specific tools, depending on the concern
- Vehicle lifting equipment, if applicable
- Diagnostic tools
- Electrical/electronic testing equipment
- Measuring equipment
- Workshop tools
- Hand tools

Some Safety Issues to Consider

- Diagnosis of this fault may require test driving the vehicle on the school grounds or on a hoist, both of which carry severe risks. Attempt this task only with full permission from your supervisor/instructor and follow all the guidelines exactly.
- **Caution:** If you are working in an area where there could be brake dust present (may contain asbestos, which has been determined to cause cancer when inhaled or ingested), wear and use all OSHA-approved asbestos protective/removal equipment.
- Lifting equipment such as vehicle jacks and stands, vehicle hoists, and engine hoists are important tools that increase productivity and make the job easier. However, they can also cause severe injury or death if used improperly. Make sure you follow the manufacturer's operation procedures. Also make sure you have your supervisor/instructor's permission to use any particular type of lifting equipment.
- Comply with personal and environmental safety practices associated with clothing; eye protection; hand tools; power equipment; proper ventilation; and the handling, storage, and disposal of chemicals/materials in accordance with federal, state, and local regulations.

- Always wear the correct protective eyewear and clothing and use the appropriate safety equipment, as well as fender covers, seat protectors, and floor mat protectors.
- Make sure you understand and observe all legislative and personal safety procedures when carrying out practical assignments. If you are unsure of what these are, ask your supervisor/instructor.

Performance Standard

0—No exposure: No information or practice provided during the program; complete training required

1—Exposure only: General information provided with no practice time; close supervision needed; additional training required

2—Limited practice: Has practiced job during training program; additional training required to develop skill

3—Moderately skilled: Has performed job independently during training program; limited additional training may be required

4—Skilled: Can perform job independently with no additional training

Name_____ Date_____ Class_____

Vehicle used for this activity:

Year_____ Make_____ Model_____

Odometer_____ VIN _____

▶ **TASK** Check emergency (spring) brake control/modulator valve, if applicable.   **NATEF 7D1.8**

CDX Tasksheet Number: H467

Time off_____

Time on_____

Total time_____

1. Check operation/functionality of the air brake system–parking brake.
    a. Research the procedure and specifications for checking the spring brake inversion system operation in the appropriate service information.

    b. Ensure that the air pressure has been completely built up; apply parking brake:
        Operational air pressure: _____ psi (kPa)

    c. Shut the engine down.

    d. Install an air pressure gauge in the spring brake air line at the brake chamber:
        Pressure reading: _____ psi (kPa)

    e. Release spring brakes from inside the cabin: Air pressure gauge reading:
        _____ psi (kPa)

    f. Apply spring brakes: Air pressure gauge reading: _____ psi (kPa)

    g. Remove test air pressure gauge and reconnect spring brake hose.

    h. Did the spring brake inversion system operate within specifications?
        Yes: _____ No: _____
        i. If no, list the problem and your recommendation(s):

        _____
        _____
        _____
        _____

2. Discuss the findings with the instructor.

Performance Rating

CDX Tasksheet Number: H467

☐	☐	☐	☐	☐
0	1	2	3	4

Supervisor/instructor signature _____ Date_____

Student/intern information:

Name_____ Date_____ Class_____

Vehicle used for this activity:

Year_____ Make_____ Model_____

Odometer_____ VIN _____

CDX Tasksheet Number: H468

Time off_____

Time on_____

Total time_____

1. Research the procedure and specifications for checking the tractor protection valve system operation in the appropriate service information.

2. Block and/or hold the vehicle by means other than the air brakes during these tests.

3. Drain vehicle reservoirs; ensure that a container(s) is placed under the drain cocks to collect any contaminants. Then close the drain cocks.

4. Disconnect vehicle emergency and service hose couplings and connect assembled hose coupling and test gauge in tractor emergency hose coupling.

5. Start engine and build up system pressure.

6. As pressure in the system builds up there should be no pressure reading on the test gauge. When system pressure reaches 30 psi (210 kPa) on the dash gauge, make and hold a foot or hand valve application and observe that no air escapes at the open service hose coupling.

7. Observe the air pressure on the test gauge: Test pressure gauge reading: _____ psi (kPa)

8. When the system pressure reaches 40 to 60 psi (280 to 420 kPa), the valve should open and the pressure reading show on the test gauge. Allow the system to build up to 100 psi (700 kPa) and shut off engine.

9. With a soap solution, coat the exhaust port of the tractor protection valve. Maximum leakage of a 1" (25mm) bubble in 3 seconds is permissible (175 SCCM).

10. Record the leakage rate: Leakage: _____ in/mm in _____ seconds

11. Remove the test air pressure gauge and reconnect the brake hose.

12. Did the tractor protection valve system operate within specifications? Yes: _____ No: _____
    a. If no, list the problem and your recommendation(s):

    _____

    _____

    _____

13. Discuss the findings with the instructor.

Performance Rating

CDX Tasksheet Number: H468

☐	☐	☐	☐	☐
0	1	2	3	4

Supervisor/instructor signature _____ Date_____

Name_____ Date_____ Class_____

Vehicle used for this activity:

Year_____ Make_____ Model_____

Odometer_____ VIN _____

▶ **TASK** Test air pressure build-up time.   **NATEF 7D1.10**

CDX Tasksheet Number: H469

Time off_____

Time on_____

Total time_____

1. Research the procedure and specifications for checking the air pressure build-up timing in the appropriate service information.

2. Block and/or hold the vehicle by means other than air brakes during these tests.

3. Drain vehicle reservoirs; ensure that a container(s) is placed under the drain cocks to collect any contaminants. Then close the drain cocks.

4. Pressure gauge reading: _____ psi (kPa)

5. Start time of air build: _____ minutes _____ seconds

6. Start engine and build up system pressure.

7. Check pressure as system builds up; record pressure when "low pressure warning device" goes out:
   a. Pressure gauge reading: _____ psi (kPa)
   b. Time to build up to shut off low pressure warning device: _____ minutes _____ seconds

8. Check pressure as system builds up; record pressure when "governor cut-out" pressure is reached:
   a. Pressure gauge reading: _____ psi (kPa)
   b. Time when "governor cut-out" pressure reached: _____ minutes _____ seconds

9. Record total time from start of pumping to reach governor cut-out pressure: _____ minutes _____ seconds

10. Did the air pressure build-up time operate within specifications? Yes: _____ No: _____
    a. If no, list the problem and your recommendation(s):

    _____

    _____

    _____

11. Discuss the findings with the instructor.

Performance Rating

CDX Tasksheet Number: H469

□	□	□	□	□
0	1	2	3	4

Supervisor/instructor signature _____ Date_____

Student/intern information:

Name_____ Date_____ Class_____

Vehicle used for this activity:

Year_____ Make_____ Model_____

Odometer_____ VIN _____

© 2017 Jones & Bartlett Learning, LLC, an Ascend Learning Company

▶ **TASK** Inspect coupling air lines, holders, and gladhands.   NATEF 7D1.11

CDX Tasksheet Number: H470

1. Research the procedure and specifications for checking and inspecting the condition and serviceability of the coupling air lines, holders, and gladhands in the appropriate service information.

    a   Inspect the coupling air lines for cracks and kinking.

        i. Condition of coupling air lines? Good: _____ Bad: _____
    Comments: _____

    _____

        ii. If the condition of the coupling air lines is bad, consult the appropriate service information for the proper procedures to repair or replace the lines. Record the procedures:

    _____

    _____

    b. Check holders for proper mounting to back of cab or frame.

        i. Condition of holders? Good: _____ Bad: _____
    Comments: _____

    _____

        ii. If the condition of the holders is bad, make repairs to properly secure them to their mounting position.

    c. Inspect gladhands for proper sealing to their counterpart and check the rubber sealing for dry rot.

        i. Condition of gladhands? Good: _____ Bad: _____
    Comments: _____

    _____

        ii. If the condition of the gladhands is bad, recommend that they be replaced.

2. Discuss the findings with the instructor.

Performance Rating

CDX Tasksheet Number: H470

☐	☐	☐	☐	☐
0	1	2	3	4

Supervisor/instructor signature _____ Date_____

Student/intern information:

Name_____ Date_____ Class_____

Vehicle used for this activity:

Year_____ Make_____ Model_____

Odometer_____ VIN _____

▶ **TASK** Check brake chambers and air lines for secure mounting and damage. | **NATEF 7D1.12**

CDX Tasksheet Number: H471

Time off_____

Time on_____

Total time_____

1. Research the procedure and specifications to carry out a visual inspection of the air brake chambers, mounting, and air lines in the appropriate service information.
    a. Inspect air brake chambers for proper mounting and condition.
    b. Inspect chambers for dents in the cans and any rust build up on the outside of the chamber.
        i. Condition of chambers? Good: _____ Bad: _____
        Comments: _____

        _____

        ii. If the condition of the chambers is bad, consult the appropriate service information for the proper procedures to repair or replace the chambers. Record the procedures:

        _____

        _____

        _____

    c. Inspect brake chamber mountings for looseness and any damage that may exist.
        i. Is there existing damage? Yes: _____ No: _____
        Comments: _____

        _____

        ii. If damage exists, make the repair to correct the problem.

2. Discuss the findings with the instructor.

Performance Rating

CDX Tasksheet Number: H471

☐	☐	☐	☐	☐
0	1	2	3	4

Supervisor/instructor signature _____ Date_____

Student/intern information:

Name_____ Date_____ Class_____

Vehicle used for this activity:

Year_____ Make_____ Model_____

Odometer_____ VIN _____

▶ **TASK** Check operation of air drier.   NATEF 7D1.13

Time off_____

CDX Tasksheet Number: H472

Time on_____

1. Following the specified procedure in the appropriate service information, check the operation of the air drier.

    a. Air drier: Serviceable: _____ Need repairs/unserviceable: _____

        i. If unserviceable/needs repairs, list the areas and your recommendation(s):

        _____
        _____
        _____
        _____
        _____

Total time_____

2. Discuss the findings with the instructor.

Performance Rating

CDX Tasksheet Number: H472

☐	☐	☐	☐	☐
0	1	2	3	4

Supervisor/instructor signature _____ Date_____

Name_____ Date_____ Class_____

Vehicle used for this activity:

Year_____ Make_____ Model_____

Odometer_____ VIN _____

▶ **TASK** Inspect and record brake shoe/pad condition, thickness, and contamination.

NATEF 7D1.14

Time off_____

Time on_____

Total time_____

CDX Tasksheet Number: H473

1. Research the procedure and specifications for inspecting the brake shoe/pad condition, thickness, and contamination. List the following specifications:
   a. Minimum lining thickness (primary): _____ in/mm
   b. Minimum lining thickness (secondary): _____ in/mm

2. Following the specified procedure, gain access to the brake shoes/pads. Perform the following measurements:
   a. Minimum lining thickness (primary): _____ in/mm
   b. Minimum lining thickness (secondary): _____ in/mm
   c. Are these measurements within specifications? Yes: _____ No: _____
      i. If no, list the problem and your recommendation(s):
      _____
      _____

3. Refit the drum and wheel assembly in accordance with the manufacturer's specifications.

4. Ensure that the wheel lug nuts are torqued to the manufacturer's specification and tightening sequence.

5. Adjust brakes per the appropriate service information.

6. If your instructor approves, road test the vehicle.

7. Discuss the findings with the instructor.

Performance Rating

CDX Tasksheet Number: H473

☐	☐	☐	☐	☐
0	1	2	3	4

Supervisor/instructor signature _____ Date_____

Student/intern information:

Name_____ Date_____ Class_____

Vehicle used for this activity:

Year_____ Make_____ Model_____

Odometer_____ VIN _____

▶ **TASK** Inspect and record condition of brake drums/rotors.   **NATEF 7D1.15**

Time off_____

Time on_____

Total time_____

CDX Tasksheet Number: H474

1. Research the procedure and specifications for determining the condition of the brake drums/rotors. List the following specifications:
   a. Maximum drum diameter: _____ in/mm
   b. Maximum drum out-of-round: _____ in/mm
   c. Minimum rotor thickness: _____ in/mm
   d. Maximum thickness variation: _____ in/mm
   e. Maximum rotor out-of-round: _____ in/mm

2. Following the specified procedure, gain access to the drum/rotor. Measure the drum/rotor and list your readings:
   a. Maximum drum diameter: _____ in/mm
   b. Maximum drum out-of-round: _____ in/mm
   c. Minimum rotor thickness: _____ in/mm
   d. Maximum thickness variation: _____ in/mm
   e. Maximum rotor out-of-round: _____ in/mm
   f. Are these measurements within specifications? Yes: _____ No: _____
      i. If no, list the problem and your recommendation(s):
      _____
      _____
      _____

   g. Reinstall the brake assembly and wheel in accordance with manufacturer's specifications.
   h. Ensure that the wheel lug nuts are torqued to manufacturer's specification and tightening sequence.
   i. Wheel lug nut torque: _____ ft-lb (Nm)
   j. Actual torque: _____ ft-lb (Nm)

3. Discuss the finding(s) with the instructor.

Performance Rating

CDX Tasksheet Number: H474

☐	☐	☐	☐	☐
0	1	2	3	4

Supervisor/instructor signature _____ Date_____

Preventive Maintenance Inspection: Frame and Chassis—Air Brakes Part 3

Student/intern information:

Name_____ Date_____ Class_____

Vehicle used for this activity:

Year_____ Make_____ Model_____

Odometer_____ VIN _____

<table>
<tr><th>Learning Objective / Task</th><th>CDX Tasksheet Number</th><th>2014 NATEF Priority Level</th><th>2014 NATEF Reference Number</th></tr>
<tr><td>• Check antilock braking system (ABS) wiring, connectors, seals, and harnesses for damage and proper routing.</td><td>H475</td><td>P-1</td><td>7D1.16</td></tr>
<tr><td>• Check operation and adjustment of brake automatic slack adjusters (ASA); check and record push rod and stroke.</td><td>H476</td><td>P-1</td><td>7D1.17</td></tr>
<tr><td>• Lubricate all brake component grease fittings.</td><td>H477</td><td>P-1</td><td>7D1.18</td></tr>
<tr><td>• Check condition and operation of hand brake (trailer) control valve, if applicable.</td><td>H478</td><td>P-2</td><td>7D1.19</td></tr>
<tr><td>• Perform antilock brake system (ABS) operational system self-test.</td><td>H479</td><td>P-1</td><td>7D1.20</td></tr>
<tr><td>• Drain air tanks and check for contamination.</td><td>H480</td><td>P-1</td><td>7D1.21</td></tr>
<tr><td>• Check condition of pressure relief (safety) valves.</td><td>H481</td><td>P-1</td><td>7D1.22</td></tr>
</table>

Time off_____

Time on_____

Total time_____

Materials Required

- Vehicle
- Vehicle manufacturer's service information
- Manufacturer-specific tools, depending on the concern
- Vehicle lifting equipment, if applicable
- Diagnostic tools
- Electrical/electronic testing equipment
- Measuring equipment
- Workshop tools
- Hand tools

Some Safety Issues to Consider

- Diagnosis of this fault may require test driving the vehicle on the school grounds or on a hoist, both of which carry severe risks. Attempt this task only with full permission from your supervisor/instructor and follow all the guidelines exactly.
- **Caution:** If you are working in an area where there could be brake dust present (may contain asbestos, which has been determined to cause cancer when inhaled or ingested), wear and use all OSHA-approved asbestos protective/removal equipment.
- Lifting equipment such as vehicle jacks and stands, vehicle hoists, and engine hoists are important tools that increase productivity and make the job easier. However, they can also cause severe injury or death if used improperly. Make sure you follow the manufacturer's operation procedures. Also make sure you have your supervisor/instructor's permission to use any particular type of lifting equipment.
- Comply with personal and environmental safety practices associated with clothing; eye protection; hand tools; power equipment; proper ventilation; and the handling, storage, and disposal of chemicals/materials in accordance with federal, state, and local regulations.

© 2017 Jones & Bartlett Learning, LLC, an Ascend Learning Company

- Always wear the correct protective eyewear and clothing and use the appropriate safety equipment, as well as fender covers, seat protectors, and floor mat protectors.
- Make sure you understand and observe all legislative and personal safety procedures when carrying out practical assignments. If you are unsure of what these are, ask your supervisor/instructor.

Performance Standard

0—No exposure: No information or practice provided during the program; complete training required

1—Exposure only: General information provided with no practice time; close supervision needed; additional training required

2—Limited practice: Has practiced job during training program; additional training required to develop skill

3—Moderately skilled: Has performed job independently during training program; limited additional training may be required

4—Skilled: Can perform job independently with no additional training

Student/intern information:

Name_____ Date_____ Class_____

Vehicle used for this activity:

Year_____ Make_____ Model_____

Odometer_____ VIN _____

▶ **TASK** Check antilock braking system (ABS) wiring, connectors, seals, and harnesses for damage and proper routing.   **NATEF 7D1.16**

CDX Tasksheet Number: H475

Time off_____

Time on_____

Total time_____

1. Research the procedure and specifications to check and inspect wiring, anti-lock brake system connectors, seals, and harnesses for damage and proper routing in the appropriate service information.

2. Consult the appropriate service information's schematics for all wiring associated with the ABS system you are working on.
   a. Inspect wiring for any rubbing or missing insulation and/or bareness.
   b. Condition of wiring? Good: _____ Bad: _____
      Comments: _____
   c. If the condition of the wiring is bad, consult the appropriate service information for the proper procedures to repair the wiring.

3. Check connectors and seals for any signs of weather related damage.
   a. Condition of connectors and/or seals? Good: _____ Bad: _____
      Comments: _____
   b. If the condition of the connectors and/or seals is bad, consult the appropriate service information for the proper procedures to repair the connectors and/or seals.

4. Inspect all harnesses for damage and proper routing.
   a. Condition of harnesses? Good: _____ Bad: _____
      Comments: _____
   b. If the condition of the harnesses is bad, consult the proper procedures to repair any damage or looseness.
   c. Are the harnesses properly routed? Yes: _____ No: _____
   d. If the harnesses are not properly routed, consult the appropriate service information for the proper procedures to repair the routing.

5. Determine any necessary actions:
   _____
   _____

6. Discuss your findings with your instructor.

   Note: Harnesses may be suspended using factory fasteners and may become loose over time.

Performance Rating

CDX Tasksheet Number: H475

☐   ☐   ☐   ☐   ☐

0   1   2   3   4

Supervisor/instructor signature _____ Date_____

Student/intern information:

Name_____ Date_____ Class_____

Vehicle used for this activity:

Year_____ Make_____ Model_____

Odometer_____ VIN _____

▶ **TASK** Check operation and adjustment of brake automatic slack adjusters (ASA); check and record push rod and stroke.

NATEF 7D1.17

CDX Tasksheet Number: H476

1. Research the procedure and specifications for checking the operation and adjustment of the automatic slack adjuster in the appropriate service information.

   a. Inspect each automatic slack adjuster for serviceability. Are they within specifications?
      Yes: _____ No: _____

      i. If no, list the problem and your recommendation(s):

      _____

      _____

      _____

   b. Apply the foundation brakes.

   c. With the brakes applied, check the push-rod stroke. Is it within specifications?
      Yes: _____ No: _____

      Comments: _____

      i. If no, adjust manual slack adjusters to come within vehicle manufacturer's specifications.

      _____

      _____

      _____

2. Discuss the findings with the instructor.

Performance Rating

CDX Tasksheet Number: H476

☐	☐	☐	☐	☐
0	1	2	3	4

Supervisor/instructor signature _____ Date_____

Student/intern information:

Name_____ Date_____ Class_____

Vehicle used for this activity:

Year_____ Make_____ Model_____

Odometer_____ VIN _____

CDX Tasksheet Number: H477

Time off_____

Time on_____

Total time_____

1. Check the lubrication requirements for slack adjusters and support components in the appropriate service information. List the specified lubricant: _____

2. Inspect all grease fittings for damage. Replace as necessary.
   a. Condition of fittings? Good: _____ Bad: _____
      Comments: _____
      Note: Some fittings may not allow grease to pass through them. Replace plugged fittings as necessary.

3. Lubricate all brake components' grease fittings.

4. List any difficulties you had while performing this task, and what you did to solve them:
   _____
   _____
   _____

5. Discuss the findings with the instructor.

Performance Rating

CDX Tasksheet Number: H477

☐   ☐   ☐   ☐   ☐

0   1   2   3   4

Supervisor/instructor signature _____ Date_____

Student/intern information:

Name_____ Date_____ Class_____

Vehicle used for this activity:

Year_____ Make_____ Model_____

Odometer_____ VIN _____

▶ **TASK** Check condition and operation of hand brake (trailer) control valve, if applicable.

NATEF 7D1.19

Time off_____

Time on_____

Total time_____

CDX Tasksheet Number: H478

1. Research the procedure and specifications for checking the condition and operation of the hand brake (trailer) control valve in the appropriate service information.

2. Inspect the hand brake (trailer) control valve. Is it within specifications? Yes: _____ No: _____
    a. If no, list the problem and your recommendation(s):

    _____

    _____

    _____

    _____

3. Discuss the findings with the instructor.

Performance Rating

CDX Tasksheet Number: H478

☐	☐	☐	☐	☐
0	1	2	3	4

Supervisor/instructor signature _____ Date_____

Name_____ Date_____ Class_____

Vehicle used for this activity:

Year_____ Make_____ Model_____

Odometer_____ VIN _____

▶ TASK Perform antilock brake system (ABS) operational system self-test. _____ **NATEF 7D1.20**

Time off_____

Time on_____

Total time_____

CDX Tasksheet Number: H479

1. Research the procedure and specifications for carrying out self-test of the ABS system in the appropriate service information.

2. A self test can be carried out by starting the engine and observing the ABS light.

3. If the light stays illuminated, there is a problem in the system.

    Note: A service tool or scan tool will be required in order to diagnose and repair any problems.

4. Carry out the self-test of the ABS system. Is it within specifications? Yes: _____ No: _____
    a. If no, list the problem and your recommendation(s):

    _____

    _____

    _____

5. Discuss the finding(s) with the instructor.

Performance Rating

CDX Tasksheet Number: H479

☐   ☐   ☐   ☐   ☐

0   1   2   3   4

Supervisor/instructor signature _____ Date_____

Name_____ Date_____ Class_____

Vehicle used for this activity:

Year_____ Make_____ Model_____

Odometer_____ VIN _____

▶ **TASK** Drain air tanks and check for contamination.   **NATEF 7D1.21**

Time off_____

Time on_____

Total time_____

CDX Tasksheet Number: H480

1. Drain the system air tanks.

2. Check the air system safety valves for operation.
   a. List your findings and your comments/recommendation(s):
      _____
      _____
      _____

3. Check the tanks for contamination.
   a. Contamination present? Yes: _____ No: _____
      Comments: _____
      _____

   b. If contamination is present, the system will have to be flushed and cleaned before operation can take place. Also, check operation of the air dryer as this can be a source of contamination.

      Note: A bad compressor can also cause contamination due to oil leaking past the rings.

4. Determine any necessary actions:
   _____
   _____

5. Discuss the findings with the instructor.

Performance Rating

                                        CDX Tasksheet Number: H480

☐	☐	☐	☐	☐
0	1	2	3	4

Supervisor/instructor signature _____ Date_____

Name_____ Date_____ Class_____

Vehicle used for this activity:

Year_____ Make_____ Model_____

Odometer_____ VIN _____

▶ **TASK** Check condition of pressure relief (safety) valves.   **NATEF 7D1.22**

CDX Tasksheet Number: H481

1. Research the procedure and specifications to check and inspect the pressure relief (safety) valves in the appropriate service information.
   a. Specified cutoff pressure: _____ psi (kPa)
   b. Specified pressure relief vavle pop off pressure: _____ psi (KPa)

2. Safety valves can be tested by adjusting governor pressure above standard cutoff pressure.
   Note: Never exceed the pressure relief valve pop off pressure by more than 5 psi (34.5 kPa) or severe injury or death may result

3. At approximately 140 psi (965 kPa), the safety valve should pop off and relieve pressure back to the system pressure of 120 psi (827 kPa).
   a. Did the safety valve exhaust excess pressure? Yes: _____ No: _____
   Comments: _____
   _____

   b. If the safety valve did not exhaust excess pressure, safety valves should be replaced or system damage may result.

4. Determine any necessary actions:
   _____
   _____
   _____

5. Discuss your findings with your instructor and record any recommendations:
   _____
   _____
   _____

Performance Rating

CDX Tasksheet Number: H481

☐	☐	☐	☐	☐
0	1	2	3	4

Supervisor/instructor signature _____ Date_____

Preventive Maintenance Inspection:
Frame and Chassis—Hydraulic Brakes

Student/intern information:

Name_____ Date_____ Class_____

Vehicle used for this activity:

Year_____ Make_____ Model_____

Odometer_____ VIN _____

© 2017 Jones & Bartlett Learning, LLC, an Ascend Learning Company

Learning Objective / Task	CDX Tasksheet Number	2014 NATEF Priority Level	2014 NATEF Reference Number
• Check master cylinder fluid level and condition.	H482	P-1	7D2.1
• Inspect brake lines, fittings, flexible hoses, and valves for leaks and damage.	H483	P-1	7D2.2
• Check parking brake operation; inspect parking brake application and holding devices; adjust as needed.	H484	P-1	7D2.3
• Check operation of hydraulic system: pedal travel, pedal effort, pedal feel.	H485	P-1	7D2.4
• Inspect calipers for, binding, and damage.	H486	P-1	7D2.5
• Inspect brake assist system (booster), hoses, and control valves; check reservoir fluid level and condition.	H487	P-1	7D2.6
• Inspect and record brake lining/pad condition, thickness, and contamination.	H488	P-1	7D2.7
• Inspect and record condition of brake rotors.	H489	P-1	7D2.8
• Check antilock braking system (ABS) wiring, connectors, seals, and harnesses for damage and proper routing.	H490	P-1	7D2.9

Time off_____

Time on_____

Total time_____

Materials Required

- Vehicle
- Vehicle manufacturer's service information
- Manufacturer-specific tools, depending on the concern
- Vehicle lifting equipment, if applicable
- Diagnostic tools
- Electrical/electronic testing equipment
- Measuring equipment
- Workshop tools
- Hand tools

Some Safety Issues to Consider

- Diagnosis of this fault may require test driving the vehicle on the school grounds or on a hoist, both of which carry severe risks. Attempt this task only with full permission from your supervisor/instructor and follow all the guidelines exactly.
- **Caution:** If you are working in an area where there could be brake dust present (may contain asbestos, which has been determined to cause cancer when inhaled or ingested), wear and use all OSHA-approved asbestos protective/removal equipment.

- Lifting equipment such as vehicle jacks and stands, vehicle hoists, and engine hoists are important tools that increase productivity and make the job easier. However, they can also cause severe injury or death if used improperly. Make sure you follow the manufacturer's operation procedures. Also make sure you have your supervisor/instructor's permission to use any particular type of lifting equipment.
- Comply with personal and environmental safety practices associated with clothing; eye protection; hand tools; power equipment; proper ventilation; and the handling, storage, and disposal of chemicals/materials in accordance with federal, state, and local regulations.
- Always wear the correct protective eyewear and clothing and use the appropriate safety equipment, as well as fender covers, seat protectors, and floor mat protectors.
- Make sure you understand and observe all legislative and personal safety procedures when carrying out practical assignments. If you are unsure of what these are, ask your supervisor/instructor.

Performance Standard

0—No exposure: No information or practice provided during the program; complete training required

1—Exposure only: General information provided with no practice time; close supervision needed; additional training required

2—Limited practice: Has practiced job during training program; additional training required to develop skill

3—Moderately skilled: Has performed job independently during training program; limited additional training may be required

4—Skilled: Can perform job independently with no additional training

Student/intern information:

Name_____ Date_____ Class_____

Vehicle used for this activity:

Year_____ Make_____ Model_____

Odometer_____ VIN _____

▶ **TASK** Check master cylinder fluid level and condition.   NATEF 7D2.1

CDX Tasksheet Number: H482

Time off_____

Time on_____

Total time_____

1. Locate brake master cylinder.

2. Clean the top of the cylinder.

3. Open master cylinder cap and check fluid level. Is it at the specified level?
    Yes: _____ Requires top up: _____

4. Collect a sample of current brake fluid.

5. Test the sample for contamination, etc.: Satisfactory: _____ Requires changing: _____
    Comments: _____

    _____

    a. If requires changing, list recommendation(s):

    _____

    _____

6. Discuss the findings with the instructor.

Performance Rating

CDX Tasksheet Number: H482

☐	☐	☐	☐	☐
0	1	2	3	4

Supervisor/instructor signature _____ Date_____

Student/intern information:

Name_____ Date_____ Class_____

Vehicle used for this activity:

Year_____ Make_____ Model_____

Odometer_____ VIN _____

▶ **TASK** Inspect brake lines, fittings, flexible hoses, and valves for leaks and damage.

NATEF 7D2.2

Time off_____

Time on_____

Total time_____

CDX Tasksheet Number: H483

1. Inspect all brake lines, both solid and flexible, for condition and security:
    a. Do they meet the manufacturer's specifications?
        Yes: _____ Require maintenance: _____
        i. If requires maintenance, list areas and recommendation(s):

        _____

        _____

        _____

2. Inspect brake valves for signs of external leakage:
    a. Do they meet the manufacturer's specifications?
        Yes: _____ Require maintenance: _____
        i. If requires maintenance, list areas and recommendation(s):

        _____

        _____

        _____

3. Discuss the findings with the instructor.

Performance Rating

CDX Tasksheet Number: H483

☐   ☐   ☐   ☐   ☐

0   1   2   3   4

Supervisor/instructor signature _____ Date_____

Student/intern information:

Name_____ Date_____ Class_____

Vehicle used for this activity:

Year_____ Make_____ Model_____

Odometer_____ VIN _____

▶ **TASK** Check parking brake operation; inspect parking brake application and holding devices; adjust as needed.

NATEF 7D2.3

Time off_____

Time on_____

Total time_____

CDX Tasksheet Number: H484

1. Research the procedure and specifications for checking the parking brake operation in the appropriate service information.
   a. Following the procedure from the appropriate service information, check and inspect parking brake application, including holding devices.
   b. Most hydraulic parking brakes are mechanically applied via cable and lever assemblies.
   c. Check to see if the cable is adjusted correctly and whether the vehicle is unable to move with it applied.
      i. Is the cable adjusted correctly? Yes: _____ No: _____
         Comments: _____
         _____

      ii. If the cable is not adjusted correctly, consult the appropriate service information for the correct procedures to adjust the parking brake. Record the procedures:
         _____
         _____
         _____

   d. Does it meet the manufacturer's specifications? Yes: _____ Requires maintenance: _____
      i. If requires maintenance, list areas and recommendation(s):
         _____
         _____
         _____

2. Discuss the findings with the instructor.

Performance Rating

CDX Tasksheet Number: H484

☐	☐	☐	☐	☐
0	1	2	3	4

Supervisor/instructor signature _____ Date_____

Student/intern information:

Name_____ Date_____ Class_____

Vehicle used for this activity:

Year_____ Make_____ Model_____

Odometer_____ VIN _____

> TASK Check operation of hydraulic system: pedal travel, pedal effort, pedal feel.

NATEF 7D2.4

Time off_____

Time on_____

Total time_____

CDX Tasksheet Number: H485

1. Research the procedure and specifications to check the operation of the hydraulic brake system in the appropriate service information.
    a. Test pedal travel and security:
        i. Does it meet the manufacturer's specifications?
            Yes: _____ Requires maintenance: _____

            Comments: _____
            _____

            a. If requires maintenance, list areas and recommendation(s):
                _____
                _____

    b. Test pedal effort:
        i. Does it meet the manufacturer's specifications?
            Yes: _____ Requires maintenance: _____

            Comments: _____
            _____

            a. If requires maintenance, list areas and recommendation(s):
                _____
                _____

    c. Check pedal free play:
        i. Does it meet the manufacturer's specifications?
            Yes: _____ Requires maintenance: _____

            Comments: _____
            _____

            a. If requires maintenance, list areas and recommendation(s):
                _____
                _____

2. Discuss the findings with the instructor.

Performance Rating

CDX Tasksheet Number: H485

☐ 0   ☐ 1   ☐ 2   ☐ 3   ☐ 4

Supervisor/instructor signature _____ Date_____

Student/intern information:

Name_____ Date_____ Class_____

Vehicle used for this activity:

Year_____ Make_____ Model_____

Odometer_____ VIN _____

▶ **TASK** Inspect calipers for leakage, binding, and damage.   **NATEF 7D2.5**

CDX Tasksheet Number: H486

1. Research the procedure and specifications for inspecting calipers for leakage, binding, and damage in the appropriate service information.
   a. Check the wheel cylinder dust seal for signs of fluid leakage:
      i. Does it meet the manufacturer's specifications?
         Yes: _____ Requires maintenance: _____

         Comments: _____
         _____

         a. If requires maintenance, list areas and recommendation(s):
            _____
            _____
            _____

   b. Check the disc brake caliper for signs of fluid leakage:
      i. Does it meet the manufacturer's specifications?
         Yes: _____ Requires maintenance: _____

         Comments: _____
         _____

         a. If requires maintenance, list areas and recommendation(s):
            _____
            _____
            _____

2. Discuss the findings with the instructor.

Performance Rating

CDX Tasksheet Number: H486

☐	☐	☐	☐	☐
0	1	2	3	4

Supervisor/instructor signature _____ Date_____

Name_____ Date_____ Class_____

Vehicle used for this activity:

Year_____ Make_____ Model_____

Odometer_____ VIN _____

▶ **TASK** Inspect brake assist system (booster), hoses, and control valves; check reservoir fluid
level and condition.   **NATEF 7D2.6**

CDX Tasksheet Number: H487

Time off_____

Time on_____

Total time_____

1. Inspect brake assist system (booster), hoses, and all brake lines, both solid and flexible, for
    condition and security:
    a. Do they meet the manufacturer's specifications?
        Yes: _____ Requires maintenance: _____

        Comments: _____

        _____

        i. If requires maintenance, list areas and recommendation(s):

            _____

            _____

            _____

2. Inspect power booster(s) and check/control valves operation:
    a. Do they meet the manufacturer's specifications?
        Yes: _____ Requires maintenance: _____

        Comments: _____

        _____

        i. If requires maintenance, list areas and recommendation(s):

            _____

            _____

            _____

3. Check reservoir fluid level and condition.
    a. Fluid level: _____
    b. Condition of fluid: _____
        Comments: _____

        _____

    c. List your recommendations:

        _____

        _____

4. Discuss the findings with the instructor.

Performance Rating

CDX Tasksheet Number: H487

☐	☐	☐	☐	☐
0	1	2	3	4

Supervisor/instructor signature _____ Date_____

Name_____ Date_____ Class_____

Vehicle used for this activity:

Year_____ Make_____ Model_____

Odometer_____ VIN _____

▶ **TASK** Inspect and record brake lining/pad condition, thickness, and contamination.

NATEF 7D2.7

Time off_____

Time on_____

Total time_____

CDX Tasksheet Number: H488

1. Research the procedure and specifications to inspect the brake shoe/pad condition, thickness, and contamination. List the following specifications:
   a. Minimum lining thickness (primary/inner): _____ in/mm
   b. Minimum lining thickness (secondary/outer): _____ in/mm
2. Following the specified procedure, gain access to the brake shoes/pads. Perform the following measurements:
   a. Minimum lining thickness (primary/inner): _____ in/mm
   b. Minimum lining thickness (secondary/outer): _____ in/mm
   c. Is contamination present? Yes: _____ No: _____ Comments:
      _____
      _____
   d. If contamination is present, this will require replacement of the brake linings.
      Note: Contamination may be present from wheel cylinder leakage of brake fluid on the linings. This requires cleaning of the entire brake assembly.

3. Are these measurements and components within specifications? Yes: _____ No: _____
   a. If no, list the problem and your recommendation(s):
      _____
      _____
      _____

4. Discuss the findings with the instructor.

Performance Rating

CDX Tasksheet Number: H488

☐ 0   ☐ 1   ☐ 2   ☐ 3   ☐ 4

Supervisor/instructor signature _____ Date_____

Student/intern information:

Name_____ Date_____ Class_____

Vehicle used for this activity:

Year_____ Make_____ Model_____

Odometer_____ VIN _____

▶ **TASK** Inspect and record condition of brake rotors.   NATEF 7D2.8

CDX Tasksheet Number: H489

Time off_____

Time on_____

Total time_____

1. Research the procedure and specifications to determine the condition of the brake rotors. List the following specifications:
   a. Minimum rotor thickness: _____ in/mm
   b. Maximum thickness variation: _____ in/mm
   c. Maximum rotor out-of-round: _____ in/mm

2. Following the specified procedure, gain access to the rotor. Measure the rotor and list your readings:
   a. Minimum rotor thickness: _____ in/mm
   b. Maximum thickness variation: _____ in/mm
   c. Maximum rotor out-of-round: _____ in/mm

3. Are these measurements within specifications? Yes: _____ No: _____
   a. If no, list the problem and your recommendation(s):

   _____
   _____
   _____

4. Reinstall the brake assembly and wheel in accordance with manufacturer's specifications.

5. Ensure that the wheel lug nuts are torqued to manufacturer's specification and tightening sequence.

6. Wheel lug nut torque: _____ ft-lb (Nm)

7. Actual torque: _____ ft-lb (Nm)

8. Discuss the findings with the instructor.

Performance Rating

CDX Tasksheet Number: H489

☐	☐	☐	☐	☐
0	1	2	3	4

Supervisor/instructor signature _____ Date_____

Student/intern information:

Name_____ Date_____ Class_____

Vehicle used for this activity:

Year_____ Make_____ Model_____

Odometer_____ VIN _____

▶ **TASK** Check antilock braking system wiring, connectors, seals, and harnesses for damage and proper routing.
                                                                          NATEF 7D2.9

Time off_____

Time on_____

Total time_____

CDX Tasksheet Number: H490

1. Research the procedure and specifications to check anti-lock braking system wiring, connectors, seals, and harnesses for damage and proper routing in the appropriate service information. Check anti-lock brake system wiring. Describe your findings.

   _____
   _____
   _____

2. Check connectors, seals, and harnesses for damage and proper routing. Describe your findings.

   _____
   _____
   _____

3. If requires maintenance, list areas and recommendations:

   _____
   _____
   _____

4. Discuss the finding(s) with the instructor.

Performance Rating

CDX Tasksheet Number: H490

☐ 0   ☐ 1   ☐ 2   ☐ 3   ☐ 4

Supervisor/instructor signature _____ Date_____

Preventive Maintenance Inspection:
Frame and Chassis—Drive Train

Student/intern information:

Name_____ Date_____ Class_____

Vehicle used for this activity:

Year_____ Make_____ Model_____

Odometer_____ VIN _____

Learning Objective / Task	CDX Tasksheet Number	2014 NATEF Priority Level	2014 NATEF Reference Number
• Check operation of clutch, clutch brake, and gearshift.	H491	P-1	7D3.1
• Check clutch linkage/cable for looseness or binding, if applicable.	H492	P-1	7D3.2
• Check hydraulic clutch slave and master cylinders, lines, fittings, and hoses, if applicable.	H493	P-1	7D3.3
• Check clutch adjustment; adjust as needed.	H494	P-1	7D3.4
• Check transmission case, seals, filter, hoses, and cooler for cracks and leaks.	H495	P-1	7D3.5
• Inspect transmission breather.	H496	P-1	7D3.6
• Inspect transmission mounts.	H497	P-1	7D3.7
• Check transmission oil level, type, and condition.	H498	P-1	7D3.8
• Inspect U-joints, yokes, drive shafts, boots/seals, center bearings, and mounting hardware for looseness, damage, and proper phasing.	H499	P-1	7D3.9
• Inspect axle housing(s) for cracks and leaks.	H500	P-1	7D3.10
• Inspect axle breather(s).	H501	P-1	7D3.11
• Lubricate all drive train grease fittings.	H502	P-1	7D3.12
• Check drive axle(s) oil level, type, and condition.	H503	P-1	7D3.13
• Change drive axle(s) oil and filter/screen, if applicable; check and clean magnetic plugs.	H504	P-2	7D3.14
• Check transmission wiring, connectors, seals, and harnesses for damage and proper routing.	H505	P-1	7D3.15
• Change transmission oil and filter; check and clean magnetic plugs.	H506	P-2	7D3.16
• Check interaxle differential lock operation.	H507	P-1	7D3.17
• Check transmission range shift operation.	H508	P-1	7D3.18

Time off_____

Time on_____

Total time_____

Materials Required

- Vehicle
- Vehicle manufacturer's service information
- Manufacturer-specific tools, depending on the concern
- Vehicle lifting equipment, if applicable
- Diagnostic tools
- Electrical/electronic testing equipment
- Measuring equipment
- Workshop tools
- Hand tools

Some Safety Issues to Consider

- Diagnosis of this fault may require test driving the vehicle on the school grounds or on a hoist, both of which carry severe risks. Attempt this task only with full permission from your supervisor/instructor and follow all the guidelines exactly.

- **Caution:** If you are working in an area where there could be brake dust present (may contain asbestos, which has been determined to cause cancer when inhaled or ingested), wear and use all OSHA-approved asbestos protective/removal equipment.

- Lifting equipment such as vehicle jacks and stands, vehicle hoists, and engine hoists are important tools that increase productivity and make the job easier. However, they can also cause severe injury or death if used improperly. Make sure you follow the manufacturer's operation procedures. Also make sure you have your supervisor/instructor's permission to use any particular type of lifting equipment.

- Comply with personal and environmental safety practices associated with clothing; eye protection; hand tools; power equipment; proper ventilation; and the handling, storage, and disposal of chemicals/materials in accordance with federal, state, and local regulations.

- Always wear the correct protective eyewear and clothing and use the appropriate safety equipment, as well as fender covers, seat protectors, and floor mat protectors.

- Make sure you understand and observe all legislative and personal safety procedures when carrying out practical assignments. If you are unsure of what these are, ask your supervisor/instructor.

Performance Standard

0—No exposure: No information or practice provided during the program; complete training required

1—Exposure only: General information provided with no practice time; close supervision needed; additional training required

2—Limited practice: Has practiced job during training program; additional training required to develop skill

3—Moderately skilled: Has performed job independently during training program; limited additional training may be required

4—Skilled: Can perform job independently with no additional training

Student/intern information:

Name_____ Date_____ Class_____

Vehicle used for this activity:

Year_____ Make_____ Model_____

Odometer_____ VIN _____

▶**TASK** Check operation of clutch, clutch brake, and gearshift. **NATEF 7D3.1**

CDX Tasksheet Number: H491

Time off_____	
Time on_____	
Total time_____	

1. Research the procedure and specifications to check the operation of the clutch, clutch brake, and gearshift in the appropriate service information.

   a. Clutch:

      i. Does it meet the manufacturer's specifications?
         Yes: _____ Requires maintenance: _____
         Comments: _____

         _____

         a. If requires maintenance, list areas and recommendation(s):

            _____
            _____
            _____

   b. Clutch brake:

      i. Start the vehicle.

      ii. Push the clutch pedal in.

      iii. Select a gear.

      iv. Is gear selection smooth? Yes: _____ No: _____
          Comments: _____

          _____

      v. If gear selection is not smooth, consult the appropriate service information for the proper procedure to replace or repair the clutch brake system. Record the procedures:

         _____
         _____
         _____

      vi. Does it meet the manufacturer's specifications?
          Yes: _____ Requires maintenance: _____
          Comments: _____

          _____

          a. If requires maintenance, list areas and recommendation(s):

             _____
             _____
             _____

          Note: The clutch brake is used to stop the input shaft from turning while stopping, starting out, and backing up in order to eliminate gear clash.

    c. Gearshift:
        i. Does it meet the manufacturer's specifications?

           Yes: _____ Requires maintenance: _____

           Comments: _____

           _____

           a. If requires maintenance, list areas and recommendation(s):

              _____

              _____

              _____

2. Discuss the findings with the instructor.

Performance Rating

CDX Tasksheet Number: H491

☐	☐	☐	☐	☐
0	1	2	3	4

Supervisor/instructor signature _____ Date_____

Student/intern information:

Name_____ Date_____ Class_____

Vehicle used for this activity:

Year_____ Make_____ Model_____

Odometer_____ VIN _____

▶ **TASK** Check clutch linkage/cable for looseness or binding, if applicable.　　**NATEF 7D3.2**

CDX Tasksheet Number: H492

Time off_____

Time on_____

Total time_____

1.　Research the procedure and specifications to check the clutch linkage/cable for looseness or binding, if applicable, in the appropriate service information.
　　a.　Clutch linkage/cable for any evidence of binding or looseness:
　　　　i.　Does it meet the manufacturer's specifications?
　　　　　Yes: _____ Requires maintenance: _____
　　　　　Comments: _____
　　　　　_____

　　　　a.　If requires maintenance, list areas and recommendation(s):
　　　　　_____
　　　　　_____
　　　　　_____

2.　Discuss the findings with the instructor.

Performance Rating

CDX Tasksheet Number: H492

☐ 0　　☐ 1　　☐ 2　　☐ 3　　☐ 4

Supervisor/instructor signature _____ Date_____

Student/intern information:

Name_____ Date_____ Class_____

Vehicle used for this activity:

Year_____ Make_____ Model_____

Odometer_____ VIN _____

▶ **TASK** Check hydraulic clutch slave and master cylinders, lines, fittings, and hoses, if applicable.

NATEF 7D3.3

Time off_____

Time on_____

Total time_____

CDX Tasksheet Number: H493

1. Research the procedure and specifications to check hydraulic clutch slave and master cylinders, lines, fittings, and hoses, if applicable, in the appropriate service information.
    a. Do they meet the manufacturer's specifications?
        Yes: _____ Requires maintenance: _____
        Comments: _____

        _____

        i. If requires maintenance, list areas and recommendation(s):

            _____
            _____
            _____

2. Check the serviceability of the hydraulic clutch cylinder lines, fittings, and hoses:
    a. Do they meet the manufacturer's specifications?
        Yes: _____ Requires maintenance: _____
        Comments: _____

        _____

        i. If requires maintenance, list areas and recommendation(s):

            _____
            _____
            _____

3. Discuss the findings with the instructor.

Performance Rating

CDX Tasksheet Number: H493

☐	☐	☐	☐	☐
0	1	2	3	4

Supervisor/instructor signature _____ Date_____

Name_____ Date_____ Class_____

Vehicle used for this activity:

Year_____ Make_____ Model_____

Odometer_____ VIN _____

▶ **TASK** Check clutch adjustment; adjust as needed. _____ **NATEF 7D3.4**

CDX Tasksheet Number: H494

Time off_____

Time on_____

Total time_____

1. Research the procedure and specifications to check the clutch adjustment in the appropriate service information. List the following specifications:
   a. Clutch pedal free play: _____ in/mm

2. Following the specified procedure, check the clutch pedal adjustment.
   a. Does it meet the manufacturer's specifications?
      Yes: _____ Requires maintenance: _____
      Comments: _____
      _____

      i. If requires maintenance, list areas and recommendation(s):
         _____
         _____
         _____

3. Discuss the findings with the instructor.

Performance Rating

CDX Tasksheet Number: H494

☐   ☐   ☐   ☐   ☐
0   1   2   3   4

Supervisor/instructor signature _____ Date_____

Student/intern information:

Name_____ Date_____ Class_____

Vehicle used for this activity:

Year_____ Make_____ Model_____

Odometer_____ VIN _____

▶ **TASK** Check transmission case, seals, filter, hoses, and cooler for cracks and leaks.

NATEF 7D3.5

Time off_____

Time on_____

Total time_____

CDX Tasksheet Number: H495

1. Research the procedure and specifications to check the transmission case, seals, filter, hoses, and cooler for cracks and leaks in the appropriate service information.
   a. Do they meet the manufacturer's specifications?
      Yes: _____ Requires maintenance: _____
      Comments: _____
      _____

      i. If requires maintenance, list areas and recommendation(s):
         _____
         _____
         _____

2. Check the condition and serviceability of the transmission filter, hoses, lines, and cooler:
   a. Do they meet the manufacturer's specifications?
      Yes: _____ Requires maintenance: _____
      Comments: _____
      _____

      i. If requires maintenance, list areas and recommendation(s):
         _____
         _____
         _____

3. Discuss the findings with the instructor.

Performance Rating

CDX Tasksheet Number: H495

☐	☐	☐	☐	☐
0	1	2	3	4

Supervisor/instructor signature _____ Date_____

Student/intern information:

Name_____ Date_____ Class_____

Vehicle used for this activity:

Year_____ Make_____ Model_____

Odometer_____ VIN _____

▶ **TASK** Inspect transmission breather.

CDX Tasksheet Number: H496

1. Research the procedure and specifications to check the condition and serviceability of the transmission breather in the appropriate service information.
   a. Remove the breather assembly.
   b. Shake it back and forth. If it feels like a ball is shaking inside, it is in good shape.
      i. Does it feel loose? Yes: _____ No: _____
         Comments: _____
         _____

      ii. If it does not feel loose, replace it.

         Note: If the breather is clogged it will allow the transmission to build pressure and damage the seals inside it.

2. Determine any necessary actions:
   _____
   _____

3. Discuss the findings with the instructor.

Performance Rating

CDX Tasksheet Number: H496

☐   ☐   ☐   ☐   ☐

0   1   2   3   4

Supervisor/instructor signature _____ Date_____

Student/intern information:

Name_____ Date_____ Class_____

Vehicle used for this activity:

Year_____ Make_____ Model_____

Odometer_____ VIN _____

▶ **TASK** Inspect transmission mounts.   NATEF 7D3.7

CDX Tasksheet Number: H497

1. Research the procedure and specifications to inspect the transmission mounts for dry rot or oil contamination in the appropriate service information.
   a. Is contamination present? Yes: _____ No: _____
      Comments: _____
      _____

   b. If contamination is present, it is good practice is to replace the mounts.

2. Determine any necessary actions:
   _____
   _____

3. Discuss the findings with the instructor.

Performance Rating

CDX Tasksheet Number: H497

☐	☐	☐	☐	☐
0	1	2	3	4

Supervisor/instructor signature _____ Date_____

Student/intern information:

Name_____ Date_____ Class_____

Vehicle used for this activity:

Year_____ Make_____ Model_____

Odometer_____ VIN _____

▶ **TASK** Check transmission oil level, type, and condition.   **NATEF 7D3.8**

CDX Tasksheet Number: H498

Time off_____

Time on_____

Total time_____

1. Research the procedure and specifications to follow all OSHA safety/environmental protection requirements in the appropriate service information.
    a. Clean around transmission filler plug to ensure no contaminants can enter the transmission.
    b. Remove the filler plug and check fluid level. Good: _____ Requires maintenance: _____
        Comments: _____
        _____

        i.   If requires maintenance, list areas and recommendation(s):
             _____
             _____
             _____

        ii. Consult the appropriate service information for the proper type of fluid to be used in this particular transmission.
             a. Type: _____
             b. Quantity: _____ gallons (liters)

    c. Collect an oil sample in a clean, sterile container to be sent for analysis.

2. Determine any necessary actions:
    _____
    _____

3. Discuss the finding(s) with the instructor.

Performance Rating

CDX Tasksheet Number: H498

☐	☐	☐	☐	☐
0	1	2	3	4

Supervisor/instructor signature _____ Date_____

Student/intern information:

Name_____ Date_____ Class_____

Vehicle used for this activity:

Year_____ Make_____ Model_____

Odometer_____ VIN _____

▶ TASK Inspect U-joints, yokes, drive shafts, boots/seals, center bearings, and mounting hardware for looseness, damage, and proper phasing.   **NATEF 7D3.9**

CDX Tasksheet Number: H499

1. Research the procedure and specifications to inspect U-joints, yokes, drive shafts, boots/seals, center bearings, and mounting hardware for looseness, damage, and proper phasing in the appropriate service information.

   a. Inspect the U-joints:

      i. Do they meet the manufacturer's specifications?

         Yes: _____ Requires maintenance: _____

         Comments: _____

         _____

         a. If requires maintenance, list areas and recommendation(s):

            _____
            _____
            _____

   b. Inspect the driveline yokes:

      i. Do they meet the manufacturer's specifications?

         Yes: _____ Requires maintenance: _____

         Comments: _____

         _____

         a. If requires maintenance, list areas and recommendation(s):

            _____
            _____
            _____

   c. Inspect the driveshafts:

      i. Do they meet the manufacturer's specifications?

         Yes: _____ Requires maintenance: _____

         Comments: _____

         _____

         a. If requires maintenance, list areas and recommendation(s):

            _____
            _____
            _____

d. Inspect the boots/seals:
   i. Do they meet the manufacturer's specifications?
     Yes: _____ Requires maintenance: _____
     Comments: _____

     _____

       a. If requires maintenance, list areas and recommendation(s):

       _____

       _____

       _____

e. Inspect the center bearing:
   i. Do they meet the manufacturer's specifications?
     Yes: _____ Requires maintenance: _____
     Comments: _____

     _____

       a. If requires maintenance, list areas and recommendation(s):

       _____

       _____

       _____

f. Mounting hardware:
   i. Do they meet the manufacturer's specifications?
     Yes: _____ Requires maintenance: _____
     Comments: _____

     _____

       a. If requires maintenance, list areas and recommendation(s):

       _____

       _____

       _____

g. Check for proper phasing for driveline:
   i. Do they meet the manufacturer's specifications?
     Yes: _____ Requires maintenance: _____
     Comments: _____

     _____

       a. If requires maintenance, list areas and recommendation(s):

       _____

       _____

       _____

2. Discuss the findings with the instructor.

Performance Rating

CDX Tasksheet Number: H499

☐   ☐   ☐   ☐   ☐

0   1   2   3   4

Supervisor/instructor signature _____ Date_____

Name_____ Date_____ Class_____

Vehicle used for this activity:

Year_____ Make_____ Model_____

Odometer_____ VIN _____

▶ **TASK** Inspect axle housing(s) for cracks and leaks.   NATEF 7D3.10

CDX Tasksheet Number: H500

Time off_____

Time on_____

Total time_____

1. Research the procedure and specifications to inspect the serviceability and condition (including any damage) of the rear axle housing(s) in the appropriate service information.
   a. Do they meet the manufacturer's specifications?
      Yes: _____ Requires maintenance: _____
      Comments: _____
      _____

      i. If requires maintenance, list areas and recommendation(s):
         _____
         _____
         _____

      Note: If axle housing is cracked, signs of leakage will be present at the source of the crack.

2. Discuss the findings with the instructor.

Performance Rating

CDX Tasksheet Number: H500

☐   ☐   ☐   ☐   ☐
0   1   2   3   4

Supervisor/instructor signature _____ Date_____

Student/intern information:

Name_____ Date_____ Class_____

Vehicle used for this activity:

Year_____ Make_____ Model_____

Odometer_____ VIN _____

▶ TASK Inspect axle breather(s).   NATEF 7D3.11

CDX Tasksheet Number: H501

Time off_____

Time on_____

Total time_____

1. Research the procedure and specifications to inspect the breather assembly in the appropriate service information. Remove the breather assembly.

2. Shake it back and forth. If it feels like a ball is shaking inside, it is in good shape.
   a. Does it feel loose? Yes: _____ No: _____
      Comments: _____

      _____

   b. If no, replace it.
      Note: If the breather is clogged it will allow the axle to build pressure and damage the seals inside it.

3. Determine any necessary actions or corrections:

   _____

   _____

4. Discuss the findings with the instructor.

Performance Rating

CDX Tasksheet Number: H501

☐ 0   ☐ 1   ☐ 2   ☐ 3   ☐ 4

Supervisor/instructor signature _____ Date_____

▶ **TASK** Lubricate all drive train grease fittings.   NATEF 7D3.12

CDX Tasksheet Number: H502

1. Research the procedure and specifications for the lubrication requirements for the drive train/axle componentry in the appropriate service information.
   a. List the specified lubricant: _____

2. Following the procedure from the service information, lubricate the appropriate components identified.

3. For reference, list all lubrication sites below.

   _____
   _____
   _____
   _____
   _____
   _____
   _____
   _____
   _____
   _____

4. Discuss the findings with the instructor.

Performance Rating

CDX Tasksheet Number: H502

☐	☐	☐	☐	☐
0	1	2	3	4

Supervisor/instructor signature _____ Date_____

Student/intern information:

Name_____ Date_____ Class_____

Vehicle used for this activity:

Year_____ Make_____ Model_____

Odometer_____ VIN _____

▶ **TASK** Check drive axle(s) oil level, type, and condition.   NATEF 7D3.13

Time off_____

Time on_____

Total time_____

CDX Tasksheet Number: H503

1. Research the procedure and specifications to follow all OSHA safety/environmental protection requirements in the appropriate service information.
   a. List the specified axle lubricant: _____

2. Clean around axle filler plug(s) to ensure no contaminants can enter the rear axle assembly.
   a. Remove the filler plug(s) and check fluid level and type.
      Good: _____ Requires maintenance: _____
      Comments: _____
      _____

      i. If requires maintenance, list areas and recommendation(s):
         _____
         _____

   b. With your instructor's approval, collect an oil sample in a clean, sterile container(s) to be sent for analysis from each axle assembly and clearly label the sample(s) identifying which axle assembly it is from.

   c. Clean the filler plug and replace; torque filler plug to manufacturer's specifications:
      i. Manufacturer's torque specification: _____ ft-lb (Nm)

3. Discuss the findings with the instructor.

Performance Rating

CDX Tasksheet Number: H503

☐	☐	☐	☐	☐
0	1	2	3	4

Supervisor/instructor signature _____ Date_____

Name_____ Date_____ Class_____

Vehicle used for this activity:

Year_____ Make_____ Model_____

Odometer_____ VIN _____

Time off_____

Time on_____

Total time_____

▶ **TASK** Change drive axle(s) oil and filter/screen, if applicable; check and clean magnetic plugs.

NATEF 7D3.14

CDX Tasksheet Number: H504

1. Research the procedure and specifications to follow all OSHA safety/environmental protection requirements in the appropriate service information.

   a. Using a collection container adequate for the amount of oil to be drained, clean around the drain plug(s).

   b. Remove drain plug(s).

   c. With your instructor's approval, collect an oil sample from each axle assembly in a clean, sterile container(s) to be sent for analysis from each axle assembly and clearly label the sample(s) identifying which axle assembly it is from.

   d. Inspect magnetic drain plug(s) for any signs of foreign particles.
   Comments: _____

   _____

   e. Clean drain plug(s).

   f. Replace drain plug(s); torque filler plug to manufacturer's specifications:
      i. Manufacturer's torque specification: _____ ft-lb (Nm)

   g. Change axle assembly oil filter(s), if applicable.

   h. Clean around axle filler plug(s) to ensure no contaminants can enter the rear axle assembly.

   i. Remove the filler plug(s) and refill differential housings with the correct type and quantity of oil:
      i. Specified oil type: _____
      ii. Specified oil quantity: _____ quarts (liters)

   j. Clean the filler plug and replace; torque filler plug to manufacturer's specifications:
      i. Manufacturer's torque specification: _____ ft-lb (Nm)

2. Discuss the findings with the instructor.

Performance Rating

CDX Tasksheet Number: H504

☐   ☐   ☐   ☐   ☐

0   1   2   3   4

Supervisor/instructor signature _____ Date_____

Student/intern information:

Name_____ Date_____ Class_____

Vehicle used for this activity:

Year_____ Make_____ Model_____

Odometer_____ VIN _____

Time off_____

Time on_____

Total time_____

▶ **TASK** Check transmission wiring, connectors, seals, and harnesses for damage and proper routing.   NATEF 7D3.15

CDX Tasksheet Number: H505

1. Research the procedure and specifications to check the transmission wiring, connectors, seals, and harnesses for damage and proper routing in the appropriate service information.

2. Consult the appropriate service information's schematics for all wiring associated with the model transmission you are working on.
    a. Inspect the wiring for any rubbing or missing insulation and bareness.
    b. Condition of wiring? Good: _____ Bad: _____
        Comments: _____
        _____
    c. If the condition of the wiring is bad, consult the proper procedures to make a repair.

3. Check connectors and seals for any signs of weather related damage.
    a. Condition of connectors and seals? Good: _____ Bad: _____
        Comments: _____
        _____
    b. If the condition of the connectors and/or seals is bad, consult the proper procedures to make a repair.

4. Inspect all harnesses for damage and proper routing.
    a. Condition of harnesses and proper routing? Good: _____ Bad: _____
        Comments: _____
        _____
    b. If the condition of the harnesses is bad or they are improperly routed, consult the proper procedures to repair any damage or looseness that exists.

5. Determine any necessary actions:
    _____
    _____

6. Discuss your findings with your instructor.

    Note: Harnesses may be suspended using factory fasteners and may come loose over time.

© 2017 Jones & Bartlett Learning, LLC, an Ascend Learning Company

Performance Rating

CDX Tasksheet Number: H505

☐ 0   ☐ 1   ☐ 2   ☐ 3   ☐ 4

Supervisor/instructor signature _____ Date_____

Name_____ Date_____ Class_____

Vehicle used for this activity:

Year_____ Make_____ Model_____

Odometer_____ VIN _____

▶ **TASK** Change transmission oil and filter, if applicable; check and clean magnetic plugs.

NATEF 7D3.16

CDX Tasksheet Number: H506

1. Research the procedure and specifications to change the transmission oil and filter, if applicable, in the appropriate service information; list the following specifications:
   a. Specified oil type: _____
   b. Specified oil capacity: _____ quarts (liters)

2. Change transmission oil filter(s), if applicable. List your observations:
   _____
   _____

3. Clean around transmission filler plug to ensure that no contaminants can enter the rear axle assembly.

4. Remove the filler plug and check it for particles. List your observations:
   _____
   _____

   a. Determine any necessary actions or corrections:
   _____
   _____

5. Refill the transmission with the correct type and quantity of oil.
   a. Actual quantity filled: _____ quarts (liters)

6. Clean the filler plug and replace; torque filler plug to manufacturer's specifications:
   a. Manufacturer's torque specification: _____ ft-lb (Nm)

7. Determine any necessary action(s):
   _____
   _____
   _____

8. Discuss the finding(s) with the instructor.

Performance Rating

CDX Tasksheet Number: H506

☐	☐	☐	☐	☐
0	1	2	3	4

Supervisor/instructor signature _____ Date_____

Name_____ Date_____ Class_____

Vehicle used for this activity:

Year_____ Make_____ Model_____

Odometer_____ VIN _____

▶ **TASK** Check interaxle differential lock operation.   NATEF 7D3.17

Time off_____

Time on_____

Total time_____

CDX Tasksheet Number: H507

1. Research the procedure and specifications to check and operate the interaxle differential lock in the appropriate service information.

2. To check the operation of the interaxle differential lock, jack up the rear differential so the rear wheels are off the ground.

   Note: On a tandem axle setup, the rear axle is the main drive axle. Once the interaxle differential is engaged, the front axle can also supply power to the ground. At this point both axles are driving the vehicle.

3. With the rear axle off of the ground, engage the interaxle differential lock. With the transmission in neutral, turn the front drive shaft manually.

4. If the axle is engaged properly, the drive shaft should not be able to turn.

5. Interaxle differential lock operation: Engaged: _____ Not engaged: _____
   Comments: _____
   _____

   a. If the lock operation is not engaged, the drive shaft will turn freely.

   b. Consult the appropriate service information for procedures to diagnose the fault.

      Note: If electronically engaged, check all wiring and solenoids. If air-operated, look for any leaks or kinked lines blocking distribution of air to the lock cylinder.

6. Determine any necessary actions:
   _____
   _____

7. Discuss your findings with your instructor.

Performance Rating

CDX Tasksheet Number: H507

☐	☐	☐	☐	☐
0	1	2	3	4

Supervisor/instructor signature _____ Date_____

Student/intern information:

Name_____ Date_____ Class_____

Vehicle used for this activity:

Year_____ Make_____ Model_____

Odometer_____ VIN _____

▶ **TASK** Check transmission range shift operation. NATEF 7D3.18

CDX Tasksheet Number: H508

Time off_____

Time on_____

Total time_____

1. Research the procedure and specifications to operate the range shift for the transmission in the appropriate service information.

2. Check the vehicle shifter by manually operating through each of the available gears.

   a. Are all gears available? Yes: _____ No: _____

   b. Is there any binding or roughness while shifting? Yes: _____ No: _____
      Comments: _____
      _____

   c. If it is an automatic transmission, check to make sure the cable is adjusted properly.
      i. Cable operation? Good: _____ Bad: _____
         Comments: _____
         _____

      ii. If electronic shift, a service tool or scan tool may be required.

3. Determine any necessary actions:
   _____
   _____

4. Discuss your findings with your instructor.

Performance Rating

CDX Tasksheet Number: H508

☐	☐	☐	☐	☐
0	1	2	3	4

Supervisor/instructor signature _____ Date_____

Preventive Maintenance Inspection:
Frame and Chassis—Suspension and Steering Systems Part 1

Student/intern information:

Name_____ Date_____ Class_____

Vehicle used for this activity:

Year_____ Make_____ Model_____

Odometer_____ VIN _____

© 2017 Jones & Bartlett Learning, LLC, an Ascend Learning Company

Learning Objective / Task	CDX Tasksheet Number	2014 NATEF Priority Level	2014 NATEF Reference Number
• Check steering wheel operation for free play or binding.	H509	P-1	7D4.1
• Check power steering pump, mounting, and hoses for leaks, condition, and routing; check fluid level.	H510	P-1	7D4.2
• Change power steering fluid and filter.	H511	P-1	7D4.3
• Inspect steering gear for leaks and secure mounting.	H512	P-1	7D4.4
• Inspect steering shaft U-joints, pinch bolts, splines, pitman arm-to-steering sector shaft, tie-rod ends, and linkages.	H513	P-1	7D4.5
• Check kingpins for wear.	H514	P-1	7D4.6
• Check wheel bearings for looseness and noise.	H515	P-1	7D4.7
• Check oil level and condition in all non-drive hubs; check for leaks.	H516	P-1	7D4.8

Time off_____

Time on_____

Total time_____

Materials Required

- Vehicle
- Vehicle manufacturer's service information
- Manufacturer-specific tools, depending on the concern
- Vehicle lifting equipment, if applicable
- Diagnostic tools
- Electrical/electronic testing equipment
- Measuring equipment
- Workshop tools
- Hand tools

Some Safety Issues to Consider

- Diagnosis of this fault may require test driving the vehicle on the school grounds or on a hoist, both of which carry severe risks. Attempt this task only with full permission from your supervisor/instructor and follow all the guidelines exactly.
- **Caution:** If you are working in an area where there could be brake dust present (may contain asbestos, which has been determined to cause cancer when inhaled or ingested), wear and use all OSHA-approved asbestos protective/removal equipment.
- Lifting equipment such as vehicle jacks and stands, vehicle hoists, and engine hoists are important tools that increase productivity and make the job easier. However, they can also cause severe injury or death if used improperly. Make sure you follow the manufacturer's operation procedures. Also make sure you have your supervisor/instructor's permission to use any particular type of lifting equipment.

- Comply with personal and environmental safety practices associated with clothing; eye protection; hand tools; power equipment; proper ventilation; and the handling, storage, and disposal of chemicals/materials in accordance with federal, state, and local regulations.
- Always wear the correct protective eyewear and clothing and use the appropriate safety equipment, as well as fender covers, seat protectors, and floor mat protectors.
- Make sure you understand and observe all legislative and personal safety procedures when carrying out practical assignments. If you are unsure of what these are, ask your supervisor/instructor.

Performance Standard

0—No exposure: No information or practice provided during the program; complete training required

1—Exposure only: General information provided with no practice time; close supervision needed; additional training required

2—Limited practice: Has practiced job during training program; additional training required to develop skill

3—Moderately skilled: Has performed job independently during training program; limited additional training may be required

4—Skilled: Can perform job independently with no additional training

Name_____ Date_____ Class_____

Vehicle used for this activity:

Year_____ Make_____ Model_____

Odometer_____ VIN _____

▶ **TASK** Check steering wheel operation for free play or binding._____ NATEF 7D4.1

CDX Tasksheet Number: H509

1. Research the procedure and specifications to check the steering wheel operation for free-play, binding, serviceability, and condition (including any damage) in the appropriate service information.
   a. Specified free play: _____ in/mm

2. Measure steering wheel free play.
   a. Actual free play: _____ in/mm
   b. Meets manufacturer's specifications? Yes: _____ Requires maintenance: _____
      i. If requires maintenance, list areas and recommendation(s):

      _____
      _____
      _____

3. Carry out full inspection of the steering components, including starting engine and rotating steering from lock to lock:
   a. Meets manufacturer's specifications? Yes: _____ Requires maintenance: _____
      Comments: _____
      _____
      i. If requires maintenance, list areas and recommendation(s):

      _____
      _____
      _____

4. Discuss the findings with the instructor.

Performance Rating

CDX Tasksheet Number: H509

☐ 0   ☐ 1   ☐ 2   ☐ 3   ☐ 4

Supervisor/instructor signature _____ Date_____

Student/intern information:

Name_____ Date_____ Class_____

Vehicle used for this activity:

Year_____ Make_____ Model_____

Odometer_____ VIN _____

▶ **TASK** Check power steering pump, mounting, and hoses for leaks, condition, and routing; check fluid level.

NATEF 7D4.2

Time off_____

Time on_____

Total time_____

CDX Tasksheet Number: H510

1. Research the procedure and specifications to check the power steering pump, mounting, and hoses for leaks, condition, and routing in the appropriate service information; check fluid level. Inspect the serviceability and condition of power steering pump.

2. Check the power steering pump for any leaks or damage.
   a. Meets manufacturer's specifications? Yes: _____ Requires maintenance/repair: _____
      Comments: _____
      i. If requires maintenance/repair, list areas and recommendation(s):
         _____
         _____

3. Inspect the security of power steering pump mounting:
   a. Meets manufacturer's specifications? Yes: _____ Requires maintenance/repair: _____
      Comments: _____
      i. If requires maintenance/repair, list areas and recommendation(s):
         _____
         _____

4. Inspect the serviceability and condition of power steering pump hoses and also for suitable routing:
   a. Meets manufacturer's specifications? Yes: _____ Requires maintenance/repair: _____
      Comments: _____
      i. If requires maintenance/repair, list areas and recommendation(s):
         _____
         _____

5. Check power steering fluid level:
   a. Meets manufacturer's specifications? Yes: _____ Requires maintenance/repair: _____
      Comments: _____
      i. If requires maintenance/repair, list areas and recommendation(s):
         _____
         _____

6. Discuss the findings with the instructor.

Performance Rating

CDX Tasksheet Number: H510

☐	☐	☐	☐	☐
0	1	2	3	4

Supervisor/instructor signature _____ Date_____

© 2017 Jones & Bartlett Learning, LLC, an Ascend Learning Company

Name_____ Date_____ Class_____

Vehicle used for this activity:

Year_____ Make_____ Model_____

Odometer_____ VIN _____

▶ **TASK** Change power steering fluid and filter.   NATEF 7D4.3

Time off_____

Time on_____

Total time_____

CDX Tasksheet Number: H511

1. Research the procedure and specifications to follow all OSHA safety/environmental protection requirements for changing power steering fluid and filter in the appropriate service information.
   a. Referencing manufacturer's specifications, record the correct type and quantity of oil:
      i. Specified oil type: _____
      ii. Specified oil quantity: _____ pints (liters)

2. Using a collection container adequate for the amount of oil to be drained, drain the power steering fluid.

3. Collect an oil sample in a clean, sterile container to be sent for analysis.

4. Remove filter and clean canister and replace filter. Comments: _____
   _____
   _____

5. Refill power steering reservoir with the correct type and quantity of oil.

6. If applicable, bleed the power steering fluid system to remove air.

7. Start and run engine; operate the power steering system and check for any leaks and secure pump mounting.

8. Rectify any leaks.

9. List how much fluid you added to the system: _____ pints (liters)

10. Discuss the findings with the instructor.

Performance Rating

CDX Tasksheet Number: H511

☐ 0   ☐ 1   ☐ 2   ☐ 3   ☐ 4

Supervisor/instructor signature _____ Date_____

Student/intern information:

Name_____ Date_____ Class_____

Vehicle used for this activity:

Year_____ Make_____ Model_____

Odometer_____ VIN _____

CDX Tasksheet Number: H512

1. Research the procedure and specifications to inspect the serviceability and condition of the steering gear in the appropriate service information.
   a. Meets manufacturer's specifications? Yes: _____ Requires maintenance/repair: _____
      Comments: _____
      _____

      i. If requires maintenance/repair, list areas and recommendation(s):
         _____
         _____
         _____

2. Inspect the mounting of the steering gear:
   a. Meets manufacturer's specifications? Yes: _____ Requires maintenance/repair: _____
      Comments: _____
      _____

      i. If requires maintenance/repair, list areas and recommendation(s):
         _____
         _____
         _____

3. Discuss the findings with the instructor.

Performance Rating

CDX Tasksheet Number: H512

☐   ☐   ☐   ☐   ☐

0   1   2   3   4

Supervisor/instructor signature _____ Date_____

Student/intern information:

Name_____ Date_____ Class_____

Vehicle used for this activity:

Year_____ Make_____ Model_____

Odometer_____ VIN _____

▶ **TASK** Inspect steering shaft U-joints, pinch bolts, splines, pitman arm-to-steering sector shaft, tie-rod ends, and linkages.   **NATEF 7D4.5**

Time off_____

Time on_____

Total time_____

CDX Tasksheet Number: H513

1. Research the procedure and specifications to inspect the steering shaft U-joints, pinch bolts, splines, pitman arm-to-steering sector shaft, tie rod ends, and linkages in the appropriate service information.

2. Start by inspecting steering shaft U-joints for excessive wear and lack of lubrication.
    a. Condition of U-joints? Good: _____ Bad: _____
        Comments: _____
        _____

3. Check the u-joint pinch bolts for looseness and oxidation or excessive rust.
    a. Condition of pinch bolts? Good: _____ Bad: _____
        Comments: _____
        _____

4. Check the steering shaft splines for any abnormal wear or stripping.
    a. Condition of splines? Good: _____ Bad: _____
        Comments: _____
        _____

    b. If the condition of the splines is bad, the steering shaft will need to be replaced.

5. Check the condition of the pitman arm and attaching sector shaft for excessive wear or looseness.
    a. Condition of pitman arm and sector shaft? Good: _____ Bad: _____
        Comments: _____
        _____

    b. If the condition of the pitman arm and/or sector shaft is bad, consult the appropriate service information for the proper procedures to repair or replace worn parts. Record the procedures:
        _____
        _____
        _____

6. Inspect the tie rod ends and attaching linkages for excessive wear and/or play.
    a. Condition of tie rod ends and linkages? Good: _____ Bad: _____
        Comments: _____
        _____

b. If the condition of the tie rod ends and/or linkages is bad, consult the appropriate service information for the proper procedures to repair or replace worn parts. Record the procedures:

_____

_____

_____

Note: Tie rod ends and linkages are a critical part of the steering system. If any parts are in poor condition, serious injury could result.

7   Determine any necessary actions or corrections:

_____

_____

8. Discuss your findings with your instructor and record the recommendations:

_____

_____

_____

Performance Rating

CDX Tasksheet Number: H513

☐   ☐   ☐   ☐   ☐
0   1   2   3   4

Supervisor/instructor signature _____ Date_____

Name_____ Date_____ Class_____

Vehicle used for this activity:

Year_____ Make_____ Model_____

Odometer_____ VIN _____

▶ **TASK** Check kingpins for wear.   NATEF 7D4.6

Time off_____

Time on_____

Total time_____

CDX Tasksheet Number: H514

1. Research the procedure and specifications to check kingpin clearance and wear in the appropriate service information. List the following specifications:
   a. Maximum kingpin play: _____ in/mm

2. Jack up the front wheels to relieve pressure from the front tires.

3. Utilizing a dial indicator, attach the base to the front axle.

4. Attach the dial pointer to the top of the spindle.

5. Utilizing a pry bar, slowly lift underneath the tire and read the dial indicator for the amount of vertical play.

6. Is there play present? Yes: _____ No: _____

7. Consult the appropriate service information for the correct amount of play allowed.
   a. Actual reading: _____ in/mm
   b. Is play within specification? Yes: _____ No: _____
   c. If play is not within specification, consult the appropriate service information for the procedures to repair or replace the kingpins. Record the procedures:

   _____
   _____
   _____
   _____
   _____

8. Discuss your findings with your instructor.

Performance Rating

CDX Tasksheet Number: H514

☐   ☐   ☐   ☐   ☐

0   1   2   3   4

Supervisor/instructor signature _____ Date_____

Student/intern information:

Name_____ Date_____ Class_____

Vehicle used for this activity:

Year_____ Make_____ Model_____

Odometer_____ VIN _____

▶ TASK Check wheel bearings for looseness and noise. NATEF 7D4.7

Time off_____

Time on_____

Total time_____

CDX Tasksheet Number: H515

1. Research the procedure and specifications to follow all OSHA safety/environmental protection requirements to check wheel bearings for looseness and noise in the appropriate service information. List the following specifications:
   a. Maximum wheel bearing end play: _____ in/mm

2. Check wheel bearings for looseness and wear:
   a. Actual movement: _____ in/mm
   b. If outside manufacturer's specifications, list recommendation(s) for rectification process:

   _____

   _____

3. Rotate wheel assemblies; check for any roughness or audible noise:
   Satisfactory: _____ Requires maintenance: _____
   Comments: _____

   _____

   a. If requires maintenance, list areas and recommendation(s):

   _____

   _____

4. Discuss the findings with the instructor.

Performance Rating

CDX Tasksheet Number: H515

☐ 0   ☐ 1   ☐ 2   ☐ 3   ☐ 4

Supervisor/instructor signature _____ Date_____

© 2017 Jones & Bartlett Learning, LLC, an Ascend Learning Company

Preventive Maintenance Inspection   **641**

Student/intern information:

Name_____ Date_____ Class_____

Vehicle used for this activity:

Year_____ Make_____ Model_____

Odometer_____ VIN _____

CDX Tasksheet Number: H516

Time off_____

Time on_____

Total time_____

1. Research the procedure and specifications to check oil level and condition in all non-drive hubs in the appropriate service information. List the following specifications.
    a. Specified type of lubricant: _____

2. Check oil level in non-drive hubs:
    a. Meets manufacturer's specifications? Yes: _____ Requires maintenance/repair: _____
        Comments: _____
        _____

        i. If requires maintenance/repair, list areas and recommendation(s):
            _____
            _____

3. Carefully examine the hub and surrounding area for any signs/sources of oil from hubs:
    Satisfactory: _____ Requires maintenance: _____
    Comments: _____
    _____

    a. If requires maintenance/repair, list areas and recommendation(s):
        _____
        _____

4. Discuss the finding(s) with the instructor.

Performance Rating

CDX Tasksheet Number: H516

☐	☐	☐	☐	☐
0	1	2	3	4

Supervisor/instructor signature _____ Date_____

Preventive Maintenance Inspection:
Frame and Chassis–Suspension and Steering Systems Part 2

Student/intern information:

Name_____ Date_____ Class_____

Vehicle used for this activity:

Year_____ Make_____ Model_____

Odometer_____ VIN _____

Learning Objective / Task	CDX Tasksheet Number	2014 NATEF Priority Level	2014 NATEF Reference Number
• Inspect springs, pins, hangers, shackles, spring U-bolts, and insulators.	H517	P-1	7D4.9
• Inspect shock absorbers for leaks and secure mounting.	H518	P-1	7D4.10
• Inspect air suspension springs, mounts, hoses, valves, linkage, and fittings for leaks and damage.	H519	P-1	7D4.11
• Check and record suspension ride height.	H520	P-1	7D4.12
• Lubricate all suspension and steering grease fittings.	H521	P-1	7D4.13
• Check toe setting.	MHT10	N/A	N/A
• Check tandem axle alignment and spacing.	MHT11	N/A	N/A
• Check axle-locating components (radius, torque, and/or track rods).	H522	P-1	7D4.14

Time off_____

Time on_____

Total time_____

Materials Required

- Vehicle
- Vehicle manufacturer's service information
- Manufacturer-specific tools, depending on the concern
- Vehicle lifting equipment, if applicable
- Diagnostic tools
- Electrical/electronic testing equipment
- Measuring equipment
- Workshop tools
- Hand tools

Some Safety Issues to Consider

- Diagnosis of this fault may require test driving the vehicle on the school grounds or on a hoist, both of which carry severe risks. Attempt this task only with full permission from your supervisor/instructor and follow all the guidelines exactly.
- **Caution:** If you are working in an area where there could be brake dust present (may contain asbestos, which has been determined to cause cancer when inhaled or ingested), wear and use all OSHA-approved asbestos protective/removal equipment.
- Lifting equipment such as vehicle jacks and stands, vehicle hoists, and engine hoists are important tools that increase productivity and make the job easier. However, they can also cause severe injury or death if used improperly. Make sure you follow the manufacturer's operation procedures. Also make sure you have your supervisor/instructor's permission to use any particular type of lifting equipment.
- Comply with personal and environmental safety practices associated with clothing; eye protection; hand tools; power equipment; proper ventilation; and the handling, storage, and disposal of chemicals/materials in accordance with federal, state, and local regulations.

- Always wear the correct protective eyewear and clothing and use the appropriate safety equipment, as well as fender covers, seat protectors, and floor mat protectors.
- Make sure you understand and observe all legislative and personal safety procedures when carrying out practical assignments. If you are unsure of what these are, ask your supervisor/instructor.

Performance Standard

0—No exposure: No information or practice provided during the program; complete training required

1—Exposure only: General information provided with no practice time; close supervision needed; additional training required

2—Limited practice: Has practiced job during training program; additional training required to develop skill

3—Moderately skilled: Has performed job independently during training program; limited additional training may be required

4—Skilled: Can perform job independently with no additional training

Student/intern information:

Name_____ Date_____ Class_____

Vehicle used for this activity:

Year_____ Make_____ Model_____

Odometer_____ VIN _____

▶ **TASK** Inspect springs, pins, hangers, shackles, spring U-bolts, and insulators.　**NATEF 7D4.9**

CDX Tasksheet Number: H517

1. Research the procedure and specifications to inspect springs, pins, hangers, shackles, spring U-bolts, and insulators in the appropriate service information. List any specifications:

   _____

   _____

2. Inspect the serviceability and condition of all leaf springs:
   a. Meets manufacturer's specifications? Yes: _____ Require maintenance/repair: _____
      Comments: _____

      _____

      i. If require maintenance/repair, list areas and recommendation(s):

         _____

         _____

3. Inspect the serviceability and condition of all pins, leaf spring hangers, and shackles:
   a Meets manufacturer's specifications? Yes: _____ Require maintenance/repair: _____
      Comments: _____

      _____

      i. If require maintenance/repair, list areas and recommendation(s):

         _____

         _____

4. Inspect the serviceability and condition of all leaf springs' U-bolts:
   a. Meets manufacturer's specifications? Yes: _____ Require maintenance/repair: _____
      Comments: _____

      _____

      i. If require maintenance/repair, list areas and recommendation(s):

         _____

         _____

5. Inspect the serviceability and condition of all suspension insulators:
   a. Meets manufacturer's specifications? Yes: _____ Require maintenance/repair: _____
   Comments: _____
   _____

   i. If require maintenance/repair, list areas and recommendation(s):
   _____
   _____

6. Discuss the findings with the instructor.

Performance Rating

CDX Tasksheet Number: H517

☐   ☐   ☐   ☐   ☐
0   1   2   3   4

Supervisor/instructor signature _____ Date_____

Name_____ Date_____ Class_____

Vehicle used for this activity:

Year_____ Make_____ Model_____

Odometer_____ VIN _____

▶ **TASK** Inspect shock absorbers for leaks and secure mounting.   NATEF 7D4.10

CDX Tasksheet Number: H518

1. Research the procedure and specifications to inspect the serviceability and condition of all shock absorbers (leaks and secure mountings) in the appropriate service information.

2. Inspect the shock absorbers for leaks, secure mounting, and damage.
   Note: If physical damage is present, the shock will have to be replaced.

   a. Meets manufacturer's specifications? Yes: _____ Require maintenance/repair: _____
   Comments: _____
   _____

      i. If requires maintenance/repair, list areas and recommendation(s):
      _____
      _____
      _____

   Note: Inspect the shocks for oil leakage and any physical damage present. If physical damage is present, the shock will have to be replaced.

3. Discuss the findings with the instructor.

Performance Rating

CDX Tasksheet Number: H518

☐	☐	☐	☐	☐
0	1	2	3	4

Supervisor/instructor signature _____ Date_____

Student/intern information:

Name_____ Date_____ Class_____

Vehicle used for this activity:

Year_____ Make_____ Model_____

Odometer_____ VIN _____

▶ **TASK** Inspect air suspension springs, mounts, hoses, valves, linkage, and fittings for leaks and damage.

NATEF 7D4.11

Time off_____

Time on_____

Total time_____

CDX Tasksheet Number: H519

1. Research the procedure and specifications to inspect air suspension springs, mounts, hoses, valves, linkage, and fittings for leaks and damage in the appropriate service information.

2. Inspect the serviceability and condition of all air suspension springs:
   a. Meets manufacturer's specifications? Yes: _____ Require maintenance/repair: _____
   Comments: _____
   _____

      i. If require maintenance/repair, list areas and recommendation(s):
      _____
      _____

3. Inspect the serviceability and condition of air suspension mounts, hoses, valves, and linkage:
   a. Meets manufacturer's specifications? Yes: _____ Require maintenance/repair: _____
   Comments: _____
   _____

      i. If require maintenance/repair, list areas and recommendation(s):
      _____
      _____

4. Inspect fittings for leaks and damage, if applicable:
   a. Meets manufacturer's specifications? Yes: _____ Require maintenance/repair: _____
   Comments: _____
   _____

      i. If require maintenance/repair, list areas and recommendation(s):
      _____
      _____

5. Discuss the findings with the instructor.

Performance Rating

CDX Tasksheet Number: H519

☐	☐	☐	☐	☐
0	1	2	3	4

Supervisor/instructor signature _____ Date_____

Name_____ Date_____ Class_____

Vehicle used for this activity:

Year_____ Make_____ Model_____

Odometer_____ VIN _____

▶ **TASK** Check and record suspension ride height.   **NATEF 7D4.12**

CDX Tasksheet Number: H520

Time off_____

Time on_____

Total time_____

1. Research the procedure and specifications to follow all OHSA safety requirements for checking ride height in the appropriate service information. List the following specifications:

    a. Manufacturer's specification of ride height: _____ in/mm

2. Carry out suspension ride height checks, ensuring that all safety measures are observed.

    a. Actual ride height: _____ in/mm

        i. Meets manufacturer's specifications?
            Yes: _____ Require maintenance/repair: _____
            Comments: _____

            _____

        a. If requires maintenance/repair, list areas and recommendation(s):

            _____

            _____

            _____

3. Discuss the findings with the instructor.

Performance Rating

CDX Tasksheet Number: H520

☐   ☐   ☐   ☐   ☐
0   1   2   3   4

Supervisor/instructor signature _____ Date_____

Name_____ Date_____ Class_____

Vehicle used for this activity:

Year_____ Make_____ Model_____

Odometer_____ VIN _____

▶ **TASK** Lubricate all suspension and steering grease fittings.   NATEF 7D4.13

Time off_____

CDX Tasksheet Number: H521

Time on_____

1. Research the procedure and specifications to check the lubrication requirements for all suspension and steering components fitted with greasing capable fittings in the appropriate service information. List the following specifications:

   a. Specified type of lubricant: _____

Total time_____

2. Carry out lubrication of all suspension and steering components greaseable fittings.

3. For reference, list all lubrication sites below.

   _____
   _____
   _____
   _____
   _____
   _____
   _____
   _____
   _____
   _____
   _____

4. Discuss the findings with the instructor.

Performance Rating

CDX Tasksheet Number: H521

☐	☐	☐	☐	☐
0	1	2	3	4

Supervisor/instructor signature _____ Date_____

Student/intern information:

Name_____ Date_____ Class_____

Vehicle used for this activity:

Year_____ Make_____ Model_____

Odometer_____ VIN _____

▶ **TASK** Check toe setting.   Non-NATEF

CDX Tasksheet Number: MHT10

Time off_____

Time on_____

Total time_____

1. Research the procedure and specifications for checking toe in the appropriate service information.
   a. Manufacturer's specification: Toe: _____

2. Prepare the vehicle for checking toe.

3. Check and record the toe reading: _____
   a. Within manufacturer's specifications: Yes: _____ No: _____
   b. If no, list the problem(s):

   _____
   _____
   _____

4. Determine any necessary action(s):

   _____
   _____
   _____

5. Discuss the findings with your instructor.

Performance Rating

CDX Tasksheet Number: MHT10

☐	☐	☐	☐	☐
0	1	2	3	4

Supervisor/instructor signature _____ Date_____

Name_____ Date_____ Class_____

Vehicle used for this activity:

Year_____ Make_____ Model_____

Odometer_____ VIN _____

▶ **TASK** Check tandem axle alignment and spacing.

Non-NATEF

CDX Tasksheet Number: MHT11

1. Research the procedure and specifications for checking tandem axle alignment and spacing in the appropriate service information.
   a. Tandem axle alignment specifications:

   _____
   _____
   _____

   b. Tandem axle spacing specifications:

   _____
   _____
   _____

2. Prepare the vehicle for checking the tandem axle alignment and spacing.

3. Check/measure the following:
   a Tandem axle alignment:

   _____
   _____
   _____

   b. Tandem axle spacing:

   _____
   _____
   _____

4. Determine any necessary action(s):

   _____
   _____
   _____

5. Discuss the findings with your instructor.

Performance Rating

CDX Tasksheet Number: MHT11

☐	☐	☐	☐	☐
0	1	2	3	4

Supervisor/instructor signature _____ Date_____

Student/intern information:

Name_____ Date_____ Class_____

Vehicle used for this activity:

Year_____ Make_____ Model_____

Odometer_____ VIN _____

▶ **TASK** Check axle-locating components (radius, torque, and/or track rods).   NATEF 7D4.14

CDX Tasksheet Number: H522

Time off_____

Time on_____

Total time_____

1. Research the procedure and specifications to follow all OSHA safety/environmental protection requirements when inspecting axle-locating components (radius, torque, and/or track rods) in the appropriate service information.

2. Inspect axle-locating components. In some cases this may require disassembly of the axle components.

3. Using an alignment machine, check the actual tandem axle alignment and all tandem axle parts: Good: _____ Require attention: _____
   Comments: _____

   _____

   a. If require attention, list areas and recommendation(s):

      _____

      _____

      _____

4. Discuss the finding(s) with the instructor.

Performance Rating

CDX Tasksheet Number: H522

☐   ☐   ☐   ☐   ☐
0   1   2   3   4

Supervisor/instructor signature _____ Date_____

Preventive Maintenance Inspection:
Frame and Chassis–Tires and Wheels

Student/intern information:

Name_____ Date_____ Class_____

Vehicle used for this activity:

Year_____ Make_____ Model_____

Odometer_____ VIN _____

Learning Objective / Task	CDX Tasksheet Number	2014 NATEF Priority Level	2014 NATEF Reference Number
• Inspect tires for wear patterns and proper mounting.	H523	P-1	7D5.1
• Inspect tires for cuts, cracks, bulges, and sidewall damage.	H524	P-1	7D5.2
• Inspect valve caps and stems; determine needed action.	H525	P-1	7D5.3
• Measure and record tread depth; probe for imbedded debris.	H526	P-1	7D5.4
• Check and record air pressure; adjust air pressure in accordance with manufacturers' specification.	H527	P-1	7D5.5
• Check wheel mounting hardware condition; determine needed action.	H528	P-1	7D5.6
• Retorque lugs in accordance with manufacturers' specifications.	MHT12	N/A	N/A
• Inspect wheels for cracks, damage, and proper hand hold alignment.	H529	P-1	7D5.7
• Check tire matching (diameter and tread) on single and dual tire applications.	H530	P-1	7D5.8

Time off_____

Time on_____

Total time_____

Materials Required

- Vehicle
- Vehicle manufacturer's service information
- Manufacturer-specific tools, depending on the concern
- Vehicle lifting equipment, if applicable
- Diagnostic tools
- Electrical/electronic testing equipment
- Measuring equipment
- Workshop tools
- Hand tools

Some Safety Issues to Consider

- Diagnosis of this fault may require test driving the vehicle on the school grounds or on a hoist, both of which carry severe risks. Attempt this task only with full permission from your supervisor/instructor and follow all the guidelines exactly.
- **Caution:** If you are working in an area where there could be brake dust present (may contain asbestos, which has been determined to cause cancer when inhaled or ingested), wear and use all OSHA-approved asbestos protective/removal equipment.

- Lifting equipment such as vehicle jacks and stands, vehicle hoists, and engine hoists are important tools that increase productivity and make the job easier. However, they can also cause severe injury or death if used improperly. Make sure you follow the manufacturer's operation procedures. Also make sure you have your supervisor/instructor's permission to use any particular type of lifting equipment.
- Comply with personal and environmental safety practices associated with clothing; eye protection; hand tools; power equipment; proper ventilation; and the handling, storage, and disposal of chemicals/materials in accordance with federal, state, and local regulations.
- Always wear the correct protective eyewear and clothing and use the appropriate safety equipment, as well as fender covers, seat protectors, and floor mat protectors.
- Make sure you understand and observe all legislative and personal safety procedures when carrying out practical assignments. If you are unsure of what these are, ask your supervisor/instructor.

Performance Standard

0–No exposure: No information or practice provided during the program; complete training required
1–Exposure only: General information provided with no practice time; close supervision needed; additional training required
2–Limited practice: Has practiced job during training program; additional training required to develop skill
3–Moderately skilled: Has performed job independently during training program; limited additional training may be required
4–Skilled: Can perform job independently with no additional training

Name_____ Date_____ Class_____

Vehicle used for this activity:

Year_____ Make_____ Model_____

Odometer_____ VIN _____

▶ **TASK** Inspect tires for wear patterns and proper mounting.　　　　　**NATEF 7D5.1**

CDX Tasksheet Number: H523

Time off_____

Time on_____

Total time_____

1. Research the procedure and specifications to follow all OSHA safety/environmental protection requirements when inspecting wheels and tires for wear patterns and proper mounting in the appropriate service information.

2. Inspect and evaluate the wear patterns of the tires fitted to your vehicle:
   Yes: _____ Requires attention: _____
   Comments: _____
   _____
   _____
   _____

   a. If requires attention, list areas and recommendation(s):
      _____
      _____
      _____

3. Inspect and evaluate proper mounting of directional tires (if applicable) fitted to your vehicle:
   a. Do they meet the manufacturer's specifications? Yes: _____ Requires attention: _____
      Comments: _____
      _____

      i. If requires attention, list areas and recommendation(s):
         _____
         _____
         _____

4. Record the specified manufacturer lug torque for the wheels and tires.
   a. Manufacturer specified lug torque: _____ ft-lb (Nm)
   b. Actual torque applied: _____ ft-lb (Nm)

5. Discuss the findings with the instructor.

Performance Rating

CDX Tasksheet Number: H523

□　　　　　□　　　　　□　　　　　□　　　　　□
0　　　　　1　　　　　2　　　　　3　　　　　4

Supervisor/instructor signature _____ Date_____

Name_____ Date_____ Class_____

Vehicle used for this activity:

Year_____ Make_____ Model_____

Odometer_____ VIN _____

▶ TASK Inspect tires for cuts, cracks, bulges, and sidewall damage. **NATEF 7D5.2**

CDX Tasksheet Number: H524

Time off_____

Time on_____

Total time_____

1. Research the procedure and specifications to inspect the serviceability and condition of all tires for cuts, cracks, bulges, and sidewall damage in the appropriate service information.

2. Inspect the tires for any damage. Do they meet the manufacturer's specifications?
   Yes: _____ Requires attention: _____
   Comments: _____
   _____
   _____
   _____

   a. If requires attention, list areas and recommendation(s):
   _____
   _____
   _____

3. Discuss the findings with the instructor.

Performance Rating

CDX Tasksheet Number: H524

☐	☐	☐	☐	☐
0	1	2	3	4

Supervisor/instructor signature _____ Date_____

Student/intern information:

Name_____ Date_____ Class_____

Vehicle used for this activity:

Year_____ Make_____ Model_____

Odometer_____ VIN _____

▶ **TASK** Inspect valve caps and stems; determine needed action. NATEF 7D5.3

CDX Tasksheet Number: H525

Time off_____

Time on_____

Total time_____

1. Research the procedure and specifications to inspect the serviceability and condition of all tire valve caps and stems in the appropriate service information.

2. Inspect the valve caps and stems to ensure that they are not damaged or missing. Do they meet the manufacturer's specifications? Yes: _____ Requires attention: _____
   Comments: _____
   _____
   _____
   _____

   a. If requires attention, list areas and recommendation(s):
   _____
   _____
   _____

3. Discuss the findings with the instructor.

Performance Rating

CDX Tasksheet Number: H525

☐ 0 ☐ 1 ☐ 2 ☐ 3 ☐ 4

Supervisor/instructor signature _____ Date_____

Name_____ Date_____ Class_____

Vehicle used for this activity:

Year_____ Make_____ Model_____

Odometer_____ VIN _____

▶ **TASK** Measure and record tread depth; probe for imbedded debris. **NATEF 7D5.4**

CDX Tasksheet Number: H526

Time off_____

Time on_____

Total time_____

1. Research the procedure and specifications to measure and record tread depth in the appropriate service information.
   a. Specification for minimum depth tread: _____ in/mm

2. Measure and record tread depth; probe for imbedded debris:

Tire Position	Actual Reading	Acceptable	Not Acceptable
L/S Front			
R/S Front			
First Drive Axle			
R/S Outer			
R/S Inner			
L/S Outer			
L/S Inner			
Second Drive Axle			
R/S Outer			
R/S Inner			
L/S Outer			
L/S Inner			
Third Axle, if Fitted			
R/S Outer			
R/S Inner			
L/S Outer			
L/S Inner			

3. Remove any embedded debris.

4. Discuss the findings with the instructor.

Performance Rating

CDX Tasksheet Number: H526

☐ 0   ☐ 1   ☐ 2   ☐ 3   ☐ 4

Supervisor/instructor signature _____ Date_____

Student/intern information:

Name_____ Date_____ Class_____

Vehicle used for this activity:

Year_____ Make_____ Model_____

Odometer_____ VIN _____

▶ **TASK** Check and record air pressure; adjust air pressure in accordance with manufacturers' specification.

NATEF 7D5.5

Time off_____

Time on_____

Total time_____

CDX Tasksheet Number: H527

1.   Research the procedure and specifications to check and record tire pressure in the appropriate service information.
     a.   Recommended tire pressure setting: _____ psi (kPa)

2.   Check and record tire pressures:

Tire Position	Actual Reading	Acceptable	Not Acceptable
L/S Front			
R/S Front			
First Drive Axle			
R/S Outer			
R/S Inner			
L/S Outer			
L/S Inner			
Second Drive Axle			
R/S Outer			
R/S Inner			
L/S Outer			
L/S Inner			
Third Axle, if Fitted			
R/S Outer			
R/S Inner			
L/S Outer			
L/S Inner			

3.   Adjust air pressure in all tires to manufacturer's specification.

4.   Discuss the findings with the instructor.

Performance Rating

CDX Tasksheet Number: H527

☐ 0   ☐ 1   ☐ 2   ☐ 3   ☐ 4

Supervisor/instructor signature _____ Date_____

Student/intern information:

Name_____ Date_____ Class_____

Vehicle used for this activity:

Year_____ Make_____ Model_____

Odometer_____ VIN _____

▶ **TASK** Check wheel mounting hardware condition; determine needed action.　　**NATEF 7D5.6**

CDX Tasksheet Number: H528

Time off_____

Time on_____

Total time_____

1. Research the procedure and specifications to check wheel mounting hardware condition in the appropriate service information.

2. Check for loose lugs and/or slipped wheels; check mounting hardware condition; determine needed action.
   a. Inspect the serviceability and condition of all wheel lugs plus any sign(s) of slipped wheels:
      i. Do they meet the manufacturer's specifications?
         Yes: _____ Requires maintenance: _____
         Comments: _____
         _____
         _____

      a. If requires maintenance, list areas and recommendation(s):
         _____
         _____

   b. Check mounting hardware condition; service as needed.

3. Retorque lugs in accordance with manufacturer's specifications.
   a. Lug nut torque specification: _____ ft-lb (Nm)
   b. Retorque lugs in accordance with manufacturer's specifications:
      i. Do they meet the manufacturer's specifications?
         Yes: _____ Requires maintenance: _____
         Comments: _____
         _____
         _____

      a. If requires maintenance, list areas and recommendation(s):
         _____
         _____

4. Discuss the findings with the instructor.

Performance Rating

CDX Tasksheet Number: H528

☐　　　☐　　　☐　　　☐　　　☐
0　　　1　　　2　　　3　　　4

Supervisor/instructor signature _____ Date_____

© 2017 Jones & Bartlett Learning, LLC, an Ascend Learning Company

Preventive Maintenance Inspection　**675**

Name_____ Date_____ Class_____

Vehicle used for this activity:

Year_____ Make_____ Model_____

Odometer_____ VIN _____

▶ **TASK** Retorque lugs in accordance with manufacturers' specifications. **Non-NATEF**

CDX Tasksheet Number: MHT12

Time off_____

Time on_____

Total time_____

1. Research the procedure and specifications for retorquing wheel lugs in the appropriate service information.
   a. Specified wheel lug torque: _____ ft-lb (Nm)
   b. Draw the specified torque pattern:

   Note: The lug contact face MUST match the contact face in the wheel. If the wheel contact face is tapered, the lug contact face MUST also be tapered to match. If the contact face in the wheel is flat, the contact face of the lug MUST be flat. If in doubt about which way the lugs should face, ask your instructor.

2. Retorque the lugs following the specified procedure.

3. To what torque did you tighten the lugs? _____ ft-lb (Nm)

4. List any lugs which were not properly torqued:
   _____
   _____
   _____

5. Discuss the findings with your instructor.

Performance Rating

CDX Tasksheet Number: MHT12

☐ 0   ☐ 1   ☐ 2   ☐ 3   ☐ 4

Supervisor/instructor signature _____ Date_____

Student/intern information:

Name_____ Date_____ Class_____

Vehicle used for this activity:

Year_____ Make_____ Model_____

Odometer_____ VIN _____

▶ **TASK** Inspect wheels for cracks, damage, and proper hand hold alignment. _____ **NATEF 7D5.7**

CDX Tasksheet Number: H529

Time off_____

Time on_____

Total time_____

1. Research the procedure and specifications to inspect wheels for cracks, damage, and proper hand hold alignment in the appropriate service information.

2. Inspect the condition of all wheels and spacer for any sign(s) of cracks or damage:
   a. Do they meet the manufacturer's specifications? Yes: _____ Requires attention: _____
   Comments: _____
   _____
   _____

   i. If requires maintenance/repair, list areas and recommendation(s):
   _____
   _____
   _____

3. Check wheels for proper hand hold alignment:
   a. Do they meet the manufacturer's specifications? Yes: _____ Requires attention: _____
   Comments: _____
   _____
   _____

   i. If requires maintenance, list areas and recommendations:
   _____
   _____
   _____

4. Discuss the findings with the instructor.

Performance Rating

CDX Tasksheet Number: H529

☐ 0   ☐ 1   ☐ 2   ☐ 3   ☐ 4

Supervisor/instructor signature _____ Date_____

Name_____ Date_____ Class_____

Vehicle used for this activity:

Year_____ Make_____ Model_____

Odometer_____ VIN _____

▶ **TASK** Check tire matching (diameter and tread) on single and dual tire applications.

NATEF 7D5.8

Time off_____

Time on_____

Total time_____

CDX Tasksheet Number: H530

1. Research the procedure and specifications to follow all OSHA safety/environmental protection requirements when checking tire matching (diameter and tread) on single and dual tire applications in the appropriate service information.

2. Check tire matching (diameter and tread) on dual tire installations:
    a. Do they meet the manufacturer's specifications? Yes: _____ Requires attention: _____
        Comments: _____
        _____
        _____
        _____

        i. If requires maintenance/repair, list areas and recommendation(s):
            _____
            _____
            _____

3. Discuss the finding(s) with the instructor.

Performance Rating

CDX Tasksheet Number: H530

☐   ☐   ☐   ☐   ☐

0   1   2   3   4

Supervisor/instructor signature _____ Date_____

Preventive Maintenance Inspection:
Frame and Chassis—Frame and Fifth Wheel

Student/intern information:

Name_____ Date_____ Class_____

Vehicle used for this activity:

Year_____ Make_____ Model_____

Odometer_____ VIN _____

Learning Objective / Task	CDX Tasksheet Number	2014 NATEF Priority Level	2014 NATEF Reference Number
• Inspect fifth wheel mounting, bolts, air lines, and locks.	H531	P-1	7D6.1
• Test operation of fifth wheel locking device; adjust if necessary.	H532	P-1	7D6.2
• Check quarter fenders, mud flaps, and brackets.	H533	P-1	7D6.3
• Check pintle hook assembly and mounting, if applicable.	H534	P-1	7D6.4
• Lubricate all fifth wheel grease fittings and plate, if applicable.	H535	P-2	7D6.5
• Inspect frame and frame members for cracks and damage.	H536	P-1	7D6.6

Time off_____

Time on_____

Total time_____

Materials Required

- Vehicle
- Vehicle manufacturer's service information
- Component manufacturer's maintenance and service information
- Wear gauge limit tool
- Manufacturer-specific tools, depending on the concern
- Vehicle lifting equipment, if applicable
- Diagnostic tools
- Electrical/electronic testing equipment
- Measuring equipment
- Workshop tools
- Hand tools

Some Safety Issues to Consider

- Diagnosis of this fault may require test driving the vehicle on the school grounds or on a hoist, both of which carry severe risks. Attempt this task only with full permission from your supervisor/instructor and follow all the guidelines exactly.
- **Caution:** If you are working in an area where there could be brake dust present (may contain asbestos, which has been determined to cause cancer when inhaled or ingested), wear and use all OSHA-approved asbestos protective/removal equipment.
- Lifting equipment such as vehicle jacks and stands, vehicle hoists, and engine hoists are important tools that increase productivity and make the job easier. However, they can also cause severe injury or death if used improperly. Make sure you follow the manufacturer's operation procedures. Also make sure you have your supervisor/instructor's permission to use any particular type of lifting equipment.
- Comply with personal and environmental safety practices associated with clothing; eye protection; hand tools; power equipment; proper ventilation; and the handling, storage, and disposal of chemicals/materials in accordance with federal, state, and local regulations.

- Always wear the correct protective eyewear and clothing and use the appropriate safety equipment, as well as fender covers, seat protectors, and floor mat protectors.
- Make sure you understand and observe all legislative and personal safety procedures when carrying out practical assignments. If you are unsure of what these are, ask your supervisor/instructor.

Performance Standard

0–No exposure: No information or practice provided during the program; complete training required

1–Exposure only: General information provided with no practice time; close supervision needed; additional training required

2–Limited practice: Has practiced job during training program; additional training required to develop skill

3–Moderately skilled: Has performed job independently during training program; limited additional training may be required

4–Skilled: Can perform job independently with no additional training

Student/intern information:

Name_____ Date_____ Class_____

Vehicle used for this activity:

Year_____ Make_____ Model_____

Odometer_____ VIN _____

▶ **TASK** Inspect fifth wheel mounting, bolts, air lines, and locks.   **NATEF 7D6.1**

Time off_____

Time on_____

Total time_____

CDX Tasksheet Number: H531

1. Research the procedure and specifications to follow all OSHA safety/environmental protection requirements when inspecting fifth wheel components in the appropriate service information.

2. Clean the fifth wheel assembly, ensuring that all environmental protection regulations are adhered to.

3. Inspect fifth wheel mounting bolts:
   a. Good condition/correct torque? _____ ft-lb (Nm)
   b. Require attention: _____
      Comments: _____

      i. If requires attention, list areas and recommendation(s):
      _____
      _____

4. Inspect fifth wheel air lines (if applicable):
   a. Yes: _____ Requires attention: _____
      Comments: _____

      i. If requires attention, list areas and recommendation(s):
      _____
      _____

5. Inspect locking mechanism on either side of a sliding coupling. Is it missing, inoperative, or excessively worn?
   a. Good/operative and not excessively worn: _____
   b. Requires attention: _____
      Comments: _____

      i. If requires attention, list areas and recommendation(s):
      _____
      _____

6. Discuss the findings with the instructor.

Performance Rating

CDX Tasksheet Number: H531

☐ 0   ☐ 1   ☐ 2   ☐ 3   ☐ 4

Supervisor/instructor signature _____ Date_____

© 2017 Jones & Bartlett Learning, LLC, an Ascend Learning Company

Name_____ Date_____ Class_____

Vehicle used for this activity:

Year_____ Make_____ Model_____

Odometer_____ VIN _____

▶ **TASK** Test operation of fifth wheel locking device; adjust if necessary. | **NATEF 7D6.2**

Time off_____

Time on_____

Total time_____

CDX Tasksheet Number: H532

1. Research the procedure and specifications to test operation of fifth wheel locking device in the appropriate service information.

2. Utilizing a fifth wheel dummy locking bar, insert it into the fifth wheel lock.

3. Secure the bar in the lock and test to see if it is good and tight.
   a. Is the bar locked securely into the fifth wheel lock? Yes: _____ No: _____
      Comments: _____
      _____

   b. If the bar is not locked securely into the fifth wheel lock, consult the appropriate service information for the proper procedures to repair or replace the fifth wheel. Record the procedures:
      _____
      _____
      _____
      _____

4. Discuss the findings with the instructor.

Performance Rating

CDX Tasksheet Number: H532

☐	☐	☐	☐	☐
0	1	2	3	4

Supervisor/instructor signature _____ Date_____

Name_____ Date_____ Class_____

Vehicle used for this activity:

Year_____ Make_____ Model_____

Odometer_____ VIN _____

▶ **TASK** Check quarter fenders, mud flaps, and brackets.   **NATEF 7D6.3**

Time off_____

CDX Tasksheet Number: H533

Time on_____

1. Research the procedure and specifications to check quarter fenders, mud flaps, and brackets in the appropriate service information.

Total time_____

2. Check quarter fenders:
    a. Meets manufacturer's specifications? Yes: _____ Requires maintenance/repair: _____
       Comments: _____
       _____

        i. If requires maintenance/repair, list areas and recommendation(s):
           _____
           _____
           _____

3. Check mud flaps and brackets:
    a. Meets manufacturer's specifications? Yes: _____ Requires maintenance/repair: _____
       Comments: _____
       _____

        i. If requires maintenance/repair, list areas and recommendation(s):
           _____
           _____
           _____

4. Discuss the findings with the instructor.

Performance Rating

CDX Tasksheet Number: H533

☐   ☐   ☐   ☐   ☐
0   1   2   3   4

Supervisor/instructor signature _____ Date_____

Student/intern information:

Name_____ Date_____ Class_____

Vehicle used for this activity:

Year_____ Make_____ Model_____

Odometer_____ VIN _____

CDX Tasksheet Number: H534

1. Research the procedure and specifications to check pintle hook assembly and mounting, if applicable, in the appropriate service information.

2. Inspect condition and serviceability of pintle hook, including any wear:
   a. Meets manufacturer's specifications? Yes: _____ Requires maintenance/repair: _____
      Comments: _____
      _____

      i. If requires maintenance/repair, list areas and recommendation(s):
         _____
         _____
         _____

3. Inspect pintle hook mounting bolts:
   a. Good condition/correct torque? _____ ft-lb (Nm)
   b. Require attention: _____
      Comments: _____
      _____

      i. If require attention, list areas and recommendation(s):
         _____
         _____
         _____

4. Discuss the findings with the instructor.

Performance Rating

CDX Tasksheet Number: H534

☐ 0   ☐ 1   ☐ 2   ☐ 3   ☐ 4

Supervisor/instructor signature _____ Date_____

Student/intern information:

Name_____ Date_____ Class_____

Vehicle used for this activity:

Year_____ Make_____ Model_____

Odometer_____ VIN _____

▶ **TASK** Lubricate all fifth wheel grease fittings and plate, if applicable._____ `NATEF 7D6.5`

CDX Tasksheet Number: H535

Note: Some fittings may not allow grease to pass through them. Replace plugged fittings as necessary.

1.   Research the procedure and specifications to lubricate all fifth wheel grease fittings and plate in the appropriate service information. List the following specifications.
     a. Specified grease: _____

2.   Lubricate all fifth wheel grease fittings and plate.

3.   Inspect all fittings for any damage and replace as necessary.
     a. Condition of fittings? Good: _____ Bad: _____
         Comments: _____
         _____
         _____
         _____

4.   Apply a thin coating of grease and spread neatly across the fifth wheel plate.

5.   Discuss the findings with the instructor.

Performance Rating

CDX Tasksheet Number: H535

☐   ☐   ☐   ☐   ☐
0   1   2   3   4

Supervisor/instructor signature _____ Date_____

© 2017 Jones & Bartlett Learning, LLC, an Ascend Learning Company

Time off_____

Time on_____

Total time_____

Preventive Maintenance Inspection **693**